ECONOMIC PRINCIPLES FOR THE HOSPITALITY INDUSTRY

"This book offers a valuable collection of economic principles that are applicable to the hospitality industry. It provides a comprehensive treatment for pricing decisions with examples germane to hotels, airlines, and theme parks. Drawing on price elasticity, applications in bundled pricing and break-even pricing are elaborated. It highlights major components of the macroeconomic environment, such as aggregate supply/demand, the business cycle, and globalization, with applications to the hospitality industry."

Anthony IpKin Wong, *Sun Yat-Sen University, China*

"This is an interesting and topical book on a very important topic. Prof. Siu showcases his expert knowledge in this area with concise and easy to follow writings, along with useful and compelling examples. Readers would be proud to own this book and use it as the authoritative guide regarding the economics of hospitality businesses."

Desmond Chee Shiong Lam, *University of Macau, China*

Economic Principles for the Hospitality Industry is the ideal introduction to the fundamentals of economics in this dynamic and highly competitive sector.

Applying economic theory to a range of diverse and global hospitality industry settings, this book gives the theory real-world context. Looking at critical issues around sustainable economic development in the hospitality industry such as diversification, technology, determinants of demand, and pricing, it enables students to effectively conduct business analyses, evaluate business performance and conduct effective improvements over time. Written in an engaging style, this book assumes no prior knowledge of economics and contains a range of features, including international case studies and discussion questions, to aid beginners in the subject.

This will be an essential introductory yet comprehensive resource on economics for all hospitality students.

Ricardo C.S. Siu is an Associate Professor in Business Economics at the University of Macau.

Hospitality Essentials Series
Series Editor: **Roy C. Wood**, Faculty of Business and Law,
University of Northampton

Hotel Accommodation Management
Edited by Roy C. Wood

Strategic Questions in Food and Beverage Management
Roy C. Wood

Improving Sustainability in the Hospitality Industry
Frans Melissen and Lieke Sauer

Managing People in the Hospitality Industry
Michael Riley

Hospitality Finance and Accounting
Essential Theory and Practice
Edited by Rob van Ginneken

Economic Principles for the Hospitality Industry
Ricardo C.S. Siu

For more information about this series, please visit: www.routledge.com/
Hospitality-Essentials-Series/book-series/RHE

ECONOMIC PRINCIPLES FOR THE HOSPITALITY INDUSTRY

Ricardo C.S. Siu

Routledge
Taylor & Francis Group

LONDON AND NEW YORK

First published 2020
by Routledge
2 Park Square, Milton Park, Abingdon, Oxon OX14 4RN

and by Routledge
52 Vanderbilt Avenue, New York, NY 10017

Routledge is an imprint of the Taylor & Francis Group, an informa business

© 2020 Ricardo C.S. Siu

British Library Cataloguing-in-Publication Data
A catalogue record for this book is available from the British Library

Library of Congress Cataloging-in-Publication Data
Names: Siu, Ricardo Chi Sen, author.
Title: Economic principles for the hospitality industry / Ricardo Chi
    Sen Siu.
Description: First edition. | Abingdon, Oxon : Routledge, 2019. |
    Series: Hospitality essentials series | Includes bibliographical
    references and index.
Identifiers: LCCN 2019009961 (print) | LCCN 2019013986 (ebook) |
    ISBN 9781315108520 (eBook) | ISBN 9781138090644
    (hardback : alk. paper) | ISBN 9781138090651 (pbk.)
Subjects: LCSH: Hospitality industry.
Classification: LCC TX907 (ebook) | LCC TX907 .S58 2019 (print) |
    DDC 338.4/791—dc23
LC record available at https://lccn.loc.gov/2019009961

ISBN: 978-1-138-09064-4 (hbk)
ISBN: 978-1-138-09065-1 (pbk)
ISBN: 978-1-315-10852-0 (ebk)

Typeset in Garamond
by Apex CoVantage, LLC

Contents

Figures

Illustrations

Tables and boxes

Table

Boxes

Acknowledgments

I would like to first and foremost thank Professor Roy C. Wood, Editor of the Hospitality Essentials Series, who gave me the opportunity to contribute to the book series. Throughout the process of completing this book, Professor Wood shared his expertise in the hospitality industry by reviewing each chapter in detail and providing valuable comments and feedback. His help undoubtedly increased the readability of the book from the perspective of the potential readers (e.g., students and practitioners in the hospitality industry, although they may not have any prior knowledge of economics).

In addition, the efforts of Emma Travis, Carlotta Fanton and Lydia Kessell at Taylor & Francis/Routledge are very much appreciated. Their mutual coordination and patience in guiding me toward the completion of the publication procedures/requirements have resulted in a book that is high in professional standards. Moreover, I would like to thank my employer, the University of Macau, for all of the supports provided which have resulted in the success of my related works and research.

Lastly, I would like to express my sincere gratitude to my wife Lina Chan and children Charmaine Siu and Chapmann Siu who have been very understanding and supportive during my preoccupation in writing this book.

Ricardo C.S. Siu
February 2019

1 Introduction

Objectives and learning outcomes

The scope of the hospitality industry in the world markets has been sub-stantially expanding and its business volume has increased likewise since the mid-20th century. This book therefore aims to provide students and practi-tioners in this field with a robust foundation by providing access to essential economic principles (as well as applications of these principles) that would be significantly helpful for their studies, business analyses and decision-making processes. In addition, this book will help students to acquire a basic knowl-edge of economics that will be an asset in their future career in the various sub-sectors of the hospitality industry. In the first chapter, an overview of the hospitality industry is presented to familiarize students with the characteris-tics, specific features and composition of this industry. In addition, economics-related thinking and reasoning that are outlined and applied in studies on the hospitality industry will be highlighted in a straightforward manner to draw the interest of students so that they can more easily benefit from the informa-tion provided in this book.

After reading this chapter, students will be able to:

- identify the specific characteristics and attributes of hospitality and the hospitality industry as a modern economic sector;
- understand the interrelationship between hospitality and other related service sectors like leisure, tourism and non-leisure;
- understand the significance of the hospitality industry in view of the world economies;
- gain an overall view on the composition of the modern hospitality industry;
- understand the economic scope of the hospitality industry (micro-economics and macroeconomics);
- gain familiarity with some of the rudiments of microeconomic and macro-economic principles; and
- have a good idea of how this book will benefit them.

Characteristics and significance of hospitality industry

Broadly speaking, hospitality refers to the provision of what people perceive as friendly and helpful services. While the provision of such services involves a process that commonly requires a set of factor inputs like labor and related facilities (e.g., hotel, restaurant, theme park, etc.), the acquisition of these services is largely due to the willingness to sacrifice resources such as time and money in exchange for such services.

Unlike the viewpoint of classical economists that

> services generally perish in the very instant of their performance, and seldom leave any trace or value behind them ... labour of some of the most respectable orders in the society is, like that of menial servants, unproductive of any value.
>
> (Smith, 1998: 192)

The rapid expansion of the service sectors (especially the hospitality industry) since the mid-20th century has gained the attention of many economists (e.g., Fuchs, 1965; Hill, 1977; Jansson, 2006; Jean and Faiz, 1998). In parallel with the modernization process in world economies, the interacting forces between consumers and producers of hospitality generate remarkable dynamics for the progression of this industry over time. This is substantiated in a report by Ernst & Young (2016: 1): "In most regional markets, hospitality is in a state of vibrant growth, and is a catalyst for economic development and job creation."

Characteristics of hospitality industry

From a historical perspective, the characteristics of the hospitality industry are largely influenced by the organized businesses that serve individuals who are seeking hospitable accommodations (mainly lodging and food services) when they are travel away from home. From the ancient Greek period at around 40 BC to the beginning of the 20th century, the "hospitality industry" was indeed the primitive form of today's "hotel industry". A good resource on this subject is a global hospitality portal called Soeg Jobs that posted an interesting article on its website which highlights the historical background and evolution of the hospitality industry; see www.soegjobs.com/2016/09/15/hospitality-industry-historical-background/. In the early period, this industry was founded mainly to meet the demands of a small group of travelers like governors, traders, and the rich who traveled to different nations and regions for political activities, business, and leisure (Soeg Jobs, 2016).

In parallel with modern development in economic societies, especially urbanization, which is associated with the widespread specific division of labor in various industries, and increases in productivity and income over time, the business characteristics of the hospitality industry have evolved from serving a relatively small social group of upscale individuals with a few types of services to a large mass of workers, and the composition of this industry has also expanded to include a wider range of services rather than just simply hotels. For example, visitors to hotels, theatres, cinemas, and parks of various forms can now choose from many different types of restaurants, as opposed to the food services that were traditionally offered. Since the mid-20th century, a broad range of hospitable services related to tourism and leisure have become major sub-sectors of the hospitality industry.

To the large mass of workers who are employed in various positions and have different work routines and income levels (e.g., blue-collar vs. white-collar workers who are employed in the different modern economic sectors like manufacturing, banking and finance, retail, or the public sector), their demand for different kinds of hospitality services has generated new opportunities for a wide range of expanded activities in the hospitality industry worldwide. For example, demand for food services with respect to breakfast, lunch, and coffee breaks, which are a part of the everyday work life of the large mass of workers, has led to the growth of restaurants and cafés of various types in our economies. In addition, as the income of this population increases, especially as the size of the above-middle-income group increases, their desire to enjoy the better things in life through increased demand for leisure pursuits such as dining in featured restaurants and bars, visiting theme parks, as well as traveling domestically or internationally, have also increased the parameters of the hospitality markets.

As depicted in Figure 1.1, the modern hospitality industry provides various types of hospitable services in many different forms which highlight the new forms of tourism, leisure, and other non-leisure businesses. Simply speaking, tourism is a part of leisure but the opposite is not necessarily true. For example, gathering with friends in bars or pubs, or having family dinners in restaurants are evidently leisure activities but they are not tourism activities. Moreover, leisure activities that are carried out at home such as "do-it-yourself" (DIY) activities and recreation are not part of the hospitality industry either (as shown in the dotted line area outside the "hospitality" solid square). In turn, though non-leisure, the demand for routine hospitality services as part of everyday life by the working population today is a non-negligible phenomenon that needs to be addressed by the hospitality industry.

Owing to technological progress, the characteristics of the hospitality industry have not necessarily evolved to simply meet the related demands of the different markets, but also created so-called demands for its services. In the 21st century, the hospitality industry has innovated by informing the community about the new ways that they could receive great hospitable services if they wanted to spend time on leisure and non-leisure activities. For example, recent developments of the hotel industry in the organization of hotel resorts or integrated resorts as a destination in themselves has clearly allowed this industry to take the lead in their business (i.e., to provide reasons for people to

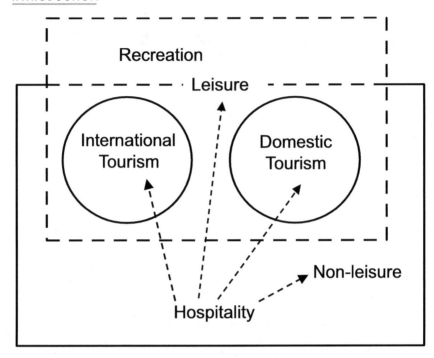

Figure 1.1 Characteristics of hospitality in relation to leisure, tourism, and non-leisure activities

travel to their properties instead of only serving those who travel). Likewise, there is the development of large-scale and premium shopping malls which not only offer shopping, but also general and featured restaurants, mini-cinemas, hair and beauty salons, etc., so that visitors can spend money on a variety of hospitality services. Probably the most unique innovative example in the hospitality industry is the cruise line industry, which has developed and provides a "moving" hotel resort experience for their customers (discussed in more detail in Chapter 7).

Lastly, the business characteristics of the hospitality industry have notice-ably evolved and expanded from services that target individual consumers to those that target business consumers. For example, the rapid development of the MICE industry since the end of the 20th century provides a wide range of hospitable services to firms to host Meetings of various forms (e.g., annual meetings of a firm for its shareholders), Incentive activities for employees (e.g., incentive travel for retreats or team building), Conferences/Conventions for different business purposes (e.g., conferences of particular topics or themes for investors or practitioners), and Exhibitions to facilitate market communi-cation (e.g., automobile or high-tech product exhibitions).

The hospitality industry and economies

In terms of the characteristics of the hospitality industry and the wide variety of businesses that characterize the business practices involved, all are affected by the performances of the local, regional and world economies and in turn affect them as well. As mentioned earlier, the hospitality industry mainly provides services to meet the desire for leisure activities, or coordinate the business demands of firms. Given that leisure activities are a non-necessity and largely influenced by changes and expected changes in income, and the demand of firms for related business services is influenced by the economic environment, related spending in the hospitality industry will therefore increase when the economic environment is good and the market atmosphere is positive, and the opposite also holds true.

The hospitality industry of a particular economy is affected by the economic environment at the local level, which may have direct impacts on industry practices. Besides, in an era of regionalization and globalization, practices of the related sub-sectors in the hospitality industry and their performance are also interrelated with the external environment and its changes especially from the perspective of tourism. For example, the slowdown of the Chinese economy since 2014 has not only reined in the rapid growth of the Chinese hotel industry, but also affected the performance of the hospitality industry in the neighboring countries/regions of Korea, Taiwan, and other Southeast Asian nations.

In these contemporary dynamic environments, the economic effects of this industry on the economic environment may be significant as the ties between the hospitality industry and the local economy are becoming more intimate. For example, according to an Oxford Economics report on "the economic contribution of the UK hospitality industry" (September 2015), in 2014, around 9 percent (2.9 million jobs) of the total employment positions in the UK were offered by its hospitality industry, which contributed to almost 4 percent of the total output of the UK (or gross domestic product (GDP); this output measure will be elaborated in the "Macroeconomic principles" section later in this chapter). In the United States in 2015, around 5.3 percent (7.6 million jobs) of the total employment was created by the travel and tourism industry, which accounted for 2.6 percent of the GDP (SelectUSA, 2016). Despite the large trade deficit of the US economy, a USD 97.9 billion trade surplus was realized through this industry from international visitors in 2015 (SelectUSA, 2016). Thus, if businesses of the hospitality industry are negatively affected during an economy downturn period, jobs and related investments may also be reduced, hence further contributing to the deterioration of the economic environment, and the opposite is also true.

Economic dimensions of hospitality industry

In considering the characteristics and related features of the hospitality industry as elucidated in the previous section, it is obvious that this industry shares

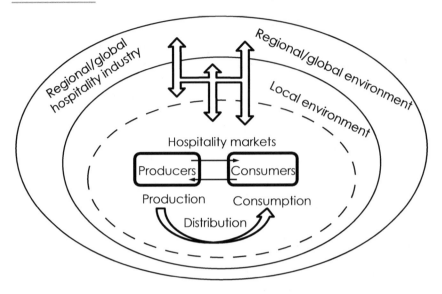

Figure 1.2 Economic dimensions of the hospitality industry

similar economic dimensions with other modern economic sectors, but has its own unique organization and business practices with many different layers. In principle, the production, consumption, and distribution of outputs (goods and services), interactions between producers and consumers in the markets, dynamic relationships with other sectors in the local economy, as well as the hospitality industry and related sectors at the regional/global levels compose the economic dimensions of the hospitality industry in a particular economy (see Figure 1.2).

Based on the economic dimensions of the hospitality industry as depicted in Figure 1.2, it is evident that related studies need to comprehensively explore the individual components of this industry on the one hand, and the environmental and contextual factors on the other hand. In other words, to be a successful manager or leader in the hospitality industry, it is necessary to acquire knowledge of the characteristics and principles of this business area, and use a macro view to examine the possible opportunities and threats that may be consequential of the external environment (at both the local and regional/global levels). To achieve these objectives, understanding economic principles is the first step.

Microeconomic principles

Economics is the study of social behavior which applies reasoning and analytical methods and tools (e.g., diagrams, tables, equations, mathematics, statistics, logic, etc.) to explore the material well-being of people. Economic studies can be simply categorized into microeconomics and macroeconomics. While the former emphasizes on the choices made by individual consumers and producers, and the interactions in the markets that give them the most benefits, the latter focuses on the performance of an economy as a whole, and the factors that may lead to changes in its performance and sustainable growth over time.

Scarcity, choices, and opportunity cost

The underlying principles in microeconomics address the issue of *scarcity* – that is, resources that are finite (e.g., time, income, raw materials, capital, technology, etc.) for any individual household or firm. As we have limited resources, we have to make *choices* on *what* types of goods and services to produce, *how* to produce them, and *to whom* the goods and services produced are to be distributed. For example, with limited resources on hand, a firm has to choose whether it will provide hospitality services through a restaurant, or a 5-star hotel, or a theme park, or a cruise ship, or any other similar businesses in a given period of time. In addition, the firm has to decide how to produce the services (e.g., scale and composition of the fixed property, as well as the source of financing for business development, etc.), and how to provide the related services to consumers (e.g., using a combination of both service workers and technology in business operations, etc.). Moreover, the firm has to decide on the service prices as a measure to determine the target consumers of its business.

In making choices, there needs to be a sacrifice of "something" in exchange for something else. In economics, the best alternative when one sacrifices to make a choice is called the *opportunity cost* (or *economic cost*) of that choice. For example, if a mother chooses to take a day off from her job to spend time with her child at a theme park, her opportunity cost is the monetary outlays on items such as transportation, admission tickets, food, etc. *plus* the income that she has to forgo for that day. It is important to point out from this example that the opportunity cost of a choice is more than the simple sum of the monetary outlays. This is because if going to work is the best alternative as compared to going to a theme park, the mother is not just able to save on the related expenditures, but has no need to forgo her income for that day.

This is the same from the perspective of a producer. For example, by choosing to run a hotel, the cost to the owner is not simply the monetary (or accounting) costs like payment for material and labor. Economically speaking, the forgone income of the business owner that could have been realized if s/he offered his or her skills in the market with his/her best expertise (e.g., as a manager in a hotel) must be included as part of the opportunity cost of the related choice. In addition, the best alternative use of the capital funds that the hotel owner has to sacrifice in order to own the hotel property (e.g., interest by depositing the same amount of funds in a bank) is included in the calculation of opportunity cost (or simply "cost" as expressed in economics).

Marginalism

To arrive at a decision in making a choice, everyone has to compare the cost and benefits. A critical way that economists do so in making a choice is to compare the *marginal* (i.e., incremental) *cost* (MC) and *marginal benefit* (MB) that follow the decision. In principle, if the MB derived from a choice is greater than its MC, the choice will increase the total well-being of the related individual.

- Comparison between MB and MC guides consideration on the feasibility of a choice.
- A choice is feasible if MB ≥ MC.

When applying the marginal principle in making an economic decision, it is important to understand that existing benefits and costs related to the decision will not be taken into consideration. For example, suppose that a restaurant is owned and operated by the same person, and during non-peak times (like certain days of a week or certain months in a year, etc.) when the operator needs to decide whether s/he should lower the prices of the dishes in order to attract more customers, and by how much, the existing prices are not necessarily relevant, nor the fixed costs paid for items such as the monthly mortgage payments to a bank for purchasing the restaurant premises a few years ago, or the regular monthly salary payments to the full-time chefs and servers, or the clerk responsible for bookkeeping and procurements, etc. of the business. To make this decision under the marginal principle, the restaurant owner has to compare the MC to serve, say, a set lunch or a happy-hour meal which includes food cost and extra operation expenditures, and the MB (i.e., marginal revenue which is determined by the new price). In economics, fixed costs are *sunk costs* which are irrelevant to a current decision (further discussion and more examples will be provided in Chapter 4).

Demand, supply, and elasticity

In the famous treatise of Sun Tzu on *The Art of War* in ancient China (5th century BC) which has been widely explored by western scholars in studies of business strategies, one of the most inspiring quotes is that "to always win the battle, we need to thoroughly understand ourselves and others". In the business world, this view could be applied in that a firm that desires to ensure its long-term success ("the battle") has to clearly understand the characteristics of its business ("ourselves") and the behavior of other firms and customers in the market ("others"). Similarly, *demand* and *supply* are the two most basic concepts in economics that any market participant should understand. A good understanding of the forces (factors) that influence demand (the behavior of consumers) and supply (the behavior of producers) in the market will allow a firm to make effective choices for its business over time, hence ensuring its long-term success.

As the factors that determine demand and supply (e.g., price, income, cost of production, etc.) may change over time, it is also important for firms to understand how they themselves and the consumers in the market will respond to changes respectively. Thus, the concept of *elasticity* in economics is a very useful tool for helping firms to understand the *responsiveness* of the market participants to changing market conditions. These principles and their applications in the hospitality industry will be presented in detail in Chapters 3 and 4.

The role of price

A central topic in economics is price, which conveys essential signals (incentives) to firms in their production decisions and consumers in their purchasing decisions. Indeed, the price of a commodity in the market reflects its degree of scarcity as related to the choices made by firms and consumers, after taking the opportunity cost of production and consumption into consideration respectively.

In addition, while the price that a consumer is willing to pay for a unit of a commodity shows the marginal benefit that s/he derives from that choice, the price at which a firm is willing to supply a unit of a commodity reflects the marginal cost of this choice to produce the commodity. Thus, price serves as a central force that guides and balances demand and supply in the market, as depicted in Figure 1.3.

Theoretically speaking, determining price is relatively routine, in which the MB equals MC. To a firm, if the MB is represented by the marginal revenue, then MR = MC is the criterion for a firm to price its output. In the real

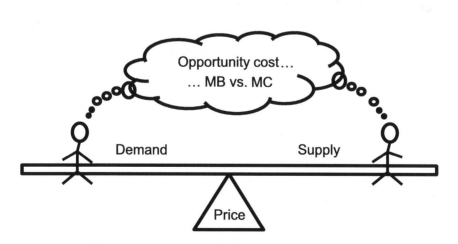

Figure 1.3 Role of price in the market

world, however, determining the price of a commodity may not be necessarily tied to the marginal principle (the technical issues, a detailed discussion and examples will be presented in Chapter 4).

Government and the markets

Despite the theoretical benefits of free markets as advocated by many economists (see for e.g., Friedman, 2002), government regulations and intervention through various means like direct and indirect taxation, minimum wages, business licensing, price control, social responsibility measures, etc. are indeed widely found in all countries. The behavior of firms and consumers in the market is therefore largely shaped by government regulations. Thus, the related effects and changes in public interest in a particular market or industry must be addressed by the related firms effectively and proactively. This is especially true in the various sub-sectors of the hospitality industry, as rapid development may lead to rising public concerns of environmental and cultural deterioration, as well as social, political, and administrative disputes, etc.

For example, as public interest and regulatory frameworks in many Asian countries, especially China, differ from those in North America and Europe, practices of international hotel brands when they are entering the Asian markets may not be identical to those practiced in their home markets. As pointed out by Qu et al. (2005), government regulations play a significant role "in driving the market orientation" of foreign hotels in Mainland China.

From the stance of the management team of a hospitality firm, gaining familiarity with the related microeconomic principles is definitely a necessary first step to effectively address the related government policies and regulations. Of course, in a service-based industry, critical thinking skills and a contextual mindset of managers and leaders with respect to the different economic societies are equally important in their decision-making process. In other words, we should note that practicing the same principles may not necessarily require the same set and sequence of action across regions and over time owing to the differences between public interest and government regulations and their changes. Some examples will be presented with reference to the related topics in the following chapters.

Macroeconomic principles

In any market, the investment and operation decisions of individual firms, and spending decisions of individual consumers are very much influenced by the economic climate at the local, regional, and global levels from the onset, and their changes over time. Thus, to make effective choices for a business, a good understanding of the macroeconomics environment and its impacts on business practices is equally important as understanding microeconomic principles.

In macroeconomics, certain common goals are formulated which are done to ensure a healthy economic environment for both business and consumer activities. To evaluate whether these goals are achieved and determine if any major segment(s) of an economy is deviating from those goals, hence affecting the economic climate, comparable indicators are constructed to project the related situations. Besides, considering the fact that the macroeconomic policies of governments (mainly fiscal and monetary policies) in modern times may have a significant influence on the different sectors of an economy, which would undoubtedly change the environment for businesses, the exploration of macroeconomic policies has become an inevitable task in macroeconomics. In addition, as the banking and financial markets are inseparable sectors in any modern economy, their practices and changes in organization may affect both microeconomic behavior and macroeconomic performance, and are hence another major area in economic studies.

Macroeconomic goals

For businesses to assess the opportunities and threats associated with the economy, four areas at the macroeconomic level have to be comprehensively and proactively considered. These four areas are indeed represented by four common goals which are pursued by the various groups (e.g., government, business firms, workers, and economists) in an economy, and they are stated below.

Four macroeconomic goals:

1   Stable growth
2   High employment levels
3   Low inflation rates
4   Stable exchange rates between local and foreign currencies

In economics, growth means an increase in the volume of the total output or income over time. *Economic growth* hence allows existing firms to increase their business scale or new firms to enter into markets to pursue business opportunities. Nevertheless, owing to the boom–recession–recovery *business cycle* as an unavoidable norm in any capitalist (or market) economy, a stable rather than soaring growth may be generally recommended by economists to reduce the likelihood that the reactive forces following a period of rapid growth may lead to significant negative effects (real, nominal, or psychological) on an economic society (the causes of business cycles and related economic debates of their heterogeneous patterns and effects across different economies will not be discussed in this book). In other words, by ensuring stable and continuous growth over time and minimizing the shocks when an economy experiences a downturn/adjustment period, improvements in the material well-being of an economy could then be realized.

In line with the objective to achieve stable growth, *high employment levels* are unquestionably, a popular goal for both governments and the general population. If the employment level is continuously low (or the unemployment rate is always high), it is possible that some of the firms are retaining some of the resources of production (surplus), and hence, they are not expanding their outputs; thus there is limited growth. Yet, when an economy approaches full employment, firms may have to raise their wages to compete for labor in the market, which thus leads to increases in production costs and output price for producing the same unit of commodity, which is defined as *inflation* in economics. If the increase in output as measured in monetary value is largely a matter of increasing price instead of the quantity of commodities, then real improvement in the material well-being of an economy is indeed lower than the growth as measured in monetary value. Thus, maintaining a lower level of inflation is another macroeconomic goal. In the real world, however, it is not difficult to see that it is often challenging to achieve these two goals simultaneously, especially when the economy is growing or booming. Indeed, as long as the inflation rate is less than the rate of growth, real economic growth is consequently ensured.

Under the context of regionalization and globalization, all economies worldwide have to interact and trade with one another in different areas and to different degrees. To ensure that there are benefits from trade between nations/regions, and hence its contribution to the economic growth of the participants, *stable exchange rates between the related currencies* are a desired macroeconomic goal. If this goal is achieved, the uncertainty associated with economic activities between nations/regions could be reduced, hence facilitating more economic activity.

For the management personnel and leaders of any business firm, including those in the hospitality industry, a good understanding of these four macroeconomic goals in an economy and the related insights as reported is necessary for effective decision-making processes.

Measurements of macroeconomic performance

To reflect the performance of their economy, governments usually construct and release measurements based on the four mentioned macroeconomic goals. These measurements and their changes over time provide essential information for investors and firms, and even consumers to make decisions in the markets. Despite the fact that different economies may apply their own rules and methods of calculation when producing the measurements, they share some common aspects that allow comparisons to be made even across different regions and periods of time.

Four measurements of macroeconomic performance:

1   Gross national product (GNP), or gross domestic product (GDP)
2   Unemployment rate

3   Inflation rate
4   Foreign exchange rates, or foreign exchange index of a currency

In the following sections, these four measurements are explained in simple terms so that students will be able quickly grasp the most important concepts and principles, which will then be elaborated in later chapters.

Measurement of output and output changes (economic growth)

To measure the growth of an economy, changes in the monetary value of the total outputs in a year (t) as compared to the preceding year ($t-1$) is a generally acceptable indicator. When the measurement is using the *current price* for the considered years (e.g., from year $t-1$ to year t) without accounting for the effect of inflation, this shows the *nominal* growth of an economy.

The *gross national product* (GNP) is defined as the monetary value of the total outputs produced by the residents of an economy (either within the boundaries of the economy or overseas) in a year, while the *gross domestic product* (GDP) is the monetary value of the total outputs produced within the boundaries of an economy (either by its residents or foreign producers). Therefore, in principle:

GNP = GDP
      + Output value by residents of an economy outside the
        boundaries of their economy   (1.1)
      – Output value by producers outside the boundaries of
        their economy.

Let the difference between the second and third terms in (1.1) be defined as the *net property income from abroad* (NPIFA), then

GNP = GDP + NPIFA   (1.2)

To measure the GDP of a particular year, there are three different methods of calculation. First, since the total output value produced within the boundaries of an economy could be represented by the *total expenditures* spent on consumption commodities and capital goods, the sum of the expenditures made by households (consumption expenditures, C), firms (investment expenditures, I), the government (public expenditures on commodities and capital goods, G), plus exports (spending of foreigners on domestic outputs of an economy, X) minus imports (spending of residents on non-domestic outputs, M) provides a generally accepted measure of GDP. This method of calculating the GDP is called the *expenditure approach*. That is,

GDP = C + I + G + (X − M)   (1.3)
or GDP = C + I + G + NX (where NX = net exports)   (1.3*a*)

Since total expenditures spent on outputs on one side of an economy actually comprise the total income received by related participants such as labor and firms on the other side of the economy, the GDP could also be measured by using the *income approach*. Lastly, the GDP may also be measured by using the *output* (or *value-added*) *approach*, which adds up the total value employed (added) by firms throughout their production process to obtain their outputs (e.g., value of labor and raw material inputs).

Based on the above measurements, the growth rate of an economy in nominal terms is:

$$\text{Nominal economic growth rate} = \frac{\text{change in GDP}_t \ (\text{or GNP}_t)}{\text{GDP}_{t-1} \ (\text{or GNP}_{t-1})} \times 100 \quad (1.4)$$

where change in $\text{GDP}_t = \text{GDP}_t - \text{GDP}_{t-1}$.

Due to inflation, the nominal growth rate may exaggerate the increase in the real quantity of outputs of an economy, hence the real level of improvement in its material well-being. To obtain the real GDP (or GNP), its nominal value has to be reduced by using the inflation rate. For example, if the GDP in Year 1 at current prices is \$100 billion and Year 2 at current prices is \$120 billion, and the average price per unit of output increases by 5% (i.e., inflation rate is 5%), then the nominal growth rate of this economy from Year 1 to 2 is (120–100) / 100 = 20%. Taking inflation into consideration, the monetary value of \$120 billion in Year 2 is indeed inflated by 5% as compared to Year 1. Thus, the real GDP in Year 2 as compared to Year 1 is only 120/(1 + 0.05) = \$114 billion, and the real growth rate is thus (114–100) / 100 = 14%. That is,

$$\text{Real economic growth rate} = \frac{\text{change in real GDP}_t \ (\text{or real GNP}_t)}{\text{real GDP}_{t-1} \ (\text{or real GNP}_{t-1})} \times 100 \quad (1.5)$$

Measurement of inflation rate

Every year, thousands of different types of commodities (goods and services) are traded in the various markets of an economy. Between the different years, the quantity of some commodities produced may increase, while others may decrease. Similarly, this also holds true for changes in the price of different commodities. To realize the measurement of real economic growth as expressed in Equation (1.5), a robust estimation of the average change in prices is thus an indispensable move to reveal the overall performance of an economy.

Despite the complications in practice which involve the continuous collection of a wide range of prices of the different commodities in the markets, which could only be done through the formal authorities of a government statistics department, the principle (*weighted average of changes*) behind measuring the changes in price is not difficult to understand. To streamline the explanation, suppose that there are only two goods and the importance (weight) of each good is the same (i.e., the weight is 50% for each good) in an economy.

In Year 1 (which is the *base year* for comparison of changes in price), the unit price of Commodity 1 is \$50 and Commodity 2 is \$80. In Year 2, the price of Commodity 1 increases to \$51 and Commodity 2 to \$82. To calculate the average change in prices, the price level in the base year is calculated as:

$$\text{Price level at the base year} = \frac{50 \times 0.5 + 80 \times 0.5}{50 \times 0.5 + 80 \times 0.5} \times 100 = 100.$$

The price level in Year 2 is:

$$\text{Price level in the succeeding year} = \frac{51 \times 0.5 + 82 \times 0.5}{50 \times 0.5 + 80 \times 0.5} \times 100 = 102.3.$$

Accordingly, the inflation rate in Year 2 as compared to the base year is $(102.3-100)/100 = 2.3\%$.

To generalize this measurement, the price index of the base year (PI_0) is always assigned an index of 100, and the price index of a succeeding year (PI_t) is:

$$PI_t = \frac{\sum_{i=1}^{n} p_i \times w_i}{\sum_{i=1}^{n} p_{i0} \times w_{i0}} \times 100 \tag{1.6}$$

where, $\sum_{i=1}^{n} p_i \times w_i = p_1 w_1 + p_2 w_2 + \ldots + p_n w_n$ (the Greek letter "Σ" or sigma is used to indicate the "sum" of a series of numbers),

p_i = price of commodity i at year t,
w_i = the weight of commodity i,
p_{i0} = price of commodity i in the base year,
w_{i0} = weight of commodity i in the base year (in general, $w_i = w_{i0}$).

In related applications, PI_t is marked as the *GDP deflator*, which is used to deflate (discount) a nominal value to its real term.

$$\text{Real value} = \frac{\text{Nominal value}}{\text{Deflator} / 100} \tag{1.7}$$

For example, if the GDP deflator as announced by the statistics department of the concerned economy is 120 in 2018 and the base year is 2010, then the inflation rate on average from 2010 to 2018 is 20%. If the reported nominal GDP in 2018 is \$120 billion, this means that the real GDP is \$100 billion (i.e., 100 / 1.2) as compared to 2010. If the GDP of this economy in 2010 is \$90 billion, the real growth from 2010 to 2018 is $(100-90)/90 = 11.1\%$, instead of a nominal growth of $(120-90)/90 = 33.3\%$.

This principle for measuring the inflation of an economy can also be applied to a particular group of commodities (e.g., the consumer price index (CPI) for the average price changes of consumer commodities), or a particular industry, like retail or wholesale (i.e., retail price index or wholesale price index), which are essential indicators for the hospitality industry.

Measurement of unemployment rate

To economists, unemployment is defined as a person who is willing and able to work but cannot secure a paid job. In the real world, unemployment is commonly measured by governments in terms of the number of able individuals who have reached legal work age and declare (e.g., by registering at the labor department) that they cannot secure a job. Thus,

$$\text{Unemployment rate} = \frac{\text{Number of unemployed}}{\text{Number of working population}} \times 100. \qquad (1.8)$$

From time to time, there must be some people who are actively looking for a job but registered as unemployed. For example, new school graduates, temporary job seekers owing to job changes for various reasons, the need of some individuals to re-train themselves to accommodate the changing structure of their industry before finding gainful employment again, etc., may always be found in the market. Thus, economists may consider a small percentage (e.g., 3% or 4%) of unemployment as an unavoidable "natural" phenomenon in any economy, which is called the *natural rate*, or *full employment rate of unemployment*. Generally speaking, economists advocate that zero percent unemployment in absolute value is not necessary for an economy, and an unemployment rate below the natural rate further impels an increase in output which may lead to higher rates of inflation, and therefore is not necessarily desirable.

Measurement of foreign exchange rate

International trade and investment are imperative factors of a global economy. Exchange rates between different currencies and their fluctuations in the market play a significant role in facilitating trade and investment among producers, consumers, and investors from different nations and regions. For example, when a hotel brand from England decided to invest in Shanghai, China in 1997, 1 British pound exchanged for 13.6 renminbi, and the brand invested 5 million pounds in exchange for 68 million renminbi for their business in China. After more than a decade of operation, the hotel made a net profit of 5 percent from its investment and decided to terminate the business in 2006 and exchange the renminbi back into pounds for a new investment opportunity in England. Would this hotel have more capital funds when it returned to England in 2006? Unfortunately, the answer is "no" because in 2006, 1 British pound exchanged for 14.9 renminbi. With total capital funds of 71.4 (68 × 1.05) million renminbi in 2006, the hotel could only obtain 4.79 (71.4 / 14.9) million pounds – indeed, there is a loss of 210,000 pounds!

Although the factors that affect the exchange rate between two currencies are beyond the scope of this book, the basic notations that show the purchasing power of one currency in terms of another currency (i.e., the foreign exchange rates) in the market are presented here as an introduction so that students will have the basic ability to understand the related market information. In the market, the foreign exchange rate between two currencies can be measured (or quoted) in two ways.

First measurement (FX_1):   Price of domestic currency in terms of foreign currency

Second measurement (FX_2):   Price of foreign currency in terms of domestic currency

For example, taking the position of a local firm in England, the British pound (GBP) is the domestic currency of this firm, while the US dollar (USD) and Japanese yen (JPY) are the foreign currencies. In the foreign exchange market, the exchange rate of the British pound is commonly quoted as GBP1 = USD1.3, or GBP1 = JPY140. This quotation is based on the measurement of FX_1. Indeed, related measurements can also apply FX_2 or both. For example, in the renowned casino resort destination of Macao, the exchange rate of the Macao dollar (MOP) is commonly quoted as USD1 = MOP8.0 instead of MOP1 = USD0.125, while its exchange with JPY is quoted as MOP1 = JPY13.5 instead of JPY1 = MOP0.074.

It is important to note that under FX_1, an increase in the foreign exchange rate of a (domestic) currency means that its purchasing power increases in the international markets, or vice versa. On the other hand, if the quotation is under FX_2, an increase in the foreign exchange rate of a (domestic) currency means that its purchasing power decreases in the international markets, or vice versa.

Government macroeconomic policies

As stated in the section on microeconomic principles, government intervention in market activities is an undeniable fact. At the macroeconomic level, government influence in the overall performance of an economy is also clearly shown in Equation (1.3) through the component G (government spending). Indeed, a government can implement two types of macroeconomic policies to stabilize the growth of its economy, hence safeguarding the related macroeconomic goals.

Two types of macroeconomic policies implemented by governments:

1   Fiscal policy
2   Monetary policy

In principle, fiscal policy refers to the discretionary adjustment by a government in its level of spending (G) and/or taxation (T) as a means to stabilize macroeconomic performance. For example, when the economy enters into a recession period where economic growth declines and the unemployment rate rises, the government can adopt a *deficit budget* to increase its spending through direct or indirect consumption, investment, employment, etc. which will be more than its fiscal income (e.g., income tax) derived from firms and work groups (i.e., G > T) so that the economic turmoil could be alleviated. In this case, the government may cover the fiscal deficit by draining its surplus from the good years or issuing fiscal debts. In contrast, when the economy is soaring and inflation is too high, the government may do the reverse by implementing a *surplus budget* to reduce its spending and raise income taxes so as to dampen economic activities in the private sectors.

On the other hand, as the legal authority for issuing money in an economy, the government (as represented by its central bank) may intervene in economic activities by altering the quantity of money (i.e., the supply of money in the market) that firms and individuals could utilize to carry out economic exchanges. In addition, the government could also modify the opportunity cost of using money (i.e., the interest rate) by the market participants. In general, an *expansionary monetary policy* to increase the money supply and/or lower the interest rate to stimulate economic activities would be undertaken by a government when the economy spirals downwards. On the contrary, to slow down economic growth during a booming period, a *contractionary monetary policy* with reduced money supply and/or increased interest rate is commonly implemented.

Despite the disputes among economists on the effectiveness of fiscal and monetary policies for addressing macroeconomic issues, these are common policies utilized by governments which have much influence on the performance of various sectors in the economy. Any firm today could hardly make business decisions without taking into consideration these policies.

Money, banking and financial markets

In economics, the primary and essential functions of money are to facilitate market transactions. To achieve this simple but essential task, and extend the functions of money to stimulate aggregate economic activities, banking and the financial markets, like security and foreign exchange markets, provide *intermediate services* between buyers and sellers, as well as borrowers and lenders. Thus, access to monetary and capital fund liquidities for consumers, firms, and investors toward their economic activities is promoted. In practice, these markets convey essential information on the prices of different types of monetary and financial products (e.g., interest rates for different types of deposits in commercial banks or credit from them, or the prices of securities of different companies, etc.) for individuals who want to lend, borrow, or invest. Consequently, as efficiency of transactions between various market participants in an economy is increased, economic growth may be stimulated.

In line with the technological advancements and further expansion of the global economies (under the context of regionalization/globalization) since the last two decades of the 20th century, more monetary and financial resources have been made available for market participants. For example, e-money and online banking have been developed to promote the spending of consumers and fund management of firms. In addition, different forms of venture capital, private equity funds, and financial derivatives allow existing firms to obtain needed financial capital from local or international markets for their business expansions or restructuring, or new firms to join a market more efficiently. Indeed, recent cross-border development of many globally renowned hotel groups or brands are expedited by the availability of new sources of capital funds. To sustain the growth of the hospitality industry, a good understanding and effective application of the different forms of banking services (e.g., online banking) and financial products/services are definitely beneficial to management teams.

Nevertheless, it is worth noting that the rapid expansion of these markets since the last two decades of the 20th century (e.g., rapid expansion of investment banking, hedge funds, etc.), and the widespread popularity of many new financial products (e.g., financial derivatives) which are innovative in theory but complicated and controversial in practice, may outpace the regulatory capacity of most governments to monitor proper operations and the integrity of the related financial activities. Unarguably, the unexpected financial problems that have emerged in a number of nations since the end of the 20th century have not only led to longstanding economic dilemmas of the related economies, but also produced domino effects at the regional and global levels. For example, the financial crisis which unfolded in Thailand in 1997 and its rapid spread to the other East Asian economies in 1997/1998, and the sub-prime crisis of the mortgage market in the United States in 2008 along with the global financial tsunami that was triggered afterwards in 2008/2009 respectively are undeniable related evidence (many studies on these two incidents can be found in both printed and web sources).

In sum, a good understanding of the aforementioned macroeconomic principles will not only allow management teams of hospitality firms to gain insights into the economic environment to make their business decisions, but are also worthwhile for evaluating the opportunities and threats that may be associated with the existing performance and prospects of their businesses. Nevertheless, as the economic structure, stages of economic development, public interest, legal system, etc. all differ across the different economic societies, the practices of the hospitality industry as a service-based economic sector may not necessarily be identical although the characteristics and principles of their businesses are the same. This attribute of the hospitality industry will be elucidated in the following chapters.

Scope of book

As an introduction to the economics principles for examining the hospitality industry, this book is not a traditional textbook which comprehensively covers topics in microeconomics and macroeconomics. If students wish to cross-check the related principles through further reading, they can simply refer to any standard textbook at the introductory level, such as Parkin (2016), Schiller and Gebhardt (2019), and Stiglitz and Walsh (2006). It is worth noting that in this book, the essential principles of economics are presented and illustrated, in order to serve as useful references and provide guidance to help students and practitioners in their work in the hospitality industry.

In considering the objectives that have been established for this book, facts and key factors associated with the evolution, practices, and progression of the hospitality industry in Western and Southern Europe, North America, and East Asia are first discussed in Chapter 2. In addition, the interrelationship between the progression of hospitality and economic performance, as well as the dynamics of the modern development of this industry are revealed. This chapter will also give students the chance to preview the information that will be introduced and discussed in the later chapters.

The related microeconomic principles that are used to explore the market behavior of consumers (demand) and producers/firms (supply) and their interactions under different circumstances are presented in Chapters 3 and 4, respectively. Factors that lead to changes in the behavior of market participants, and their influence on consumption and production decisions in the markets are also examined. Besides, the important concept of elasticity and various forms of elasticity in economic analyses are given an introduction. Then, the economic rationales of applying price elasticity in revenue management and showing the consequences of expenditure taxes imposed by a government, as well as various forms of pricing strategies like price differentiation, bundled pricing and break-even pricing, are clarified with reference to the practices of the hospitality industry. In Chapter 4, various forms of the cost of production and their roles/functions in business decisions are identified and discussed as well.

A discussion on the composition of the macroeconomic environment and business cycle which are highly interactive with firm performance in the markets is provided in Chapter 5. To stabilize the macroeconomic environment, a common practice of governments is to implement a fiscal policy (mainly carried out through government spending and taxation) based on the changes in the aggregate performance of their economies. Thus, the economic arguments for implementing a fiscal policy and its implications on business decisions are presented and highlighted. Besides, the connotations of regionalization and globalization to the macroeconomic environment of the world economies and the implications for the hospitality industry are also highlighted.

Since money and banking are indispensable intermediaries that facilitate modern industrial growth and development, the characteristics and advancement of the monetary and banking systems are closely examined in Chapter 6. Much like the discussions on fiscal policy in Chapter 5, the economic rationales and business implications of a monetary policy that is implemented by the central bank of a nation to adjust the market interest rate and modify reserve requirements in the banking system, and change its open market operations, are examined. In addition, the rapid progress of e-money and online banking apps since the 2000s, and the related economic importance to market practices in general and the hospitality industry in particular are presented.

In Chapter 7, the economic notions of technology, and its progression and changing recognitions in economic and business studies are explained. In addition, economic insights around innovation, and its interrelationship with and differences from technological advancement are emphasized. The recent advancements of cruise lines (such as "floating" hotel resorts) are elaborated to illustrate the importance of innovation in the hospitality industry in the 21st century. Indeed, the economic innovativeness of cruise lines in the hospitality industry (e.g., the increasing importance placed on technology for organizing purposes, the cost of production, and product differentiation) may enlighten other sectors in the industry to learn from their innovativeness and secure their own competitiveness and continual growth.

The rapid growth and development of the hospitality industry since the mid-20th century mean that its practices have indeed greatly contributed to the consumption of limited resources on Earth. On top of the longstanding negative impacts of the secondary industries like energy and manufacturing, the practices of the hospitality industry have undoubtedly further deteriorated the environment and ecosystem both directly and indirectly. In the face of global concerns, the concept and importance of sustainable development as compared and contrasted to economic growth and development are elaborated in Chapter 8. Common efforts of the hospitality industry (and future efforts) and the challenges that they face to ensure their sustainable development are elucidated. In addition, the ongoing efforts and the primary areas that need to be addressed by this industry are discussed.

Did you know?...

Before moving on to Chapter 2 and the remaining chapters of this book, please see Box 1.1 below to determine if you are able to apply the knowledge presented in this chapter as a means for understanding some of the real world situations.

Box 1.1 Contribution of the hospitality industry to the UK economy

As commissioned by the British Hospitality Association, Oxford Economics conducts detailed research work and has provided a series of reports since 2010 on the contribution of the hospitality industry in the UK to its economy. In the 2010 report, it is estimated that the "total number in employment through the British hospitality economy" would increase from 2.44 million in 2010 to 2.76 million in 2015 (British Hospitality Association, 2010: 2). In the 2015 report, they indicated that the total number of employment positions in this industry had reached 2.919 million in 2014 (Oxford Economics, 2015: 25).

It was also pointed out that indirect and induced employment generated from the hospitality industry to other local economic sectors was 1.717 million. For example, to meet the demand of the hospitality firms for goods and services as inputs of their businesses, employment opportunities were made available by related local suppliers (i.e., indirect employment). On the other hand, employees of the hospitality industry will spend a part of their income on locally produced commodities which create jobs that are consequently offered by the related producers (i.e., induced employment).

When assessing the potential economic contributions of the UK hospitality industry to the UK economy between 2015 and 2020, the 2015 report stated that "proactive and supportive government intervention leads to stronger visitor growth than would otherwise have occurred" (Oxford Economics, 2015: 26).

Discussion questions:

1   By referring to the above information and using Equation (1.3), discuss how and in what ways the UK hospitality industry had influenced the economic growth of the nation between 2010 and 2014.
2   What kinds of "proactive and supportive government intervention(s)" in practice could lead to "stronger visitor growth" in the UK (or in the economy of your home country)?
3   Other than employment, what other ways could the hospitality industry contribute to the UK economy?

Conclusions and remarks

As a global industry which significantly contributes to the domestic output of an economy, employment, investment and business opportunities, etc., effective management of the hospitality industry is vital to allow interest groups to gain from the related economic benefits and ensure the sustainable growth of this industry. For this purpose, economics provides relevant and robust grounds to managers and leaders in this industry to better understand the markets (their consumers, competitors, and their own firm), in order to evaluate their business performance, and assess the changing opportunities and threats from the external environment on the practices and growth of their business, hence making effective and proactive business decisions in a dynamic world.

Yet, it is also important to emphasize that economic principles may not necessarily inform practitioners on how they should operate their everyday business, or promote or package their services, etc. In other words, one should not expect this to be a book about business management or marketing for the hospitality industry. Instead, this is an essential textbook (or reference source) for management teams to gain a concrete understanding of the characteristics and practices of their business, hence to address the changing business environment and make effective decisions so that they can amend business routines, and ensure that they continue to maintain a competitive edge over other firms. To the academics, interpretations of certain economic principles in the context of the hospitality industry could be seen as controversial, but keep an open mind: there is always room for another perspective in the economics literature for furthering related studies in the service economics.

References and further reading

British Hospitality Association, November 2010. Creating jobs in Britain – A hospitality economy proposition. Available http://dip9shwvohtcn.cloudfront.net/wordpress/wp-content/uploads/2013/08/BHA-Economic-Report-Nov2010FINAL.pdf

British Hospitality Association, October 2011. Hospitality: driving local economy. Available https://dip9shwvohtcn.cloudfront.net/wordpress/wp-content/uploads/2013/08/ENGLAND-HOSPITALITY-DRIVING-LOCAL-ECONOMIES-REPORT-FINAL-OCT-11.pdf

Ernst & Young, 2016. Global Hospitality Insights: Top 10 thoughts for 2016. Available www.hospitalitynet.org/file/152006075.pdf

Friedman, M., 2002. *Capitalism and Freedom*, 40th anniversary edition. University of Chicago Press, Ltd., Chicago, IL, USA.

Fuchs, V.R., 1965. The growing importance of the service industry. *Journal of Business*, 38 (4), 344–373.

Hill, T.P., 1977. On goods and services. *Review of Income and Wealth*, 23 (4), 315–422.

Jansson, J.O., 2006. *The Economics of Services: Development and Policy*. Edward Elgar, Northampton, UK.

Jean, G., Faiz, G., 1998. The provider–customer interface in business and professional services. *The Service Industries Journal*, 18 (2), 1–15.

Langford, G., Weissenberg, A., 2018. 2018 travel and hospitality industry outlook. Deloitte Development LLC, Oakland, USA. Available https://

www2.deloitte.com/content/dam/Deloitte/us/Documents/consumer-business/us-cb-2018-travel-hospitality-industry-outlook.pdf

McNeilly, M.R., 2012. *Sun Tzu and the Art of Business: Six Strategic Principles for Managers*, revised edition. Oxford University Press, New York, USA.

Oxford Economics, September 2015. The economic contribution of the UK hospitality industry. The British Hospitality Association, Oxford, UK. Available www.bha.org.uk/wordpress/wp-content/uploads/2015/09/Economic-contribution-of-the-UK-hospitality-industry.pdf

Parkin, M., 2016. *Microeconomics*, 12th edition. Pearson Education Limited, Harlow, UK.

Qu, R., Ennew, C.T., Sinclair, M.T., 2005. The impact of regulation and ownership structure on market orientation in the tourism industry in China. *Tourism Management*, 26 (6), 939–950.

Schiller, B.R., Gebhardt, K., 2019. *The Economy Today*, 15th edition. McGraw-Hill Education, New York, USA.

SelectUSA, 2016. The travel, tourism and hospitality industry in the United States. Available www.selectusa.gov/travel-tourism-and-hospitality-industry-united-states

Smith, A., 1998. *An Inquiry into the Characteristics and Causes of the Wealth of Nations*, A Select Edition. Oxford University Press, Oxford, UK.

Soeg Jobs, 2016. Background of the hospitality industry. Available www.soegjobs.com/2016/09/15/hospitality-industry-historical-background

Stiglitz, J.E., Walsh, C.E., 2006. *Principles of Macroeconomics*, 4th edition. Norton & Company, London, UK.

Sutter, T., Sauvage, E., Bost, C.E., Laroche, O. 2013. Seizing advantage in hospitality's new frontier. A.T. Kearney, Inc. Available www.atkearney.at/documents/10192/2969082/Seizing+Advantage+in+Hospitalitys+New+Frontier.pdf

2 Hospitality industry in the world economies

Objectives and learning outcomes

A good understanding and grasp of the historical forces that have contributed to the evolution and modern development of hospitality businesses may enhance the overall knowledge of management teams and hospitality sector leaders about this industry, and hence their decision-making process. For this purpose, this chapter will familiarize students with the forces that have driven the evolution of the hospitality industry, and the factors that contribute to the modern development of this industry worldwide. In particular, historical evidence from Western and Southern Europe (hereinafter "Western Europe" unless specified otherwise), North America (including the United States of America and Canada), and East Asia (including Northeast and Southeast Asia) is summarized and analyzed. Thereby, students will gain insights into the differences in the paths of development and performance of the hospitality industry worldwide across different eras and economies.

Besides, factors that promote the rapid growth and business innovations of this industry since the mid-20th century are elucidated so that students will understand the dynamics and changing attributes of the modern development of the hospitality industry, as well as its interactive relationship with other sectors in related industries. Indeed, the historical evidence which is summarized and discussed in detail in this chapter will provide a comprehensive knowledge foundation for practitioners to better assess the opportunities and threats associated with their business in a highly dynamic environment in the 21st century.

After reading this chapter, students will:

- understand the origins of the hospitality industry and its evolution into an organized sector in the early periods;
- be able to compare and contrast the different paths of development of the hospitality industry in various world economies;
- understand how the progression of industrialization has brought about the dawn of and rise in mass societies in the world economies;

- be able to recognize the essential role of an expanding mass society to the modern and large-scale development of the hospitality industry;
- be able to recognize how the modernization of an economic society further boosts and stimulates the growth of the hospitality industry;
- understand the interrelationship between business innovation and growth in market size for the hospitality industry;
- understand how the hospitality industry may develop interactively with other industry sectors in parallel, hence contributing to overall growth in the world economies; and
- have a better understanding of the primary uncertainties that may inhibit the growth and performance of the hospitality industry.

A snapshot from history

In respect of the historical and societal developments of the hospitality industry, hospitality as an organized business and economic industry first emerged in Western Europe (primarily in Greece, Italy, France, the United Kingdom, and the Netherlands). Indeed, progression of this industry from the 13th century onward could be viewed as the result of the evolution of capitalism. Then, technological advancements and the dawn of a mass society (increasing incomes and improved living conditions of the mass workers) from the last quarter of the 19th century facilitated the modern development of the hospitality industry. Unfortunately, war and economic chaos in the first half of the 20th century stunted the progress that should have continued in Western Europe.

Following the tide of migration from Europe to North America in the second half of the 19th century, and widespread technological and business innovations which led to the rapid growth of the US economy since the turn of the 20th century, the world economic leadership was gradually transferred from Western Europe to North America (or in particular, from the UK to the USA). Subsequently, the development of the hospitality industry further ensued in a new continent, and advanced as the most dynamic market in the world in the second half of the 20th century.

On the other side of the world, the development of hospitality as an industry in nations/regions in Asia only emerged after World War II (WWII) because Asia lagged behind the social, political, and economic progress of Western Europe and North America prior to the mid-20th century (except for Japan as its modern development commenced in the mid-19th century). Despite that, family-operated and small-scale inns and eateries were found in some of the Asian regions in the earlier periods, they were haphazardly set up. Nevertheless, the rapid development of the Asian economies from the 1950s onwards, and the booming economy in Mainland China since the 1980s have generated the impetus for the flourishing of the hospitality industry in East

Asia. In the 21st century, the evident performance and continuous growth of the hospitality industry in East Asia have obviously gained the attention of the world.

Evolution and modern development of hospitality industry in Western Europe

Often highlighted in the related literature on the origins of the hospitality industry is the word "hospitality", which originated from the French word "hospice" and means "taking care of the travelers" (Global Hospitality Portal, 2016). Generally speaking, in the early periods between ancient Greece at around 40 BC and the Middle Ages from the 5th to the 15th century, hospitality services were provided to those who had to travel away from home for religious, political, military, or business activities (ibid.). In other words, hospitality services in the early ages were coordinated and provided to those who were largely mandated to travel, or traveled for some formal and necessary purpose rather than traveling for leisure.

Hospitality as a formal business with the emergence of capitalism

Owing to the emergence of merchant capitalism (Guy, 1984), which was the earliest form of capitalism in Western Europe around the 12th century, demand for hospitable lodgings, food and beverage, and related services by merchants during their business travels led to the evolution of hospitality as a formal and organized business. For example, according to an online article (posted by Alassaf, 2016), inns were established in the 1280s in Italy and then Rome as a formal business to meet the demands of the growing number of merchants. Indeed, related establishments could be considered as the prototype of the modern-day hospitality industry, which continued to expand into other European nations like the UK and France between the 16th and 18th centuries. In addition to venues that provided lodgings and food, "coffee-houses became extremely popular in Europe and were incorporated into many of the inns" in the 18th century (ibid.).

Nevertheless, prior to the last quarter of the 19th century, the hospitality business remained privy to a small group of upper-class individuals and merchants who had the purchasing power to use these services. As for the general community, very few were privileged to enjoy these services as income was low and work hours were long. For example, although the Industrial Revolution started in the UK in the mid-18th century and significantly increased productivity, and hence their national macroeconomic growth, which was also the case for some of the other Western European countries in the following century, the income and living conditions of the workers deteriorated (e.g., long work hours, poor work environment, and low pay).

Growth from evolution of mass society

Along with the continuous and interactive progression of science and technology in Western Europe and North America, the second Industrial Revolution at the end of the third quarter of the 19th century to 1914 (marked as the outbreak of World War I (WWI)) led to crucial advancements in production methods and accelerated industrial innovations. The second Industrial Revolution can be largely differentiated from the first Industrial Revolution in terms of inventions that offered much more efficiency in energy as well as production methods that used electric power, new types of materials, and communication technology (see, e.g., Mokyr, 1999). In addition to further increases in productivity, a major transformation took place in economic society so that "living standards and the purchasing power of money increased rapidly, as the new technologies reaches like never before into the daily lives of the middle and working classes" (ibid.).

Parallel to the emergence and spread of the *mass society* (Spielvogel, 2012) – the middle class – a new era in the modern development of the hospitality industry began, which served the increasing demand for *mass leisure* at the end of the 19th century (Spielvogel, 2012; Larrabee and Meyersohn, 1958). In addition, the evolving "industrial system – evening hours after work, weekends" (Spielvogel, 2012: 700), in which mass workers had the discretion of spending some of their time to acquire hospitable services, such as leisure, instituted a new culture in society. For example, pubs, bars, and amusement parks were expanding to meet the increasing demand for leisure by mass workers. Another contributing factor, and probably a key point that led to the growth of the hospitality industry, was the changing leisure culture of society for tourism, especially short trips that lasted one or two days over the weekend, or regular holidays at the turn of the 20th century, which were evidently different in terms of the characteristics of "travelers" in ancient Greece and medieval times.

Modern development in the mid-20th century

Despite the beneficial advances of the hospitality industry at the turn of the 20th century, its growth in Western Europe stagnated from the mid-1910s to the mid-1940s. While the economic difficulties experienced by the European nations in the decade following WWI (e.g., increased inflation and unemployment, and declines in real economic growth) prevented the initial advancement of society, the global Great Depression in the 1930s, then the outbreak of war again in Europe in 1939 hit the European economies hard, and hence negatively impacted the growth of their hospitality industry.

To rebuild European societies and economies through cooperative efforts among nations and avoid political conflicts; that is, future wars, six European nations (France, Italy, West Germany, Belgium, the Netherlands, and

Luxembourg) formed the European Coal and Steel Community (ECSC) in 1951 under the Treaty of Paris. In considering the initial success of the ECSC, these nations furthered their economic cooperation by establishing the European Economic Community (EEC) under the Treaty of Rome which was signed in 1957. Apart from the various contentions that followed the progression and expansion of the EEC (e.g. increasing number of member states), thereafter, the modern development of Europe in the mid-20th century generated real and noteworthy efforts that revitalized the growth of the hospitality industry.

For example, although the UK government passed the Holidays with Pay Act in 1938 as a measure to ensure that millions of workers would be entitled to paid holidays, their real income did not increase due to the social and economic problems that took place between the end of the 1930s and the mid-1940s. Thus, the willingness and ability of the mass workers to spend on leisure and hospitality services were indeed limited. After WWII, the real income of workers increased while the number of work hours fell. This phenomenon heralded in a new culture of leisure that eventually evolved and expanded to provide new business opportunities in the hospitality industry which led to its further development and expansion. In particular, the working or middle class embarked on holiday camps with their family during holidays in the coastal areas of England which contributed to the development of seaside resorts in the UK, such as Warners on Hayling Island founded by Harry Warner in 1931 and later, Warner's protégé, Billy Butlin launched his first camp in Lincolnshire in 1936. As Dawson (2007: 280) has noted, these two seaside resorts "gained national recognition through advertising and their ability to accommodate thousands of campers each week of the holiday season". In addition, a renowned chain of tea shops and restaurants, Lyons, also took the opportunity to expand their business conglomerate to hotels in response to the increasing demand for leisure (see, e.g., McCracken, 2005).

In the 1960s, the growth of the hospitality industry in Europe on the one hand benefited from the expansion of the mass society due to increasing income and reduced annual work hours of workers. On the other hand, more regional economic cooperation among the member states of the European Community in infrastructure development and trade facilitated increased flow in population and capital in the region as a whole. Thus, in addition to the increasing demand from the mass workers for leisure and non-leisure services, growth in domestic and cross-border tourism all together contributed to the rapid growth of the hospitality industry in the second half of the 20th century. For example, Jones (1986) discusses the progression of the leisure industry in the UK after WWII due to the expanding business opportunities resultant of the changing "working-class culture" for leisure and tourism in the hospitality industry in terms of their desire for hotels, night clubs, and restaurants.

Other than hotels, restaurants, coffee shops, bars, and pubs, amusement parks with various themes and features also became popular and spread throughout Western Europe in the 1970s. For example, the Leolandia which opened in Italy in 1971, Popeye Village in Malta in 1980, and Paultons Park, Alton Towers, and The Milky Way Adventure Park in the UK in the 1980s, are some of the more well-known parks where European families spent their weekends and holidays. In addition, the opening of related theme parks under the worldwide trademark of Legoland in Denmark in 1968 and England in 1996 also contributed to the modern development of the hospitality industry in Europe. Obviously, related establishments increased the scale and scope of this industry as compared to the pre-WWII period in Europe. Besides, expansion of the hospitality business in various forms primarily as the result of the increased demand for mass leisure in the second half of the 20th century produced a dynamic environment for interactive development between the various associated sectors in this industry.

Same principles with progressive changes in North America

The mass migration from Europe to North America in the 19th century not only involved the transfer of culture and business to a new land full of hope for new endeavors, but most importantly, transported capital goods and production methods derived from a long process of technological innovation in Europe for application and further business opportunities in North America. In addition, the increase in trade between North America and Western Europe in the last quarter of the 19th century, and rapid growth of business activities and productivity in North America altogether brought about remarkable opportunities for the development of the hospitality industry.

Despite that the principle of this industry is to provide hospitable services to travelers when they are away from home, its organization and practices underwent innovative and progressive changes in North America in the 20th century. For example, the development of hotel resorts (including casino resorts) in addition to the conventional offering of inns and hotels (and gaming venues) and large-scale theme parks, as well as integration of hospitality with different forms of catering and entertainment as a leisure package to the expanding mass society all led to a new chapter in this industry.

Dynamics in early stages

In comparison to its historical development in Western Europe, the development of the hospitality industry in North America was largely influenced by business travel rather than religious or political activities in the first place. The growing market for mass leisure as a result of rapid and continuous increases in productivity in the domestic economy also contributed to the dynamics of the advancement of this industry. Following the increase in trade volume with Western Europe, and related business activities between the east and west coasts and the inland, business travelers in North America not only demanded traditional lodgings and food services, but also larger-scale entertainment events and leisure activities to strike a balance between their physical and mental health, or make use of their free time between different trips. All these activities offered considerable business opportunities toward the modern development of the hospitality industry.

Besides, economic development in North America (in particular, the USA and parts of Canada) in the 1920s and 1930s progressed smoothly because North America was an independent power during the WWI period, and had a primary role of supplying war-time materials and funds to related European nations for the war. After the war, it was estimated that the "United States received about $1 billion on war debt account between mid-1926 and mid-1931" (Eichengreen, 1992: 224). Thus, since North America was not directly affected by the war in its homeland and benefited from related business for the war, the income and wealth of North American firms and the mass society increased notably. Similar to the experiences in Europe at the end of the 19th century, a direct consequence of the expansion of the mass society in North America was the increase in demand for mass leisure, which included individual travel (tourism) and dining for leisure purposes. As Markert (1993: 1076) has said: "Mass leisure has its roots in the mass production of goods that began in the 1920's [sic] in the United States." In contrast to the path of development of Europe, that of mass leisure in North America in its early stages was largely stimulated by the development of its roadway system and automobile population (Soule, 1957; Jakle and Sculle, 2009), which obviously increased the ability of the general public to reach out and enjoy the related hospitality services.

As the conventional and also the largest sector in the hospitality industry, hotels in the USA developed rapidly. For example, state-wide or nation-wide hotel chains expanded rapidly from three in 1896 to 25 in 1918 and then to over 500 in 1996 (Ingram, 2001). Among the best-known multinational hotel chains today, many were founded between the 1910s and the 1930s (e.g., Hilton in 1919 and the Marriott in 1927). Indeed, the development of the hotel industry produced positive effects which further contributed to mass society in terms of better-paying jobs in local communities, hence facilitating their purchasing power and desire for hospitality services, which, in turn, sustained the related businesses in the industry.

Nevertheless, the progression of the hospitality industry in North America was not without difficulty. The industry was hit hard by the Great Depression in the 1930s which had negative impacts on income and wealth, and thus affected demand for business travel and individual leisure. After a rapid period of growth from the 1910s to the 1930s, a substantial number of hotel rooms were available in the market. It was estimated that there were "some 25,900 hotels in the United States in 1928 ... [which] contained more than 1,525,000 guest rooms" (Williamson 1930, cited in Jakle and Sculle, 2009: 4). Thus, a decade-long slump in the local and world economies significantly hindered the growth of the hospitality industry. For example, "Hilton suffered massive losses during the Great Depression and narrowly avoided bankruptcy" (Terzeon, 2014). Aside from the extensive bankruptcy of various hotels in the USA, the situation in Canada was no different, in that "occupancy levels dropped from 71 per cent in 1928 to 50 per cent in 1932" (Kostuch Media, 2013).

Revitalization and progressive changes after WWII

Although Europe and Asia suffered massive losses in WWII, the USA itself was not directly under attack (except for the Pearl Harbor naval base, which was destroyed by Japan's raid at the end of 1941). Besides, by assuming a similar role as that in WWI – that is, the USA was a supplier of war materials to the Allies, and then providing funds for the post-war reconstruction of the involved nations – the USA affirmed itself as a leader in the world economy after WWII. Despite a reported brief recession in 1946 (around -10% of the real GDP growth) due to significant reductions in government spending on military products, and hence output from the related industries, private-sector businesses recovered and expanded rapidly after the Great Depression. Indeed, the US economy entered a long-term growth period in the 1950s and the 1960s, except for a few short (less than a year) recessions which were considered as part of the business cycle.

Revitalization of the US economy in the post-WWII period also generated new opportunities for the further development of the hospitality industry. In addition, continuous improvements in the national infrastructure system (especially the inter-state highway system and inland airports) and accelerated urbanization made many new desires (demand) real for the hospitality industry. For example, short trips during weekends and public holidays undertaken by the mass workers translated into considerable spending power which motivated the launch of motels and restaurants along thousands of major highway exits and airports throughout the USA (as well as Canada). Besides, fast-food franchises like McDonald's also flourished, although they were largely intended to provide "grab and go" food, with minimal hospitality services (and might not necessarily be even considered as part of the hospitality industry), unlike the tea shops and restaurants.

As the business sector and the mass society continuously expanded in parallel, the make-up of the hospitality industry experienced a stage of progressive changes and innovative developments. For example, the Walt Disney theme park, Disneyland, which opened in California in 1955, and then in Florida in 1971, represented an innovative landmark development in the hospitality industry. In contrast to the set-up of traditional amusement parks in Europe and North America during that time, all-inclusive large-scale accommodations, food services, entertainment, and leisure services based on a unique theme were installed by Disney in a single venue for family leisure. In addition, technology was also widely applied to enhance the experience of the visitors, thereby adding value to the business. Actually, Disneyland created a new mass leisure culture in American society, which further promoted the many facets of the hospitality industry.

Another landmark development in the hospitality industry is the innovative integration of casino gaming and destination resort for everyone in the adult community, from the rich to the working class and business travelers as well. The successful reorganization of Las Vegas from Sin City to a renowned casino resort destination in the 1970s, and the expansion of casino resorts across many other states in the USA and Canada from the end of the 1980s contributed significantly to the hospitality industry and its growth in North America. On the one hand, the concept of a casino resort (or mega-casino resort) was derived to sustain business turnovers and the long-term growth of large-scale and all-inclusive hospitality properties through the profits from casino gaming. On the other hand, the aim of the facilities was to provide the opportunity for the community to spend their holidays in a colorful destination where memorable entertainment and leisure services could be enjoyed. As shown in Illustration 2.1, visitors to Las Vegas can enjoy water activities in the desert, replicas of renowned attractions both in the USA and around the world (like the Arc de Triomphe in Paris), and the excitement of gaming. It is evident that the development of casino resorts in North America can be likened to the progressive rebirth of Monte Carlo in Monaco in Europe.

Illustration 2.1 Innovative development of Las Vegas as a casino resort destination

From monotony to excitement in East Asia

Historically, simple taverns which provided lodging, food, tea, and wine services were first found in some of the cities in various dynasties of ancient China (a simple Chinese tavern is shown in Illustration 2.2 – serving food on the ground floor and providing rooms for lodging upstairs). For example, following the emergence of the "merchant class" and marketplaces in the "commercial streets of cities" in the Warring States Period (around 481 BC to 403 BC), "shops selling jewellery … as well as taverns and gambling houses") were established (WorldHistory.Biz, 2015). However, China was a feudal society until the beginning of the 20th century (China's last dynasty, the Qing Dynasty, ended in 1912), and the emphasis for thousands of years was on agricultural production (the merchant class was only a small group

Illustration 2.2 A simple tavern in ancient China (the four Chinese characters mean "Lucky Tavern")

Source: Tochi Leung

over time), so that taverns remained simple and there was little change prior to the 20th century. Aside from some individual inns and hotels which were initiated by the Europeans in parallel with the expansion of their business ventures in Asia in the mid-19th century (e.g., the first "western" hotel – Richards' Hotel and Restaurant, was established by a Scottish merchant called Peter Richards in 1846 in Shanghai, China; see Wikipedia, 2017), the modern development of the hospitality industry in Asia, especially as a business sector which was organized for the masses only emerged in the mid-20th century.

Other than the simple taverns found in ancient China and some of its neighboring regions, another early form of lodging which provided lodging services to travelers was the ryokan in Japan (see Japan Ryokan & Hotel Association, n.d.). Indeed, Japanese ryokans were commonly referred to as part of the nation's culture, which evolved as "free rest houses" offered by groups of individuals such as the "Buddhist monks" to travelers in the 8th century. Related lodgings then transformed into small-scale "cheap inns" which offered only accommodations but no meals in the 12th century. Following the development of a "money economy" and the expansion of the merchant class in the 17th century, ryokans formally started to provide hospitable accommodation services including meals and the use of hot springs to the upper-middle- and upper-class travelers (ibid.). After WWII, as domestic tourism and leisure activities were promoted by the Japanese government as a measure to stimulate economic growth in Japan (Kaven, 1992), ryokans expanded notably at a larger scale and were designed in a modern style.

Although the modern development of the hospitality industry in Asia lagged behind that in Western Europe and North America, the rapid economic growth in East Asia post-WWII has impressed the world. Indeed, the development of the economy of Japan, the Four Little Dragons (Hong Kong, Taiwan, Singapore, and South Korea) and the Four Little Tigers (the Philippines, Thailand, Malaysia, and Indonesia) from the mid-1950s onward have not only led to the "Asian economic miracle", but also provided the economic conditions for the modern and rapid development of their hospitality industry.

Driving forces

After WWII, the East Asian economies entered a period of boom (except for Mainland China until the start of the 1980s), largely due to:

1   the involvement of the US government and American firms with political and economic developments in Japan, Taiwan, South Korea, and the Philippines;
2   the extended traditions of the British government and British firms in pursuing their business interests in Hong Kong, Singapore, and Malaysia;

3   the dynamic interactions between foreign and local parties to pursue eco-
     nomic interests which generated significant positive effects back into the
     related economies.

As social communication and business volume with the outside world
increased, and the income/wealth of the mass society also increased as a result
of rapid economic growth, the modern development of the hospitality industry in East Asia underwent rapid expansion, mimicking the characteristics of
the "West" (including Western Europe and North America).

The hotel industry of two of the world's most open economies, Hong Kong
and Singapore, is largely western in nature due to modern development.
Although some of the more renowned local brands like Shangri-La Hotels
and Resorts were established in the 1960s and expanded during the 1970s,
the design of the related properties and business operations was fundamentally acquired from western inspirations. In addition, western style restaurants,
bars and pubs opened over time to meet the increasing demand from Westerners who visited and worked there, and pursued related business opportunities offered by the changing culture and desire of local people (especially the
increasing working-class population, who were becoming better educated) to
enjoy modern hospitality services as part of their leisure activities. For example,
the development of Lan Kwai Fong, a well-known bar and restaurant street in
Hong Kong, and various seafood restaurants that cropped up along Long Beach
on the east coast of Singapore are two of the many typical examples in East Asia.

Another interesting westernization phenomenon of the hospitality industry in Asia is "McDonaldization". Although takeaway or self-serve fast-food
restaurants may not be formally considered as a sector of the hospitality industry, the expansion of McDonald's in East Asia is not solely a "takeaway" business; instead, some of the customers are paying for hospitable services, such
as birthday parties for their children, or special gatherings of youth groups
(Illustration 2.3 shows a banner posted by a McDonald's in Hong Kong when
it organized a birthday party for one of its customers). Thus, it is evident
that with different cultures and social contexts, increase in the population
and spending power of the masses in different societies may indeed produce
new opportunities that enrich the business context of the modern hospitality
industry.

Continuous driving forces

Through westernization (and imitation), the development of the hospitality
industry in East Asia in the 1950s accelerated as compared to its evolution in
the western societies. Specifically, business environment and technology were
ripe for the modern development of this industry. Thus, much of the time that
would have been spent on technological innovation and business development
was saved, which allowed the industry to rapidly transform from the traditional to a modern mode.

Illustration 2.3 A birthday party banner posted by a McDonald's in Hong Kong

Nevertheless, westernization by itself was not sufficient to sustain the long-term growth and continuous development of the hospitality industry in East Asia. Indeed, several forces were interacting in parallel in the last quarter of the 20th century, which further facilitated and stimulated its growth. First, rapid economic growth over a period of two decades starting from the post-WWII period positioned domestic and inter-regional tourism activities as a new leisure culture among the mass workers. Other than the aforementioned tourism growth in Japan as part of the national strategy to stimulate domestic consumption, the development of tourism was also facilitated by related public and private interests in other East Asian countries/regions as new forces to sustain economic growth and boost foreign exchange from inbound tourists. Subsequently, new hospitality facilities packaged with the unique attributes of a region or a nation (e.g., attractions of the "Orient" or Asian sceneries and architecture), as well as theme parks with new features, were established over time. For example, the launch of well-known hospitality brands like the first hotel resort in Genting Highlands in Malaysia in 1971, Everland in South Korea in 1976, Ocean Park in Hong Kong in 1977, Leofoo Village Theme Park in Taiwan in 1979, and Tokyo Disneyland in Japan in 1983, all represent landmarks of the development of the hospitality industry in East Asia.

In the 1980s, the market vitality and capacity of the hospitality industry were further enhanced and increased as a result of the success of the Chinese government in reforming and opening up the Mainland Chinese economy in 1978. For example, according to various sources, the number of hotels (all stars) in Mainland China significantly increased from 137 in 1978 to 710 in 1985, then to 7,035 in 1999, and almost 19,000 in 2015. Owing to the great success of economic reform and development, the spending of Mainland

Chinese tourists in various forms of hospitality services has caused excitement among domestic and foreign hospitality firms, both inside and outside Mainland China. Aside from hotels, other sectors of the hospitality industry also experienced rapid growth in Mainland China in the last decade of the 20th century, which was undoubtedly significant enough to sustain the overall prosperity of the industry in East Asia. Indeed, another milestone was the opening of two additional Disneylands in East Asia; one in Hong Kong in 2005 and the other in Shanghai in 2016, so that including Japan there are three Disneyland theme parks, as compared to only two in North America and one in Western Europe.

Last but not least, in considering the various uncertainties that have limited the prospects of western societies and their economies in the 21st century, it is commonly anticipated that East Asia will dominate any further growth and development of the hospitality industry. This is also expected to extend to Central Asia, with India as another economic power that is emerging in the global community.

Summary of development of world economies and hospitality industry

The discussed evidence and facts in the context of Western Europe, North America, and East Asia in this chapter evidently show that the evolution of the hospitality industry as an organized business and modern industrial sector is indeed a reflection (and a consequence) of the modern development of an economy. Due to differences in historical, societal, and economic contexts, the relationship between the rate of economic development and the progression of the hospitality industry across different regions in the world would not be the same and hardly quantifiable. Nevertheless, the role of the hospitality industry in general and its relationship with the development of the world economies in some of the key stages are depicted in Figure 2.1.

In Figure 2.1, the term "industrialized economic society" does not simply refer to the economy in Western Europe following the Industrial Revolution in the second half of the 19th century (which is the common understanding in most literature). The different world economies may go through industrialization in different periods of time at different scales and with different compositions. For example, the level of industrialization was higher and speed was more rapid in North America, even though it took place after that in Western Europe. Besides, when the Four Little Dragons in East Asia went through industrialization in the 1950s, they were dubbed as "newly industrialized economies". Yet, the timeline and scale of their industrialization and the respective influence on the progression of their hospitality industry are not identical. Similarly, in the last quarter of the 20th century, the advancement of industrialization in China, India, Brazil, and South Africa also situated these countries as the world's "newly industrialized economies". Besides, in the 21st century, many individual world economies are still emerging from

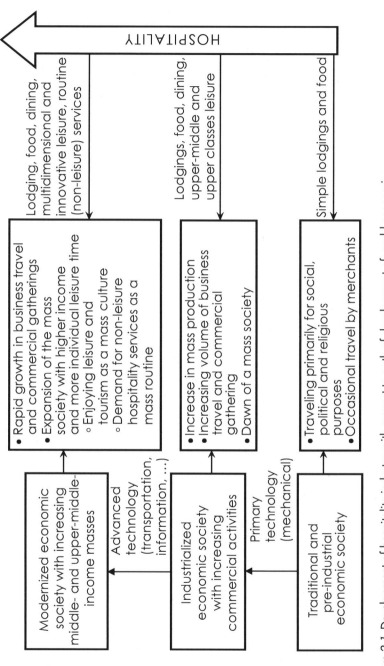

Figure 2.1 Development of hospitality industry with respect to path of development of world economies

their own industrialization and are situated in different phases, so that they transform into modernized nations in different timeframes.

Therefore, two propositions can be made on the development of the hospitality industry in the world economies based on the flow diagram in Figure 2.1.

Propositions on development of hospitality industry

1   The potential market size during the development of the hospitality industry of a certain country/region is jointly determined by the scale and scope of the business activities (at both the domestic and international levels) and the size of the mass society.
2   The transition of an economy from industrialization to modernization will produce driving forces that accelerate the progression and diversification of the hospitality industry.

A careful examination of these two propositions, which are associated with various economies, may assist practitioners in the industry to formulate effective plans and strategies to secure sustainable growth and a competitive edge for their business.

As emphasized by O'Gorman (2009) in his study on the origins of the commercial hospitality industry, "learning from the past will help to inform the future" (O'Gorman, 2009: 777). In applying O'Gorman to the focus of this chapter, gaining familiarity on the historical relationship between the paths of development of the world economies and the hospitality industries will be useful to management teams and leaders for exploring potential opportunities and threats that may affect their business over time. This is especially true when they wish to assess whether to increase their business scale, introduce new business elements, invest in new technology and business innovations, or enter a new market.

Economic dynamics of modern hospitality industry

After the end of the 1980s, the development of the hospitality industry was no longer simply or largely determined merely by the development of the world economies as historically evidenced, but through the simultaneous development and macroeconomic performance of related economies. In terms of capital investment, direct and indirect job opportunities, expenditures in domestic consumption, and international trade in related services, their economic dynamics triggered by the rapid growth of the hospitality industry significantly contributed to the economic development of a nation in real terms. For example, as presented in Box 1.1, the evidence cited from the UK clearly shows the economic dynamics of the hospitality industry toward the growth of its local economy.

In addition, the sectors of the industrial market (including the chains of pro-duction, supply and distribution) from agricultural, manufacturing, whole-sale and retail, banking and finance, transportation and logistics to agency services developed along with the advancement of the hospitality industry. These positive effects from the hospitality industry to other local economic sectors have been largely acknowledged by many, including academics.

A comprehensive report released by Ernst & Young (2013) indicates that there are substantial economic contributions from the hospitality industry to 31 European countries in the 21st century, although the level of significance across the different countries may not be the same. At the aggregate level, it is estimated that in 2010, the hospitality industry "directly employ[ed] 10.2m [million] people in Europe" (Ernst & Young, 2013). In addition, the "turnover across the hospitality sector [was] over €1.0tn [trillion], equal to approximately 8.1% of total economic output, with gross value added ... of more than €460bn [billion], or 3.7% of the GDP" (ibid.). Consequently, vari-ous local sectors, including "transportation, tourism, culture, construction, and brewing" (ibid.: 8) obviously benefit from the continuous growth of the hospitality industry.

Dynamics between hospitality industry and tourism

To maintain the vitality of the hospitality industry and its overall contribu-tions to the growth of an economy, interactive and innovative relationships cultivated with the related industries, especially tourism and routine leisure for society, are a necessary aspect in the 21st century. As mentioned earlier, the development of tourism since the mid-20th century is largely due to the new and fast growing culture of mass societies around the world. This trend has indeed facilitated substantial driving forces which enhance the interrela-tionship between the hospitality industry and tourism, and is in line with the related discussions as summarized in Figure 1.1 in Chapter 1.

On the one hand, most tourist activities involve demand for hospitable services of one form or another in a tourism market/destination (e.g., from regular meals to fine dining, and routine lodging services to all-inclusive accommodation and entertainment services in a single package). In turn, the variety and quality of related services as provided by the hospitality sector undoubtedly help to increase the stay time of tourists and stimulate their desire to spend money, as well as their inclination to return, hence increasing market penetration simply through "word of mouth". Thus, the related driv-ing forces will mutually intensify their contributions to the local economy.

Actually, there is much evidence from tourism destinations worldwide that can be cited to emphasize the dynamics of the hospitality industry toward their long-term growth and joint contributions to the local economies. For example, despite that the foundation of the economic success of Las Vegas lies in casino tourism, its modernization process in the 1970s and success which was used as a benchmark for the development of many other destinations in North America and worldwide, could hardly have been achieved without large-scale investment in all-inclusive and innovative hospitality facilities. Following the decades-long expansion of the casino-hotel resorts in Las Vegas, and introduction of multifarious and innovative hospitality services with effective applications of different technologies, a well-known business philosophy of Philip Satre, Chief Executive Officer (CEO) of a nation-wide casino-hotel resort called Harrah's in 1994, appropriately summarizes the economics dynamics of the hospitality industry: "If you build it, they will come" (Loveman, 2003),

Other than the case of casino tourism in Las Vegas, economic dynamics produced from effective interactions between tourism in general and the hospitality industry are widely recognized by various governments and related business firms around the world, and provide them with an attractive proposition to vitalize local economies. For example, the hospitality aspects of the tourism industry such as diversity and quality of facilities and services have been emphasized by interest groups in different Canadian provinces in the 21st century to facilitate the contributions from tourism in which: "the GDP and employment from tourism spending is felt across Canada in every province and territory. Tourism represents more of Canada's GDP than agriculture, forestry and fisheries combined" (Rural Alberta Business Centre: Rocky Mountain House, 2013).

Since many of the countries/regions in East Asia (especially China) are in the process of transforming from an industrialized to a modernized economy, both mass society and tourism culture are expanding, and this trend will continue. As anticipated by Goh et al. (2013: 2; see Figure 1 in that volume), the "mid-scale and budget hotel segment in China will experience the greatest growth" while the high-end hotel segment will still show a positive growth between 2015 and 2022. As national policies to boost expenditures on leisure and tourism consumption have been adopted by the Chinese government, it is anticipated that "China's hospitality market will be among the most important – if not the most important – markets for global operators" (ibid.: 4).

In addition, the overseas investment made by Mainland Chinese investors in the global hotel real estate and hospitality between 2012 and 2016 is rated as "the largest spend on hotel transaction stemming from any one country other than the United States" (Ferroni, 2017). Despite the anticipation that related investments may be "reset in 2017 as Chinese regulators look to cool capital outflows amid a weakening currency" (ibid.), interactive business dynamics between the Chinese economy and the world hospitality industry is not likely to stop anytime soon.

Hurdles to growing dynamics

Despite the upsides and optimistic expectations for the growth of the hospitality industry in the world economies, there remain uncertainties. In short, the outputs from this industry are largely non-necessities to mass societies. To business consumers, their spending on related services is very much affected by the economic environment at both the local and international levels. In considering the different social, political, and economic unrests since the end of the 20th century (e.g., economic downturns and difficulties experienced by many of the Western European countries, financial turmoil in the global major markets, rising protectionism in global advanced economies, unexpected changes in public policies related to social and economic factors, and increasing threats of terrorism), the momentum of the hospitality industry may stagnate in one form or another.

According to *The Travel & Tourism Competitiveness Report 2015* (Oaten et al., 2015: 47): "operating in a globally inter-connected and consumer-led environment, the hotel industry is exposed to various risks of business interruption". Among the factors that may lead to various uncertainties, recessions related to macroeconomic cycles (especially those found in the Eurozone), and political and terrorism risks since the dawn of the 21st century have the greatest impacts on the "complex make-up" of the hotel industry. In addition, the "impact of pandemics such as SARS, swine flu and Ebola on the hotel industry" (ibid.: 49) could "trigger deeper declines" (ibid.) in the industry, although it may recover sooner or later. Indeed, concerns that are raised in the hotel industry may also be applicable to other sectors like restaurants and theme parks in the hospitality industry, which deserve careful and strategic consideration by the management teams and leaders of related firms.

Did you know? ...

The evolution, modern development, and outstanding performance of the hospitality industry in Las Vegas are unique to the historical, cultural, institutional, and economic contexts of the USA. Box 2.1 provides the crucial facts and factors at the macroeconomic level which have brought about the evolution and dynamics of significant growth in the non-gaming hospitality sectors of Las Vegas, especially large-scale hotel facilities and various forms of leisure. Thus, students may gain more insights into the path of development that has led to the success of the hospitality industry in Las Vegas, and further explore related areas of interest in their studies.

Box 2.1 Growing dynamics of hospitality industry in Las Vegas

In *Suburban Xanadu: The Casino Resort on the Las Vegas Strip and Beyond* (Schwartz, 2003), the development of a casino resort (i.e., the Xanadu) in Las Vegas as "an opulent, exotic locale" (ibid.: 3) for Americans to take part in casino gambling and various forms of entertainment as part of their leisure activities is analyzed with a historical perspective. It is ascertained that the early development of Las Vegas was resultant of the desire of "suburban Americans ... to gamble in insular resorts" (ibid.) far away from home, and approved by the government.

The rapid growth of Las Vegas in the 1930s was largely due to the development of this city as a "regional commercial and political center" (ibid.: 27). This "twin engines of the city's economy in the postwar period" (ibid.) then coincidentally brought about "all of the ingredients needed for a tourist economy" (ibid.). On this occasion, Las Vegas was further expanded into a casino resort and tourism destination in which a wide range of hospitality services were provided together with casino gaming to mass tourists.

Nevertheless, due to lax crime control and other socially controversial activities, Las Vegas was labeled as Sin City until the late 1960s, when the Nevada state government took serious measures to rectify the issue. In addition, by promulgating the Corporate Gaming Act in 1969 which allowed modern, well-organized, and large-scale hospitality enterprises to introduce their nation-wide trademark to Las Vegas, extensive capital investment was injected into the development of non-gaming attractions and high-quality hospitality facilities in the 1970s (Eadington, 1999). Consequently, an entirely new era of modern and innovative development in Las Vegas was showcased to the general public in North America and around the world.

After decades-long development in the non-gaming hospitality sectors, their business revenue in Las Vegas has been reported to be higher than that of gaming revenue since 1999. For example, while only 39% of the reported revenue on the Las Vegas Strip in 1990 was derived from non-gaming activities, this increased to 64% in 2012. Indeed, the primary force that has led to this change is the evolution of Las Vegas "into a more complete tourist destination with hotel, entertainment, retail, and F&B/fine dining becoming increasingly important revenue drivers ... the Strip now has 150K hotel rooms and room supply has growth +100% over the past 20 years" (Ro, 2013).

With considerable expansion in the number of non-gaming hospitality facilities, and targeting revenue from expenditures of the mass society, the business performance of Las Vegas has not been without challenges, and obviously affected by macroeconomic cycles. For example, the recent recession in 2009 had significantly adverse impacts on the industry. Most hotels had to reduce their prices to maintain occupancy levels and secure visitors for their related hospitality businesses, including gaming. Despite doing so, the profitability of the casino hotels and resorts still slumped significantly. Yet even with unavoidable cyclical fluctuations in the economy, business practitioners in Las Vegas were still optimistic about the future of the industry. As presented in the title of an article which interviewed the leaders of the industry: "Las Vegas embodied the motto 'If you build it, they will come', recession forged new motto 'If you slash prices, they will come'" (Robison, 2010).

Discussion questions:

1   Identify and discuss in detail the two major factors that simultaneously led to the phenomenal performance of the non-gaming hospitality businesses in Las Vegas since the 1970s.
2   Why are "slashed prices" for attracting more visitors used to "forge a new motto" for the casino resorts in Las Vegas? Does this mean that the use of the marginal principle in making an economic decision as discussed in Chapter 1 is incorrect?
3   Could the successful experiences in Las Vegas be duplicated in other cities? Why or why not?

Conclusions and remarks

To realize the economic forces that would facilitate the advancement of the hospitality industry, its changing organization and effects on the world economies over time are not simply relevant to academics, but also essential to management teams and leaders in the industry. Indeed, historical experiences have provided real and informative grounds for practitioners to better understand the forces that have led to the changes, thus helping them to make more objective, effective and proactive decisions in their business endeavors.

Based on the essential evidence that has been summarized and discussed in detail in this chapter, it is evident that the development of the hospitality sector into a modern industry with diverse business components in different economies around the world has common attributes. In sum, advancements in technology which increase productivity, expansion of the mass society and notable changes in their purchasing power and leisure culture for tourism, leisure and routine services, as well as related government policies, play crucial interactive roles in promoting the progression and increasing the scale of the hospitality industry in the mid-20th century. Nevertheless, it is worth emphasizing that due to the differences in social and economic development stages and public interests, business strategies and routines applied respectively in well-developed and modernized or emerging and developing economies, and in societies with different historical contexts and cultures, will not be the same in any given period of time.

To further understand the business practices in the hospitality industry, important economic principles and applications for analyzing the behavior of the mass consumers of hospitality services and modern hospitality firms, as well as their interactions in the markets will be discussed in the next three chapters.

References and further reading

Alassaf, F., 2016. The history of hospitality industry. Available www.linkedin.com/pulse/history-hospitality-industry-fadi-alassaf

Dawson, S., 2007. Working-class consumers and the campaign for holidays with pay. *Twentieth Century British History*, 18 (3), 277–305.

Eadington, W.R., 1999. The economics of casino gambling. *Journal of Economic Perspectives*, 13 (3), 173–192.

Eichengreen, B., 1992. *Golden Fetters: The Gold Standard and the Great Depression, 1919–1939*. Oxford University Press, New York, USA.

Ernst & Young, 2013. The hospitality sector in Europe – An assessment of the economic contribution of the hospitality sector across 31 countries. Available www.ey.com/Publication/vwLUAssets/The_Hospitality_Sector_in_Europe/$FILE/EY_The_Hospitality_Sector_in_Europe.pdf

Ferroni, L., 2017. Hospitality & tourism investment: Forces for the future. In: *Travel & Tourism: Global Economic Impact & Issues 2017*, 19, World Travel & Tourism Council, London, 2017, p. 8. Available www.wttc.org/-/media/files/reports/economic-impact-research/2017-documents/global-economic-impact-and-issues-2017.pdf

Global Hospitality Portal, 2016. Background of the hospitality industry. Available www.soegjobs.com/2016/09/15/hospitality-industry-historical-background/

Goh, M.F., Gan, C.W., Kim, D., 2013. China's hospitality industry – Rooms for growth. A.T. Kearney, Inc. Available www.atkearney.com/documents/10192/982632/Chinas_Hospitality_Industry.pdf/72ed00fb-1cad-4798-a1a1-1552604bc72e

Guy, R., 1984. Chapter 3: Merchant capitalism. In: R. Guy, *Economics – An Alternative Text*. Sheridan House Inc., Scarsdale, USA, pp. 24–33.

Ingram, P., 2001. Changing the rules: Interests, organization and institutional change in the U.S. hospitality industry. In: M.C. Brinton, V. Nee (eds), *The New Institutionalism in Sociology*. Stanford University Press, Stanford, CA, USA, pp. 258–276.

Jakle, J.A., Sculle, K.A., 2009. *America's Main Street Hotels: Transiency and Community in the Early Auto Age*. University of Tennessee Press, Knoxville, USA.

Japan Ryokan & Hotel Association (n.d.). Origins and History of the Japanese Ryokan. Available www.ryokan.or.jp/past/english/pdf/origins_and_history.pdf

Jones, S.G., 1986. Trends in the leisure industry since the Second World War. *The Service Industries Journal*, 6 (3), 330–348.

Kaven, W.H., 1992. Japan's hotel industry: An overview. *The Cornell H.R.A. Quarterly*, April, 26–32.

Kostuch Media, 2013. Looking back at the hospitality industry in the '30s and '40s. Available www.hoteliermagazine.com/looking-back-at-the-hospitality-industry-in-the-30s-and-40s

Larrabee, E., Meyersohn, R. (eds), 1958. *Mass Leisure*. The Free Press, Glencoe, IL, USA.

Loveman, G.W., 2003. Diamonds in the data mine. In *Harvard Business Review*, May, 1–5. Available http://www2.fiu.edu/~ereserve/010019214-1.pdf

Markert, J., 1993. Leisure. In: F. Magill (ed.), *Survey of Social Science: Sociology Series*, Salem Press, Pasadena, CA, USA, pp. 1075–1080.

McCracken, S., 2005. Chapter 8: Voyages by teashop: An urban geography of modernism. In: Brooker, P. Thacker, A. (eds), *Geographies of Modernism*. Routledge, London, UK.

Mokyr, J., 1999. The second industrial revolution, 1870–1914. Available https://en-econ.tau.ac.il/sites/economy_en.tau.ac.il/files/media_server/Economics/PDF/Mini%20courses/castronovo.pdf

Oaten, S., Quesne, K.L., Segal, H., 2015. Chapter 1.2 Adapting to uncertainty – The global hotel industry. In: *The Travel & Tourism Competitiveness Report 2015*, World Economic Forum, Geneva, Switzerland, pp. 47–51. Available http://www3.weforum.org/docs/TT15/WEF_Global_Travel&Tourism_Report_2015.pdf

O'Gorman, K.D., 2009. Origins of the commercial hospitality industry: From the fanciful to factual. *International Journal of Contemporary Hospitality Management*, 21 (7), 777–790.

Ro, S., 2013. Las Vegas hasn't been about gambling since 1999. *Business Insider*, March 8. Available www.businessinsider.com/las-vegas-gaming-vs-non-gaming-revenue-2013-3

Robison, J., 2010. Las Vegas embodied the motto "If you build it, they will come", recession forged new motto "If you slash prices, they will come". *Las Vegas Review-Journal: McClatchy – Tribune Regional News*, January 31. Available www.hotel-online.com/News/PR2010_1st/Feb10_LasVegasSlogan.html

Rural Alberta Business Centre: Rocky Mountain House, 2013. Tourism & hospitality industry profile. The Business Link, Alberta, Canada. Available www.rockymtnhouse.com/DocumentCenter/View/327

Schwartz, D.G., 2003. *Suburban Xanadu: The Casino Resort on the Las Vegas Strip and Beyond*. Routledge, New York, USA.

Siu, R.C.S., 2018. Institutional change and evolution of the world leisure industry. *Journal of Economic Issues*, 52 (2), 378–386.

Soule, G., 1957. The economics of leisure. *The Annals of the American Academy of Political and Social Science*, 313 (1), 16–24.

Spielvogel, J.J., 2012. Chapter 23: Mass Society in an "Age of Progress", 1871–1894. In: J.J. Spielvogel, *Western Civilization – Volume II: Since 1500* (8th edition). Cengage Learning, Boston, MA, USA, pp. 678–709.

Terzeon, J., 2014. How the world's biggest hotel chains began. Available www.elinapms.com/blog/2014/how-the-worlds-biggest-hotel-chains-began

Wikipedia, 2017. Astor House Hotel (Shanghai). Available https://en.wikipedia.org/wiki/Astor_House_Hotel_(Shanghai)

Williamson, J., 1930. *The American Hotel: An Anecdotal History*. A.A. Knopf, New York, USA.

WorldHistory.Biz, 2015. Ancient China. Available www.worldhistory.biz/sundries/46261-ancient-china.html

3 Economic attributes of consumers and firms

Objectives and learning outcomes

Chapter 1 demonstrated that a good understanding/mastering of the characteristics of one's business, and the behavior of consumers and other related firms in the market is necessary to ensure the effectiveness of business decisions. This chapter will examine the most fundamental and essential principles at the microeconomic level to assist students with the development of basic knowledge on the characteristics and practices of a market, and the skills to analyze the changes in the state of this market. Thus, the concepts and principles of demand and supply and their elasticity are comprehensively explained in terms of their general aspects and by applying examples from the hospitality industry. In addition, factors which influence the behavior of consumers and firms respectively, and the interacting forces that may be generated which change the price and business volume in the markets are explicated so that students have the ability to manage different possible scenarios in the real world.

After reading this chapter, students will be able to:

- understand the concepts of both demand and supply;
- understand the factors that influence the spending decisions of consumers;
- understand the factors that influence the output decisions of firms;
- express how price and quantity exchanged in the market are determined through the interactions between consumers and firms;
- express how price and quantity exchanged in the market may be changed when the choices of consumers or firms or both have changed;
- understand the differences among price, income elasticity, and cross-price elasticities, as well as their simple applications; and
- apply the related concepts and principles to explore some common business decisions faced by hospitality firms.

Economic concepts of demand and supply

In every society, economic activities originate from demand and supply. Without the interaction of these two forces, markets would not exist. Thus, a good understanding of the attributes of demand and supply is indispensable for the management team and leaders of any firm to gain better insights into not only the nature and practice of their own business, but also the behavior of their existing and potential customers, and other competing firms.

In economics, demand and supply are the two most fundamental concepts which are applied by economists to explore the respective consumption and production behaviors/decisions of consumers (households) and producers (firms) in the markets. The principle of these two concepts is provided below.

Demand: The willingness and ability of a person to buy a commodity (an economic good or service) at various prices.

Supply: The willingness and ability of a producer (or business person) to produce or sell a commodity at various prices.

Based on these principles, three factors have to be in place simultaneously to make demand and supply real. They are willingness, ability, and price. For example, a person is traveling away from home, and requires accommodation. S/he is willing to pay for a hotel room and has the ability to spend up to $30 a night. If the lowest price of a hotel room at his/her destination is $50, then his/her demand will not count in the market because s/he is not able to pay for this hospitality service. On the other hand, if s/he is able to spend up to $80 a night, then his/her demand becomes real. Consider another scenario in which this individual has a budget of $80 for a hotel room. However, s/he prefers and chooses to stay with a friend to save the money for shopping instead. Thus, s/he is not willing to pay for a hotel room and hence, his/her demand for a hotel room also fails to materialize.

To any business firm in the market, a reasonable estimation of the potential demand for their outputs serves as essential grounds for related decisions on the quantity to be produced at various prices. In other words, a firm should not solely refer to the number of people who "like" or "want" to buy its commodities, or merely estimate the number of people who have the purchasing power to buy its commodities, but carefully examine the market size of those who are "willing and able to" buy at various prices in planning for the scale of their business. This is especially true for businesses that produce non-necessities or luxury commodities like hospitality firms. By the same token, the presence of these three factors are also vital for supply to be realized. That is, the interest (willingness) of an individual to go into business to organize the production of a commodity at various prices is not sufficient to supply this commodity in the market. S/he must have in place the required knowledge, organizational skills, physical and financial resources (the abilities) simultaneously to implement production.

Determinants of quantity demanded and demand

To further explore the demand behavior of a consumer, it is necessary to understand the factors that enter into his/her decision process on the quantity to be purchased. The concept of demand exemplifies that the quantity of a commodity that a consumer is willing and able to buy is directly determined by price.

Price and quantity demanded

In applying the concept of marginalism in the behavior of people as discussed in Chapter 1, it is generally assumed that if a person has never had the opportunity to access a certain commodity (or not for quite a while), and then s/he gains the purchasing power to enjoy this commodity, s/he would be willing to pay the highest possible price for the first unit. After s/he enjoys the first unit of consumption of the commodity, his/her desire to have the second unit is less than that for the first one and so on and so forth for more units. This is a law of economics called *diminishing marginal utility*, which is derived from the successive consumption of a commodity, and the decline in satisfaction with more units of consumption.

A consumer may assign a total amount or *a budget* that will be spent on a commodity within a certain period of time (e.g., a year) in accordance with his/her preference (i.e., like or dislike, or anywhere in between liking and disliking) toward a commodity (e.g., a buffet meal at a 5-star hotel), income, and wealth. Based on his/her willingness and budget, the quantity demanded is then simply determined by dividing the budget by the market price of the commodity.

For example, if a consumer is willing and able to spend a budget of $300 a year to enjoy buffet dinners at a hotel, and if the price of each buffet dinner is on average $30, s/he will pay for ten buffet dinners a year. If the price is lower, say, $20, his/her quantity demanded will increase by five visits to 15 buffet dinners per year. Or if the price is further reduced to $15, s/he would enjoy 20 buffets per year. This negative relationship could also be explained with two simple concepts: the *income effect* and *substitution effect*.

By referring to the example, the purchasing power (i.e., with the same amount of income or budget) of the consumer increases when the price of the hotel buffet dinner is reduced, so that s/he could buy more dinners; this is the income effect which results with changes in purchasing power. On the other hand, when the price of the hotel buffet dinner is reduced, the consumer may see this as a good opportunity to enjoy more buffet dinners instead of, say, steak dinners with wine in fine dining restaurants; this is the substitution effect which results with changes in consumption due to changes in the relative price.

In economics, a negative relationship between the *quantity demanded* (i.e., the number of units consumed) and *price* is governed by the *law of demand*.

Law of demand: *Ceteris paribus**, there is a *negative relationship* between changes in *price* and *quantity demanded*. That is, when the price increases, the quantity demanded is reduced, and vice versa.

* *Ceteris paribus*: The assumption that when discussing the influence from the change of one factor (e.g., market price) to another factor (e.g., quantity demanded), the behavior (or quantity) of all the other factors (e.g., taste and income) remains unchanged. The objective of this assumption is to simplify the related discussions and show the direct relationship between two factors that are considered in the first place.

Demand curve/schedule

To show the relationship between price and quantity demanded, a demand curve (or demand schedule) is plotted to facilitate related discussions and analyses of the market behavior of a consumer with respect to changes in price. For example, as shown in Figure 3.1, the line that is labeled D slopes downward from left to right, which is a simple demand curve (D$_1$ and D$_2$ are also demand curves and related discussions will be provided in the next section).

In economics, the price (P) of a commodity is placed on the vertical axis while the quantity (Q) of a commodity is placed on the horizontal axis. In principle, any point along a demand curve (e.g., Point *a* on D in Figure 3.1) shows the quantity demanded (q$_1$) with respect to a particular price (p$_1$) of the commodity. According to the law of demand, if the price increases (say, from p$_1$ to p$_2$), the consumer buys less of this commodity and quantity demanded

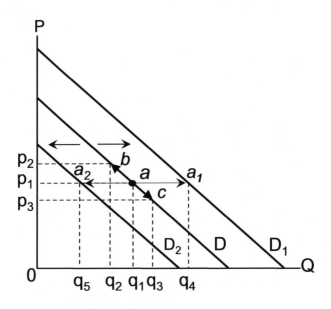

Figure 3.1 Demand curve (schedule) and its changes

decreases (from q_1 to q_2). On the contrary, if the price decreases (say, from p_1 to p_3), the quantity demanded increases (from q_1 to q_3).

Non-price determinants of demand

Apart from price, the quantity that a consumer chooses to buy may also be determined by other non-price factors. Traditionally, these factors include income, taste, price of substitutes and complements, and expected changes in price and income respectively. In addition to these conventional factors, time is also a crucial factor which determines the behavior of a consumer in demand for hospitality services.

Ceteris paribus, while changes in price lead to a movement along a unique demand curve (e.g., from Point *a* to *b*, or *a* to *c* as depicted in Figure 3.1), changes in a non-price factor lead to a shift in the demand curve (e.g. from D to D_1, or D to D_2). Generally speaking, if the changes of a non-price factor (e.g., income) increase the quantity that a consumer purchases at every possible price, the demand curve shifts to the right (or outward). For example, if income increases, a consumer will increase his/her demand for a commodity, say, from q_1 (Point *a* on D) to q_4 (Point a_1 on D_1) at the same price p_1. If this change in the demand is the same for all other prices on D, it is represented by a parallel shift of D to D_1. In contrast, if the income of a consumer decreases, s/he will reduce consumption from q_1 to q_5 (Point a_2 on D_2) at p_1 and similarly with all other prices, and hence D shifts to the left (or inward).

Changes in quantity demanded and demand:
A short note

The terms "quantity demanded" and "demand" are commonly applied to differentiate between the influences of price and non-price determinants on the changing quantity that a consumer purchases. In principle, price increases are expressed as "quantity demanded decreases" to reflect a downward movement along the demand curve (e.g., from *a* to *b*), and vice versa. Increases in the value of a non-price determinant (e.g., income) are expressed as "demand increases" to reflect an outward shift of the demand curve (e.g., from D to D_1), and vice versa.

Major non-price determinants of demand

The quantity of a commodity that a consumer acquires at any given price is primarily determined by six determinants of demand, including:

1   income;
2   taste/preference;
3   the price of substitutes and complements;
4   expected changes in income;

5   expected changes in price; and
6   time.

Income and taste/preference

As mentioned earlier, changes in income will affect the purchasing power of a consumer, and hence the quantity that s/he is able to buy. On the other hand, when the taste/preference of a consumer for a commodity has changed, so will his/her demand for the commodity. For example, if the preference of a consumer has changed from eating dinner at home every night to spending one or two evenings each week to relax and enjoy dinner out, then his/her demand for restaurant services increases. Throughout the modernization process of any society (as discussed in Chapter 2), a common phenomenon emerges in which the increased income of the various mass workers allows them to realize their preference for more leisure and other non-leisure activities, and hence reflects the increasing demand for related hospitality services.

Price of substitutes and complements

In general, a commodity can be a substitute or a complement of some other commodity.

Thus, a change in the price of a commodity will not only change the quantity demanded of this commodity, but also the demand for its related commodities. For example, 3- and 4-star hotel rooms could be a substitute for many travelers. If the rate of a room at a 4-star hotel increases, its quantity demanded will decrease, and demand for 3-star hotel rooms may increase (i.e., consumers choose to substitute the 4-star hotel room with a 3-star hotel room), or vice versa.

On the other hand, since most travelers will use hotel and restaurant services on their trips, these two categories of hospitality services are complementary. Therefore, if the room rate of hotels at a destination decreases during the low season, the quantity of hotel rooms demanded will increase, and the demand for restaurant services (both in the hotels or within their proximity) may also increase. Another example could be travel-related costs like the price of gasoline and their impacts on the demand for certain types of hotels. A study by Walsh et al. (2004) finds that when the price of gasoline increases, Americans travel less so that the "demand for certain lodging products" is reduced, especially mid-scale hotels in resort areas that do not offer food and beverage (Walsh et al., 2004: 505).

Therefore, to generalize these effects:

1   if two commodities, A and B, can substitute for each other, and the price of A increases, then the demand for B will increase, and vice versa; and
2   if two commodities, X and Y, are complements, and the price of X increases, then the demand for Y will decrease, and vice versa.

Impacts of changing expectations

In any modernized economy, the expectations of consumers on possible changes in their income or the price of various commodities in the foreseeable future may have significant impacts on their current consumption behavior. In principle, if a consumer is expecting an increase in his/her income in the coming months because of, say, an increase in salary, s/he may decide to spend more for his or her own enjoyment before the increment actually happens. This is done by changing his/her current consumption volume in terms of saving less or borrowing more (e.g., through credit).

In terms of the price of a commodity, if it is expected that the price will go up in the near future, the consumer will in principle buy more now at the current price level. For example, if the price of admission tickets to a theme park is expected to increase at the beginning of next year, the consumer (especially locals) may decide to visit the theme park a few more times now, (i.e., demand increases) before the price is increased.

Time: An essential determinant of demand for hospitality

In considering the nature and particular characteristics of the hospitality services as an economic commodity, its demand is explicitly determined by the amount of time that a consumer has to enjoy or receive the related services. In other words, in addition to having the financial means, time is an indispensable factor which jointly determines the ability of a consumer to spend money on hospitality services. *Ceteris paribus*, a positive relationship between time and demand for various forms of hospitality services could generally be expected. Nevertheless, applications of this relationship need to be contextual.

For example, in the hotel industry, one should not simply expect that when more time is available to consumers for leisure, say, due to an extra two-day paid statutory holiday, that their demand for "hotel services" will increase because they may take the opportunity to travel. Indeed, they may choose to spend their vacation by traveling further away from home. However, they may end up spending more time in traffic or traveling instead of in a hotel. Besides, the effects of the demand for hotels located in different local regions versus those overseas may be quite different, or may even not necessarily present a positive relationship. In the event that people choose to spend more on trips that are further away from home, or even overseas, the demand for hotels in the local market may indeed decrease.

Determinants of quantity supplied and supply

Parallel to the aforementioned discussions on demand, the quantity that a firm may produce for sale in the market in any given period of time is determined by its *willingness* and *ability* to produce. Thus, one has to understand the impacts from price and non-price factors on the decision of a firm on whether they will enter into a business, and the quantity that will be produced if the firm decides to take part in the business.

Price and quantity supplied

In principle, higher priced commodities in the market not only provide more incentive for profit-making firms to produce but also increase their willingness to do so. In other words, the price that a firm is willing to accept to implement production reflects its marginal cost of production (including different forms of opportunity costs and a normal profit to the producer). Due to scarcity (limited resources), a concept which was elaborated in Chapter 1, it is generally assumed that when a firm expands its quantity of output, the incremental costs of producing the succeeding unit is higher than those of the preceding unit, and so on and so forth. In other words, a higher price is necessary for a firm to cover the increasing marginal costs of production when more units are produced. To this extent, the supply curve also reflects the marginal cost curve of a firm with respect to the various quantities to be supplied. This relationship between price and quantity supplied is called the law of supply.

> **Law of supply:** There is a *positive relationship* between changes in *price* and *quantity supplied*. That is, when the price increases, the quantity supplied increases, and vice versa.

Supply curve/schedule

A typical supply curve (or supply schedule) S is illustrated in Figure 3.2. In contrast to the demand curve that is presented in Figure 3.1, the supply curve slopes upward from the left to the right, which shows a positive relationship between price and quantity supplied. As with the description of a demand curve, any point along a supply curve (e.g., Point *a* on S in Figure 3.2) shows the quantity supplied (q_1) with respect to a particular price (p_1) of the commodity. According to the law of supply, if the price increases (say, from p_1 to p_2), a firm will produce more of this commodity so that quantity supplied increases (from q_1 to q_2). Or, to cover the increasing marginal costs of production for extra units, a firm has to charge a higher price when a higher quantity is to be supplied. On the contrary, if the price decreases (say, from p_1 to p_3), the quantity supplied also decreases (from q_1 to q_3).

Non-price determinants of supply

Other than price, the production (or business) decisions of a firm and the level of output at various price levels are also determined by a number of non-price factors. *Ceteris paribus*, while a change in price leads to movement

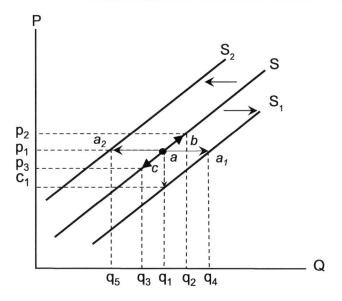

Figure 3.2 Supply curve (supply schedule) and its changes

along a unique supply curve (e.g., from Point *a* to *b*, or *a* to *c* as depicted in Figure 3.2), changes in a non-price factor lead to a shift of the supply curve (e.g. from S to S_1, or S to S_2). In principle, if the change in a non-price factor leads to an increase in the quantity to be produced by a firm at every possible price, the supply curve shifts to the right (or outward), say, from q_1 (Point *a* on S) to q_4 (Point a_1 on S_1) at the same price p_1. Conversely, the supply curve shifts to the left (or inward) if supply decreases from q_1 to q_5 (Point a_2 on S_2) at p_1 and similarly to all other prices.

Major non-price determinants of supply

In the production process, a number of factors may change the quantity of output of a firm at any given price level, or influence its willingness to produce a given level of output by accepting different prices. In general, these factors mainly include:

1   cost of production/business;
2   technology;
3   price of substitutes and complements in production/business;
4   unexpected shocks; and
5   public policies.

Cost of production/business

While an upward sloping supply curve illustrates the rising marginal cost of production as quantity supplied (or business volume) increases, a proportionate change in the cost of production for every level of output implies that the supply curve shifts. For example, when input costs like raw materials or labor are reduced, the marginal cost to a firm of producing q_1 units (as shown in Figure 3.2) will be lowered (say, from a level represented by p_1 to c_1). In other words, with a lower cost of production, a firm is willing to produce q_1 units by accepting a lower price (c_1), or increase the supply from q_1 to q_4 at the existing price level of p_1. As this change applies to all other levels of production like q_2, q_3, and so on and so forth, the supply curve (S) shifts to the right (e.g., S_1). In contrast, an increase in the cost of production shifts the supply curve to the left (e.g., from S to S_2).

Technology

Advancements in technology generally reduce the cost of production/doing business. For example, the availability of different kinds of "apps" in the market today allows hotels and restaurants to approach more customers with lower marketing and operations costs, and hence increase the quantity sold (e.g., increase the occupancy rate of their facilities) at the same price. In other words, technological progress leads to a right shift of the supply curve (from S to S_1). Nevertheless, as technological set-up costs (e.g., hardware of computers and servers, subscription to databases) could be expensive, ineffective installation of technology may indeed cause an increase in the average cost of production (especially for small firms), and hence a left shift of the supply curve (e.g., from S to S_2).

Price of substitutes and complements in production/business

As firms have limited resources for producing different kinds of commodities, the supply decisions of a profit-seeking firm for any commodity are influenced by the prices of related substitutes and complements in the market. In principle, two commodities can substitute for each other for production purposes if they can be produced with the same type of material. On the other hand, two commodities are complements if they can be produced together.

Take for example, the hotel industry. If the daily rate for a 3- or 4-star hotel room shows an increasing trend while that for a full-service 5-star hotel room is stagnant or offers a higher discount to achieve a balanced occupancy rate, it is likely that the supply of 3- or 4-star hotel rooms will increase. Simultaneously, the supply of mid-range hotel-related facilities such as restaurants, bars, and shops will also increase.

Unexpected shocks

In the production process, the occurrence of some unexpected and uncontrollable events may increase or reduce the quantity of output of a firm. In the agricultural sector, for example, natural disasters or unexpected good weather changes the quantity of output of a product at any existing price level. To the hospitality industry, natural disasters such as earthquakes and storms, accidental events like fires, and catastrophes such as political and social chaos (including terrorism attacks) may adversely affect the supply of a firm.

Public policy: An essential determinant of supply of hospitality services

In contrast to the production of agricultural and manufacturing products, the supply of hospitality services is more directly framed and influenced by the related public policies in the market and their changes over time. For example, if a government wants to boost tourism in their country through supportive policies such as lowering the business taxes of hospitality firms and for new investments in related facilities, it is reasonable to expect that the supply of hospitality services by individual firms will increase. Besides, under supportive public policies, more new firms may also enter the market so that the supply as a whole will further increase. However, if restrictive policies related to environmental protection and/or licensing requirements are imposed, the supply will decrease.

In most microeconomic discussions, the supply of a commodity of a firm in any given period of time is also determined by the expected changes in price. Generally speaking, if a firm expects that the price of its output will increase in the near future, this firm will stock up on some of its products today so that supply in the short term will fall. However, one of the unique features of the hospitality industry is the non-storability of services. This means that stocking up on unoccupied facilities for related services is not an option in this industry. For example, a hotel with a maximum capacity of 1,000 hotel rooms cannot stock up on, say, 500 unsold rooms during the non-peak season to increase its total number of rooms to 1,500 during the peak season.

Market equilibrium

To understand how the price of a commodity is determined in the market, an introduction will be first given on the market demand and market supply curves. In principle, the market demand and supply can be obtained respectively by summing the quantity that consumers and producers will buy and sell at various prices. For example, if there are only two firms in the market and they will produce 600 and 800 units respectively at a price of $10, then the market supply at $10 is 1,400 units, and so on for different prices so that a market supply curve can be obtained. This principle also applies to obtaining the market demand curve of any private consumer good.

Given the market demand and supply schedules for a commodity, consumers and producers will adjust their quantity demanded and supplied respectively in accordance with changes in price. By reverting to the laws of demand and supply, changes in price will ultimately balance the quantity demanded and supplied since the response of consumers and producers to changes in price is in the opposite direction. In this situation, the market achieves an *equilibrium*. As shown in Figure 3.3, market equilibrium (e) occurs when quantity demanded equals quantity supplied ($q_d = q_s = q^*$) at price p^* (where p^* is the *equilibrium price* and q^* is the *equilibrium quantity*).

If the market price is above or below the equilibrium price (e.g., p_1 or p_2 as depicted in Figure 3.4), the market faces *disequilibrium*. If the market price is above the equilibrium (e.g., $p_1 > p^*$), profit-seeking firms may decide to increase their quantity output (say, from q^* to q_1). However, at p_1, consumers only demand q_2 and not q^*, so that there is a *surplus* or *excess supply* (i.e., $q_1 - q_2$) in the market. If so, then the commodity will be conventionally tagged "on sale" or "discounted". When the price is adjusted downward, existing firms will produce fewer units (moving from q_1 to q^*) while consumers will buy more units (moving from q_2 to q^*). As shown in the downward arrows in Figure 3.4, the market will adjust back to equilibrium.

In contrast, if the market price (e.g., P_2) is set below the equilibrium price, *shortage* or *excess demand* is presented in the market as many consumers see that the item is a good deal and want to buy the item, but producers may not find it profitable to increase the supply of the commodity (say, to q_1) and may even reduce the output (say, to q_2). Thus, market price will adjust upward so

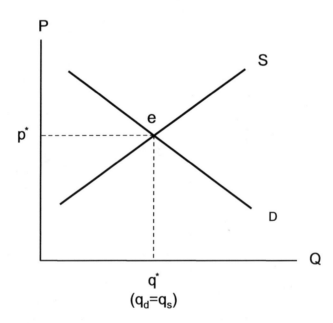

Figure 3.3 Derivation of equilibrium price (p^*) and quantity (q^*) in the market

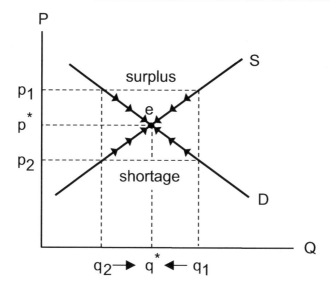

Figure 3.4 Market adjustment when price deviates from equilibrium

that market equilibrium can be restored. (Although it is not presented in this book, a competitive market in which the existence of many consumers and producers is a pre-condition for efficient adjustments is shown in Figure 3.4.)

Interactions between demand and supply in market

In any market, changes in the behavior of consumers and/or firms will shift either the demand or supply, or both, and hence change the equilibrium quantity and price.

Changes in demand or supply

To illustrate the possible changes in the market, Figure 3.5 shows two of the simplest situations where only demand or supply changes. These changes are shown in Figures 3.5a and 3.5b respectively.

For example, in certain peak seasons when the demand for flights increases, say, from D to D_1 as depicted in Figure 3.5a, the airlines may increase the number of flights from q^* to q_1 with existing aircraft (i.e., quantity supplied is to be increased while S remains unchanged). By doing so, marginal costs such as required maintenance for aircraft and labor will increase so that the price charged for the higher demand (D_1) has to be increased, say, from p^* to p_1, and the market equilibrium is adjusted from e to e_1. If the demand for

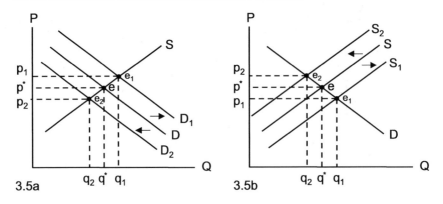

Figure 3.5 Effects from changes in demand or supply to p* and q*

flights is reduced from q^* to q_2 (i.e., demand shifts downward from D to D_2), the market equilibrium will adjust from e to e_2 in which the equilibrium price will be lower from p^* to p_2, and quantity supplied is reduced from q^* to q_2 for the reduced demand in the market.

On the other hand, if the cost of fuel to airlines increases from the current equilibrium level (e), the supply shifts upward from S to S_2 as depicted in Figure 3.5b. Consequently, a higher price has to be charged at any given level of demand (D) to cover the higher operation costs. When the price increases from p^* to p_2, the quantity demanded for flights decreases from q^* to q_2. Thus, the market equilibrium adjusts from e to e_2. In contrast, if the cost of fuel falls, the price charged by the airlines will also adjust accordingly; say, from p^* to p_1, and the extent of the market will increase from q^* to q_1 in a new equilibrium at e_1.

Simultaneous changes in demand and supply

Simultaneous changes in demand and supply are commonly observed in the real world. Therefore, their combined effects on equilibrium quantity and equilibrium price may not necessarily be unique. Generally speaking, both the direction and relative degree of changes between demand and supply determine how quantity and price would change when the market has adjusted to a new equilibrium. As demand or supply could either simultaneously increase or decrease, four possible situations may occur which are illustrated in Figure 3.6.

Increase in both demand and supply

Intuitively, if demand and supply both increase, the scale of the market will increase from q^* (as depicted in Figure 3.6a). However, the extent of the

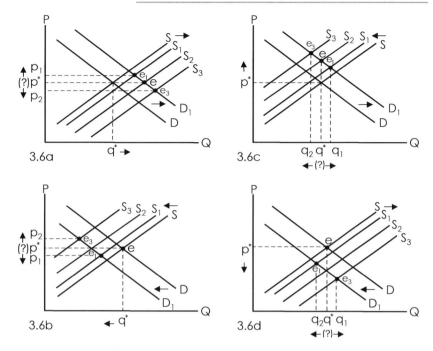

Figure 3.6 Effects from simultaneous changes in demand and supply to p* and q*

changes in quantity and the price level will be determined by the amount of increase in supply as compared to the increase in demand (D_1). If the increase in supply is less than $D_1 - D$ (e.g., from S to S_1 as shown in Figure 3.6a), the new equilibrium price (p_1) at e_1 is higher than the original price (p^*) at e. Alternatively, if the increase in S is more than $D_1 - D$ (e.g., from S to S_3), the new equilibrium price (p_2) at e_3 is less than p^*. Moreover, in a particular circumstance when the increase in supply is the same as $D_1 - D$ (i.e., from S to S_2), the market price remains the same at p^*.

With reference to the example of airplane flights, it can be inferred that during the peak season when demand increases, if the increase in supply is restricted by the small number of extra aircraft that can be used or high operation costs due to high fuel prices, then the increase in flights is associated with a higher price (say, at p_1) than the existing situation (at p^*). On the other hand, if supply increases more than demand as, say, the price of fuel falls rapidly and more budget (low-cost) airlines expand their services, then more flights may be available in the market at lower prices (say, at p_2).

Decrease in both demand and supply

In contrast to the above situation, if both demand and supply decrease, the scale of the market will decrease from q^* (as depicted in Figure 3.6b).

Similarly, the impacts on price depend on the amount of change in supply as related to demand. Herein, if demand falls at a higher rate than supply (i.e., $D_1 - D$ versus $S_1 - S$ as shown in Figure 3.6b), the price under the new equilibrium e_1 is less than e. On the other hand, if supply falls at a higher rate than demand (i.e., $S_3 - S$ versus $D - D_1$), the price under the new equilibrium e_3 is higher than e.

Increase in demand but decrease in supply

Aside from movement in the same direction, demand and supply may change in different directions. For example, when demand for air travel increases in the summer season and supply is reduced due to increasing operation costs or shutdown of a budget airline (e.g., as depicted in Figure 3.6c; when D shifts outward to D_1, S shifts inward), the market price of flight tickets on average will be pushed upward. In the new equilibrium, however, whether the quantity transacted in the market is more or less than the original amount at e is dependent on the amount of change in supply as related to demand. If the decrease in supply is less than the increase in demand (i.e., $S_1 - S$ versus $D_1 - D$ in Figure 3.6c), more flights (at q_1) will still be made available in the market but at higher prices. Otherwise, even if the price is higher, fewer services (at q_2) will be provided.

Decrease in demand but increase in supply

Lastly, if demand decreases and supply increases, the equilibrium price in the market will fall (e.g., as shown in Figure 3.6d). In this case, the effects on quantity at the new equilibrium will depend on whether the increase in supply is more or less than the decrease in demand. If the increase in supply is less than the decrease in demand, the new equilibrium quantity (e.g., q_2 at e_1 in Figure 3.6d) is less than q^*. On the other hand, if supply increases more than the decrease in demand, more goods (e.g., q_1) will be exchanged in the market at a much lower price in a new equilibrium (e.g., e_3).

Principle of elasticity

Apart from the above discussions on demand, supply and their interactions in the market, there is also the need to understand the degree of *responsiveness* of a consumer or a firm with respect to any changes in the major determinants of their choice. For this purpose, the measurement of elasticity is a common approach. In principle, elasticity measures the percentage changes in a variable (say, Y) with respect to a 1 percent change in another variable (say, X), which is shown in Equation (3.1).

$$\text{Measurement of elasticity: } \varepsilon = \frac{\%\Delta Y}{\%\Delta X} = \frac{\dfrac{Y_{new} - Y_{original}}{Y_{original}}}{\dfrac{X_{new} - X_{original}}{X_{original}}} = \frac{\dfrac{\Delta Y}{Y}}{\dfrac{\Delta X}{X}} = \frac{\Delta Y}{\Delta X} \cdot \frac{X}{Y} \quad (3.1)$$

Mathematically, Δ (delta) denotes "change" (e.g., ΔY means the change in the value of Y: $Y_{new} - Y_{original}$), while ε (epsilon) is commonly used to denote the elasticity (responsiveness) of a variable (e.g., Y) with respect to the change in another variable (e.g., X). For example, if Y denotes the quantity of admission tickets purchased by consumers to a theme park in one day, and X denotes the ticket price, then ε_p denotes the *price elasticity of demand* of the admission tickets, which shows the percentage change in the quantity of tickets demanded when there is a 1 percent change in the price.

Generally speaking, the numerical value of ε could be either positive (i.e., $\varepsilon > 0$ when changes in X and Y are in the same direction) or negative (i.e., $\varepsilon < 0$ when changes in X and Y are in the opposite direction). For example, if $\varepsilon = +1.5$, this means that when the value of X increases by 1%, the value of Y increases by 1.5%, and vice versa. Or if $\varepsilon = -1.5$, then a 1% increase in the value of X corresponds to a 1.5% decrease in the value of Y, and vice versa. Besides, it is also possible that ε may have a particular value like zero ($\varepsilon = 0$ when Y does not change at all), infinity ($\varepsilon = \infty$ when X does not change at all), or one ($\varepsilon = \pm 1$ when X changes 1%, as with Y).

In addition, if the responsiveness of Y is greater than the change in X (i.e., when X changes 1%, Y changes by more than 1%, regardless of whether the change is in the same or opposite direction), ε is referred to as *elastic*. If the responsiveness of Y is lower than the change in X (i.e., $\%\Delta Y < \%\Delta X$), ε is referred to as *inelastic*. In other words, if $\varepsilon > 1$ (or $\varepsilon < -1$), it is elastic, and if $0 < \varepsilon < 1$ (or $-1 < \varepsilon < 0$), it is inelastic.

Three forms of elasticity in economics

In economics and business applications, there are three forms of elasticity, which are:

1 price elasticity (of demand and supply respectively);
2 income elasticity of demand; and
3 cross-price elasticity of demand.

These different forms of elasticity convey essential information about the market behavior of consumers and hence, assist with the business decisions of firms, as discussed below.

Price elasticity of demand

During the low season, the management team of a hospitality firm such as a hotel or a theme park would usually consider lowering prices or offering discounts for their services to attract more business. In contrast, prices are commonly adjusted upward during the peak season. To be more effective in the related decisions, the initial step would be probably to estimate the likely response of consumers to the change in prices. By substituting Y in Equation (3.1) with the quantity demanded (Q_d), and X with price (P), we get Equation (3.2) which shows the price elasticity of demand (ε_p^d):

$$\varepsilon_p^d = \frac{\%\Delta Q_d}{\%\Delta P} = \frac{\Delta Q_d}{\Delta P} \cdot \frac{P}{Q_d} \qquad (3.2)$$

A concrete example would be to suppose that the average room rate currently charged by a hotel is $120 per night and the number of rooms sold (which is equivalent to the quantity demanded for its rooms) is 140 a day. When the room rate is reduced to $100 per night, the number of rooms sold increases to 180. Thus,

$$\varepsilon_p^d = \left(\frac{180-140}{140}\right) \bigg/ \left(\frac{100-120}{120}\right) = -1.7.$$

Since -1.7 is less than -1 (or without considering the negative sign, 1.7 is greater 1), the demand for the rooms at this hotel is price elastic. This also means that at the current price level, when the price is reduced by 1%, the quantity demanded increases by 1.7%. The negative sign is indeed consistent with the behavior of the consumers as shown by the law of demand.

In the hospitality industry, reasonable estimates and a good understanding of the price elasticity of demand for the related services are a good reference source for the management team in making business decisions, especially when determining the relationship between pricing and total revenue. For example, Wood (2013) shows that a good understanding of the price elasticity of demand for hotel rooms is essential to hotel managers when pricing their rooms effectively, so that they can maximize their business revenue (a related analysis will be presented in Chapter 4).

Price elasticity of supply

By the same token, the price elasticity of supply can be measured by substituting Q_d in Equation (3.2) with the quantity supplied (Q_s), so that we get Equation (3.3) which shows the price elasticity of supply (ε_p^s).

$$\varepsilon_p^s = \frac{\%\Delta Q_s}{\%\Delta P} = \frac{\Delta Q_s}{\Delta P} \cdot \frac{P}{Q_s} \qquad (3.3)$$

According to the law of supply, the numerical value of ε_p^s is in principle positive, while ε_p^d is negative since the quantity supplied changes in the same direction as price (see Figure 3.3 and related discussion).

Income elasticity of demand

By measuring the responsiveness of a consumer's demand for a commodity when his/her income changes, it becomes possible to identify the importance of this commodity to the consumer. If the quantity of a commodity that a consumer buys (Q_d) with respect to different income levels (Y) is given, the income elasticity of demand (ε_Y) is determined by Equation (3.4).

$$\varepsilon_Y = \frac{\%\Delta Q_d}{\%\Delta Y} = \frac{\Delta Q_d}{\Delta Y} \cdot \frac{Y}{Q_d} \tag{3.4}$$

In principle, if consumers buy more of a commodity when their income increases, and vice versa (i.e., when Y and Q_d change in the same direction), the income elasticity of demand is positive ($\varepsilon_Y > 0$), and the commodity in consideration is a *normal good*. On the other hand, if consumers buy less of a commodity when their income increases (i.e., Y and Q_d change in the opposite direction $\varepsilon_Y < 0$), this commodity is an *inferior good*.

Besides, if the income elasticity of demand for a commodity is positive and less than 1 ($0 < \varepsilon_Y < 1$), this commodity is a *necessity*. If income elasticity is greater than 1 ($\varepsilon_Y > 1$), this commodity is a *luxury*. Generally speaking, most hospitality services are luxuries to consumers.

Suppose that the monthly income of a family increases from \$5,000 to \$6,000, and their visits to theme parks increase from two to three times a year. Accordingly, the income elasticity of demand for theme parks is:

$$\varepsilon_Y = \left(\frac{3-2}{2}\right) \bigg/ \left(\frac{6000-5000}{5000}\right) = 2.5,$$

which means that theme parks are a luxury commodity for this family. In this situation, a 1% increase in income provides a 2.5% increase in quantity consumed.

On the other hand, suppose that there are four members in this family and they increase their consumption of haircuts at a barber shop from 40 to 44 times a year. The income elasticity for the barber shop service is:

$$\varepsilon_Y = \left(\frac{44-40}{40}\right) \bigg/ \left(\frac{6000-5000}{5000}\right) = 0.5,$$

which means that the barber shop service is a necessity for this family. In this situation, a 1% increase in income provides about a 0.5% increase in quantity consumed.

Cross-price elasticity of demand

As mentioned earlier, changes in the price of one commodity may impact the quantity consumed of a related commodity (e.g., a substitute or a complement). Thus, if commodities m and n are related commodities in consumption, the responsiveness of demand for m when the price of n changes is calculated by using Equation (3.5).

$$\varepsilon_{m,n} = \frac{\%\Delta Q_m}{\%\Delta P_n} = \frac{\Delta Q_m}{\Delta P_n} \cdot \frac{P_n}{Q_m} \tag{3.5}$$

where $\varepsilon_{m,n}$ denotes the cross elasticity of demand for m with respect to change in price of a related commodity n.

Based on the related discussions under "Major non-price determinants of demand" above, the cross-elasticity of commodity m with respect to change in price of n is positive ($\varepsilon_{m,n} > 0$) if the two commodities are substitutes (e.g., 3-star and 4-star hotel rooms). The cross-price elasticity is negative ($\varepsilon_{m,n} < 0$) if the two commodities are complements (e.g., theme park admission tickets and on-site catering services).

A business application: Demand, supply, and price elasticity of demand in pricing decision

Business practitioners will find that mastering the principles of demand, supply, and various forms of elasticity well enough will have positive impacts on their business decisions, especially in pricing decisions. These principles also provide the essential grounds to react effectively to changing market conditions.

In the hotel industry, a common pricing strategy is to charge different room rates during low and high seasons, or normal days and holidays, or weekdays and weekends. As depicted in Illustration 3.1, the room rate set by a hotel to visitors who check-in on a Monday which happens to be New Year's Eve is over three times the rate of a regular Monday. Is the hotel a profiteer in this case?

For a better understanding of the pricing strategies of hotels (or other hospitality firms), the principles of demand, supply and elasticity provide a simple and useful framework for related discussions. As illustrated in Figure 3.7, the number of rooms available for sale by a hotel in any given period of time is a fixed quantity (q). Its everyday operations require a minimum cost for items such as frontline service and housekeeping staff, supplies for rooms that have

Illustration 3.1 A profiteer?

Source: Tochi Leung

been occupied and their maintenance before they can be sold again on another day, extra charges in utilities, etc. Accordingly, if the room rate that this hotel can charge (e.g., P_{min} as indicated in Figure 3.7) is below this minimum cost outlay, the hotel should not sell any rooms. Otherwise, the hotel may stand to lose more when more rooms are sold.

To attract visitors on a normal day so that business can continue, a relatively lower rate (e.g., p_n) will be offered in accordance with the anticipated demand (say, $D_{normal\ day}$) in the market. When demand increases on the weekends ($D_{weekend}$), the hotel may offer more rooms for sale (e.g., an increase from q_n to q_w) with higher marginal costs like extra part-time workers, and hence, charge a higher room rate (e.g., p_w). During major public holidays or long weekends, there may be a large number of reservations (e.g., demand further increases to $D_{major\ public\ holiday}$) and the hotel approaches the maximum number of rooms that can be sold. Therefore, the room rate will be substantially increased

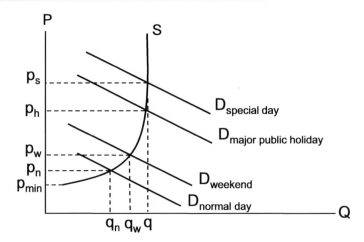

Figure 3.7 Demand and supply analysis of different hotel room rates charged on different days

(e.g., p_h) as compared to a normal day. Furthermore, on certain extra special days of the year (e.g., New Year's Eve as shown in Illustration 3.1), demand could be beyond the capacity of the hotel ($D_{special\ day}$) so that the room rate will be increased even higher (e.g., p_s).

The principle of elasticity of demand is applied to further the discussions of Illustration 3.1 and Figure 3.7. *Ceteris paribus*, when the price increases as a result of increases in demand, consumers who are less flexible to price change (i.e., price inelastic in demand) may be willing to pay a higher price to obtain the commodity, while those who are more flexible (i.e., price elastic in demand) may postpone their consumption. For example, if the hotel has 1,000 rooms and anticipates from past experience that the demand will be 1,500 rooms or more on New Year's Eve, a substantial increase in the room rate will allow those who have the highest preference (as measured by their willingness and ability to pay) to enjoy the related hospitality services. Besides, when the room rate increases, some of the consumers may postpone or withdraw their demand, and the shortage of hotel rooms in the market could then be reduced, or even eliminated so that the limited resources could be allocated more efficiently.

Did you know? ...

Tourism and the related hospitality services are largely luxuries to consumers. Recently, many studies have shown that on average, the income elasticity of demand for these services is greater than 1. Box 3.1 presents evidence on the demand for tourism in EU countries.

Box 3.1 Demand for tourism as a luxury

A study by Konovalova and Vidishcheva (2013) shows that when spending on tourism and related hospitality services, "consumers are usually sensitive to the change in their income". One example is the global financial crisis in 2008 and 2009, in which the "number of tourism nights spent in collective tourist accommodations in the EU countries fell by 0.6% and 2.8%" (ibid.: 85) respectively in those two years. By referring to the "Tourism trends" statistics released by Eurostat, they further indicate that this percentage rebounded in 2010 when the adverse effects from the financial crisis were reduced. In addition, they indicate that on average, the income elasticity of demand by some countries like Germany, France, Ireland, and the USA for tourism in the UK ranges from 1.35 in Germany to 2.01 in the USA (ibid.: 86).

As consumption expenditure on tourism and related hospitality services brings about substantial economic benefits (e.g., in terms of the share of a country's GDP and employment opportunities provided to the local labor market), Konovalova and Vidishcheva emphasize in their study that "understanding the theory behind demand and its elasticity is very important for policymakers and companies" (ibid.: 88).

Discussion questions:

1   Why did the financial crisis in 2008 and 2009 reduce the number of nights spent in collective tourist accommodations?
2   With reference to the discussions on the changes in demand and supply and their possible impacts on market equilibrium, explain how the market might have adjusted shortly after the financial crisis in 2008 and 2009.
3   Can you think of any reasons why the income elasticity of demand of the Americans for tourism in the UK is higher than that of the Germans?

Conclusions and remarks

Despite the differences in business practices across the different industries, the behavior of consumers and firms in any market share a number of common attributes. The determinants of demand and supply as discussed in this chapter provide the essential grounds for students and practitioners to comprehend these attributes. Besides, illustrations of the various consequences that may result from the changes in demand and/or supply offer a set of simple and useful principles for envisaging the possible changes in the price and/or quantity of a commodity in the market when the related condition(s) change.

In addition, three forms of elasticity (i.e., price, income, and cross-price elasticities) have been introduced, which would undoubtedly broaden current understanding on how consumers might respond to the changes in the major determinants of their consumption behavior. Based on the magnitude of their responsiveness to the changes in a particular commodity in the market, the importance of the commodity can then be identified, which provides important information and guidance to firms in their production and business decisions.

As a service-based economic sector which is composed of a wide range of inter-dependent industries, effective management in the hospitality industry not only requires a good understanding of the basic principles of demand, supply, and elasticity, but also their particular applications for different business purposes. With reference to the materials that have been provided in this chapter, some of the related applications for the hospitality industry will be further elaborated and discussed in Chapter 4.

References and further reading

Becken, S., Lennox, J., 2012. Implications of a long-term increase in oil prices for tourism. *Tourism Management*, 33 (1), 133–142.

Bharucha, J., 2016. Effect of price elasticity of demand on airline tickets. *Asian Journal of Research in Business Economics and Management*, 6 (11), 1–11.

Blake, A., Crotez-Jimenez, I., 2007. The drivers of tourism demand in the UK. Available http://tourismanalysis.yolasite.com/resources/Drivers_of_Tourism_Demand.pdf

Camilleri, M.A., 2018. Chapter 8: Tourism demand and supply. In: M.A. Camilleri, *Travel Marketing, Tourism Economics and the Airline Product: An Introduction to Theory and Practice*. Springer Nature, Cham, Switzerland, pp. 139–154.

Corgel, J., Lane, J., Woodworth, M., 2012. Hotel industry demand curves. *Journal of Hospitality Financial Management*, 20 (1), Article 6. Available https://scholarworks.umass.edu/jhfm/vol20/iss1/6

Gustavo, N., 2013. Marketing management trends in tourism and hospitality industry: Facing the 21st century environment. *International Journal of Marketing Studies*, 5 (3), 13–25.

Hayes, A., n.d. Economics basics: Supply and demand. Available www.investopedia.com/university/economics/economics3.asp

Kenton, W., 2018. Change in demand. Available www.investopedia.com/terms/c/changeindemand.asp

Koh, Y., 2013. The income elasticity of demand and firm performance of US restaurant companies by restaurant type during recessions. *Tourism Economics*, 19 (4), 855–881.

Konovalova, A.A., Vidishcheva, E.V., 2013. Elasticity of demand in tourism and hospitality. *European Journal of Economic Studies*, 4 (2), 84–89.

Parkin, M., 2016. *Microeconomics*, 12th edition. Pearson Education Limited, Harlow, UK.

Skyscanner, n.d. Price elasticity & air fares: Analysing the low cost long haul opportunity. Available https://partners.skyscanner.net/price-elasticity-a-long-haul-low-cost-opportunity-awaits/thought-leadership

Tran, X.V., 2015. Effects of economics factors on demand for luxury hotel rooms in the U.S. *Advance in Hospitality and Tourism Research*, 3 (1), 1–17.

Walsh, K., Enz, C.A., Canina, L., 2004. The impact of gasoline price fluctuations on lodging demand for US brand hotels. *Hospitality Management*, 23, 505–521.

WikiBooks, n.d. Microeconomics/Supply and Demand. Available https://en.wikibooks.org/wiki/Microeconomics/Supply_and_Demand

Wood, P., 2013. Price elasticity and demand change indicators. *Hotel Business Review*, October 06, 2013. Available www.hotelexecutive.com/feature_focus/3606/

Videos

(From the Khan Academy (www.youtube.com/khanacademy) for related economic concepts.)

Khan Academy, n.d. Change in demand versus change in quantity demanded – AP Macroeconomics. Available www.youtube.com/watch?v=iC9hkhbIimA

Khan Academy, n.d. Change in supply versus change in quantity supplied – AP Macroeconomics. Available www.youtube.com/watch?v=NrlF8mMHfLE

Khan Academy, n.d. Cross elasticity of demand – Elasticity – Microeconomics. Available www.youtube.com/watch?v=Ngv0Be9NxAw

Khan Academy, n.d. Elasticity of supply – Elasticity – Microeconomics. Available www.youtube.com/watch?v=AAWsuFXojgo

Khan Academy, n.d. Income elasticity of demand – AP® Microeconomics. Available www.youtube.com/watch?v=RDcf5L6o0mI

Khan Academy, n.d. Law of demand – Supply, demand, and market equilibrium – Microeconomics. Available www.youtube.com/watch?v=ShzPtU7IOXs

Khan Academy, n.d. Law of supply – Supply, demand, and market equilibrium – Microeconomics. Available www.youtube.com/watch?v=3xCzhdVtdMI

Khan Academy, n.d. Market equilibrium – Supply, demand, and market equilibrium – Microeconomics. Available www.youtube.com/watch?v=PEMkfgrifDw

Khan Academy, n.d. Price elasticity of demand using the midpoint method – Elasticity – Microeconomics. Available www.youtube.com/watch?v=slP8XZ6Nq40

CHAPTER

4 Price and output decisions of firms

Objectives and learning outcomes

To any profit-making firm, raising business revenue with a given level of inputs, or reducing the required volume of inputs to achieve a given level of business revenue is a common objective of the management team. To achieve these goals, the principles of demand, supply, and elasticity as outlined in Chapter 3 provide a comprehensive and useful framework for the related discussion in this chapter. Thus, these principles are further elaborated in this chapter in a more practical manner, especially illustrating the price and output decisions of a firm in general and in the hospitality industry. Particularly, the importance of estimating the price elasticity of demand when a firm is trying to adjust the price of its commodity to improve business performance is explicated. In addition, common applications of the related principles by a firm in its price differentiation and bundled pricing strategies, as well as to understand the impacts of a government-imposed expenditure tax on market exchanges, are elucidated.

On the supply side, the relationships between output and different categories of cost (i.e., fixed, variable, and marginal costs) are identified to enhance the understanding of students on how the cost structure of a firm may affect its choice on the business scale. With reference to the cost structure of a firm, price and output decisions in non-peak seasons or on slow business days are also discussed through the basic principle of break-even pricing.

After reading this chapter, students will be able to:

*   understand the specific role of price elasticity of demand on the changes in total revenue when the price of a commodity is adjusted;
*   understand the principles behind price differentiation and the related applications;
*   understand the principle behind bundled pricing and the related applications;
*   understand the impacts and distribution of an expenditure tax on consumers and firms respectively;

- gain familiarity with the cost structure of firms and the changes in various types of costs with respect to the changes in output level; and
- apply break-even pricing for price and output decisions when business is slow.

Price elasticity of demand and total revenue

In the hospitality industry, revenue management (also known as yield management) is an essential aspect of any related firm and its management team. To increase the total revenue of a firm (e.g., a hotel) during a given period of time, managers can take advantage of economic principles, which are generalized propositions that can be used to help them reach a decision with fewer uncertainties. As indicated by Haynes and Egan (2017: 67), for example,

> the dominant areas of interest in the past … were on market analysis of supply and demand, pricing, elasticity of demand, and market segmentation. All these areas are of central importance to revenue management and still impact on hospitality businesses today.

Despite the complexities involved when applying the related economic principles in practical studies to increase the total revenue of a firm, the first question that a manager usually asks is probably whether the price of a commodity (e.g., the rate of a hotel room or the price of an admission ticket to a theme park) should be increased or reduced. In practice, this question could hardly be addressed accordingly without a good understanding of likely consumer response to the proposed change in price. That is, in price and output decisions, it is important that managers have a good grasp of the principles behind the price elasticity of demand and its applications in the first place.

Intuitive reasoning

Since the total revenue (TR) derived from the production of a commodity is measured by multiplying its price and the quantity sold (i.e., TR = price × quantity = pq), and if *demand is price-elastic*, a small reduction in price will therefore attract a higher proportionate increase in the quantity demanded (related principles are provided in Chapter 3) so that the total revenue is increased. In other words, one may assume that if demand is price-elastic, consumers are rather sensitive (responsive) to how much they consume with respect to the changes in price. Thus, if the price of a commodity is reduced by 1%, consumers will buy more than the 1% in quantity. This means that the additional revenue received by a firm from the existing quantity sold exceeds the decrease in revenue due to a lower price charged, so that total revenue is increased.

In contrast, if a firm raises the price of its commodity when demand is price-elastic, customers may react more proportionately to the price change by "walking away" from buying the commodity. Therefore, the gain in revenue due to a price increase may be outweighed by the loss in revenue as the quantity sold is reduced, and thus the total revenue of this firm is decreased.

On the other hand, when *demand is price-inelastic*, consumers are less responsive to a change in price. Accordingly, when a firm raises the price of its commodity, the decrease in quantity demanded is less proportionate to the increase in price so that its total revenue increases. However, if a firm lowers the price of its commodity when demand is price-inelastic, its total revenue is indeed decreased because consumers may not react to the fall in price by buying more of the commodity.

Generalization of the relationship[1] between changes in price and total revenue

In principle, the impacts of price elasticity of demand on total revenue when the price of a commodity changes can be generalized with some simple mathematical operations. Given that TR = pq, if price of a commodity is slightly adjusted by Δp, the quantity demanded will change by Δq, so that the total revenue after the change in price is $(p + \Delta p) \times (q + \Delta q)$. Thus, the changes in the total revenue (ΔTR) is calculated as:

$$\Delta TR = \underbrace{(p + \Delta p)(q + \Delta q) - pq}$$ ↳ Total revenue before price change

Total revenue after price change (4.1)

$$= (pq + p\Delta q + q\Delta p + \Delta p\Delta q) - pq$$

$$\Delta TR = p\Delta q + q\Delta p + \Delta p\Delta q$$

Suppose that when the price slightly changes, so will the change in quantity, and hence, the influence from the product of two small numbers (i.e., $\Delta p\Delta q$) to the change in total revenue as presented in Equation (4.1) can be ignored (i.e., let $\Delta p\Delta q = 0$ to simplify the related calculations). Therefore,

$$\Delta TR = p\Delta q + q\Delta p$$ (4.2)

To determine the change in total revenue with respect to the change in price, both sides of Equation (4.2) are divided by Δp.

$$\frac{\Delta TR}{\Delta p} = \frac{\Delta q}{\Delta p}p + q$$ (4.3)

Generally speaking, Equation (4.3) shows the change in total revenue with respect to the change in price by 1 unit (e.g., per dollar increase or decrease in price). By referring to Equation (3.2) in Chapter 3 in which the price elasticity of demand $\varepsilon_d = \dfrac{\%\Delta q_d}{\%\Delta p} = \dfrac{\Delta q_d}{\Delta p} \cdot \dfrac{p}{q_d}$, Equation (4.3) can be rewritten as:

$$\frac{\Delta TR}{\Delta p} = q\left(\frac{\Delta q}{\Delta p}\frac{p}{q} + 1\right)$$

Thus, $\dfrac{\Delta TR}{\Delta p} = q(\varepsilon_d + 1)$ 　　　　　　　　　　　　　　　　　(4.4)

If *demand is price-elastic* (i.e., when the price changes by 1%, the quantity demanded changes in the opposite direction by more than 1%, so that $\varepsilon_d < -1$), then $(\varepsilon_d + 1)$ is negative. As the quantity sold in the market (q) is a positive number, $q(\varepsilon_d + 1)$ in Equation (4.4) is negative. So, $\Delta TR/\Delta P < 0$, which means that the *change in price and the change in total revenue move in the opposite direction*. In other words, when the change in the price of the commodity is positive (*increasing*), the change in the total revenue is negative (*decreasing*), and vice versa.

On the other hand, if the *demand is price-inelastic* (i.e., when the price changes by 1%, the quantity demanded changes in the opposite direction by less than 1%, so that $-1 < \varepsilon_d < 0$), $q(\varepsilon_d + 1)$ in Equation (4.4) is positive. This means that $\Delta TR/\Delta P > 0$, *and the change in price and the change in total revenue are moving in the same direction*. Accordingly, when the price increases, the total revenue also increases, and vice versa. These relationships are summarized in Table 4.1.

Applications in practice

The relationships between the change in price and change in total revenue as summarized in Table 4.1 provide important (although not the only)

Table 4.1 Relationships between changes in price and total revenue under different price elasticities of demand

Price elasticity of demand (ε_d)	Change in price (Δp)	Change in total revenue (ΔTR)
Elastic $(\varepsilon_d < -1)$	Increase (+)	Decrease (−)
	Decrease (−)	Increase (+)
Inelastic $(-1 < \varepsilon_d < 0)$	Increase (+)	Increase (+)
	Decrease (−)	Decrease (−)

grounds for business managers and scholars when they are making related decisions or conducting related studies. Indeed, this is a common topic that is included in most, if not all introductory economics textbooks to illustrate business applications. For example, in the well-known *Economics* text written by Samuelson and Nordhaus (2002: 72), a simple presented example is that

> business travelers have an inelastic demand for air travel, so an increase in business fares tends to raise revenue. By contrast, leisure travelers have much more elastic demand for air travel because they have much more choice about where and when they are traveling. As a result, raising leisure fare tends to decrease revenue.

In the latest edition of their book, it is further indicated that "understanding demand elasticities is worth billions of dollars each year to U.S. airlines" (Samuelson and Nordhaus, 2010: 70).

In many academic studies and industry practices that focus on the topics of revenue management and price decisions of hospitality firms, the principle of price elasticity demand is commonly included or emphasized. For example, the price elasticity of demand is a popular measure that researchers use to understand why discounted room rates may increase the occupancy rate but lower the total revenue in many hotels (Enz et al., 2004), or show the success of revenue management and pricing strategies, such as those of the Carlson Rezidor Hotel Group (Enz et al., 2004). In addition, the application of this same principle is also commonly found in related topics of studies on theme parks and cruise ships (e.g., Adhikari et al., 2013; Heo and Lee, 2009; Vogel, 2009).

Simply put, the relationship between the changes in price and total revenue can be applied in a way that is a useful reference for related business decisions. Indeed, this could be determined by considering that the relationships in Table 4.1 move in the opposite direction. In some economic textbooks, this is known as the "total revenue test" (Parkin, 2016: 126) for the price elasticity of demand.

Since business is ongoing, a firm may apply this principle to test the responsiveness of consumers by pricing its goods and services with slight differences on certain days or in certain seasons. If the total revenue increases when price is adjusted upward in several trials under the similar context (e.g., weekends or particular holidays), it is possible that the price elasticity of demand is inelastic. In contrast, if the price is reduced on select normal days and during non-peak seasons yet the total revenue is increased, it is reasonable to infer that the price elasticity of demand is elastic. Otherwise, demand is price-inelastic and attempts to lower the price on select normal days to improve business turnover may not be a wise decision.

Price differentiation

In practice, an essential application of the price elasticity of demand is to use a pricing strategy in which different groups of consumers whose elasticity of demand for a commodity differ (i.e., price differentiation for different consumer groups) are charged different prices. Indeed, the previous example in Samuelson and Nordhaus (2002) on airlines that charge business and leisure travelers different air fares is a form of price differentiation. In the hospitality industry, some other common examples include "happy hour" prices for food and beverage versus the price of regular meals, early booking versus walk-in rates of hotels, express (fast-track) versus normal tickets in theme parks, adult versus elderly and child fares for admission fees, and discounts on normal days given to locals for attractions.

In principle, suppose that consumers are familiar with the general market price of a commodity, and a particular group may be more responsive to the quantity purchased due to a change in price than another group, owing to, say, differences in their time, income, and wealth. Thus, if a lower price is offered exclusively to this group, the total revenue received by the vendor may increase as compared to charging the same price to all consumers. For example, students in general may have a lower budget than the working population for recreation, but are more flexible in time, especially during the summer season and on some of the regular weekends. Accordingly, a theme park may consider it worthwhile to offer them discounted tickets in certain months or on certain days to increase its business turnover. In contrast, if those who are inelastic in their demand can be identified, they would be subjected to a higher price without incurring a substantial reduction in their consumption which would then increase the total revenue.

Conditions for price differentiation

Based on the principle of price elasticity of demand and its relationship with total revenue, the effectiveness and efficiency of various price differentiation schemes in practice simultaneously depend on three conditions. The absence of one or more of these conditions may greatly reduce the potential gain in total revenue from price differentiation.

Determining price elasticity of demand of major consumer groups/ segments and anticipated consumption volume

The effectiveness of formulating and practicing a price differentiation scheme relies on the ability of a firm to clearly identify the primary consumer groups whose price elasticity of demand is either elastic or inelastic (or even the magnitude of the elasticity). Besides, the targeted groups who are charged different prices should be relatively large in scale so that their consumption volume are worthy of validation. This is the first important condition that allows a firm to anticipate the likely outcome of its total revenue by charging different prices to different consumer groups.

Efficiency of reducing costs for different consumer groups

As the ultimate goal of a firm in raising its total revenue is to increase its profit, and profit is derived from deducting the total cost from total revenue, the real economic benefits that a firm can receive may be reduced in one form or another if a large sum of additional funds and/or more time is required to execute the price differentiation scheme. Thus, a price differentiation scheme should not be overly complex and should be able to be carried out efficiently within business operations. For example, it is a common practice of theme parks to offer student and non-student admission prices, but not different prices with small differences for all of the different age groups, nor for different nationalities.

Non-transferability of commodity between different consumer groups

To reach the desired end state of price differentiation, it is important to ensure that those who pay a lower price for the commodity cannot (and will not) resell the commodity to those who are charged a higher price. Otherwise, only a few would actually pay the higher price so that the total revenue may not increase very much. Even worse, there might be a fall in profits if the extra cost to carry out the scheme cannot be fully covered.

Applications in hospitality industry

Originally, the idea of price differentiation was introduced by an economist in the 19th century called Jules Dupuit (1804–1866) under the term "price discrimination". The fundamental goal was to investigate the different pricing schemes that could be applied by a government monopoly in providing various forms of public goods and services like "roads, bridges, and water systems" (Brue and Grant, 2013: 236) to different users. In the hospitality industry, extensive applications of this concept were initially in the airline industry in the late 1970s, which were then found in the hotel, car rental and restaurant industries (Kimes, 1989; Heo and Lee, 2009). Kimes (1989) stated that owing to the increasing levels of competition in the US airline industry after its deregulation in the late 1970s, the industry became "the birthplace of yield management" which started to apply the principle of price differentiation to sell "the right seat to the right customer at the right price so as to maximize yield" (Kimes, 1989: 15).

In echoing Kimes (1989), Heo and Lee (2009) reiterate that revenue management "is basically a form of price differentiation and market segmentation", which is mainly carried out by "charging premium prices to the less price-sensitive market segments … and at the same time charging discounted prices to a price-sensitive market segment to encourage increased sales …" (Heo and Lee, 2009: 448). By comparing the similarities and differences among the traditional hospitality industries (such as the hotel and airline industries) with the modern theme park industry, Heo and Lee (2009) further explore and propose other applications of revenue management (like "demand-based pricing policy" and "variable admission price policy" (ibid.: 451)) for theme parks to maximize their total revenue. In their study, price differentiation evidently serves as one of the major guiding principles.

Lastly, following the rapid advancement of technologies since the advent of the 21st century (especially under the wide applications of digital-based information technology and Big Data), more subdivided market segments and more tailored price differentiation schemes have been identified and used by the various sectors in the hospitality industry. Generally speaking, technological advancement not only allows firms to reduce their marginal cost when implementing price differentiation schemes, but also identify different market segments more efficiently.

Bundled pricing

In the hospitality industry, another common strategy that firms use to increase business turnover is to bundle a package of services and consumable goods to sell for a single price. For example, many hotels may promote a single price that would allow their guests to also enjoy various dining and entertainment services during their stay, like that shown in Illustration 4.1. This is also a unique feature of the cruise industry as shown in Illustration 4.2.

On the other hand, some of the hospitality firms may provide an alternative (choice) to consumers to pay for itemized services or products such as a resort fee and room services on top of their basic hotel room fee. In contrast to bundled pricing, this is known as partitioned pricing. For example, resort fees

Eat, Drink & Stay all for one price!
One price, endless experiences … Book your package and receive a hotel stay in one of our suites, breakfast, lunch and dinner at some of our most popular outlets and beverages … during your stay!

Illustration 4.1 Bundled pricing offered by a hotel in Las Vegas, USA

Source: www.caesars.com/rio-las-vegas/hotel/all-inclusive-package (retrieved on April 8, 2018)

Best Cruise Lines for the Money
Since a cruise is basically a package deal, with
lodging, food and entertainment all included in one
price, a vacation at sea is often better value than a
land-based getaway

Illustration 4.2 Example of bundled pricing in the cruise ship industry

Source: https://travel.usnews.com/cruises/best-cruise-lines-for-the-money/ (retrieved on April 8, 2018)

that are charged separately by many hotels have been a common strategy of partitioned pricing (see, e.g., O'Neill and Quadri-Felitti, 2016; Repetti et al., 2015). Despite the pros and cons of bundled pricing and partitioned pricing, their strategies and practices are influenced by the principles of demand, supply, and elasticity.

Principles and practices

Chapter 3 discussed how the demand of a consumer reflects his/her willingness and ability to pay for a commodity in the market. Thus, his/her perceived benefit derived from the enjoyment of the commodity is represented by the area below the demand curve. In turn, s/he pays a price for enjoying the commodity. If a consumer pays on average a market price that is less than his/her highest willingness to pay, s/he obtains a net gain. In economics, this gain from consumption is called *consumer surplus*.

As illustrated in Figure 4.1, given that the demand schedule of a consumer for hotel rooms is D_h, and if the room rate is p_1, this consumer will purchase q nights of the hotel room service. To enjoy q nights in the hotel, this consumer is willing to pay the highest amount that is equal to the area of $hdqo_h$. Since the room rate is p_1, s/he pays p_1dqo_h. Therefore, s/he enjoys a consumer surplus represented by the area of hdp_1.

To increase total revenue, a hotel may consider bundling its hotel room service with another commodity, say, a breakfast buffet for a single price, to capture part of the consumer surplus. Generally speaking, although this bundled price is higher than the hotel room rate itself (e.g., p_b as compared to p_1 as depicted in Figure 4.1), a consumer may feel that the bundled price is less in comparison to the sum of the prices of the two commodities.

For example, if the listed price of a breakfast buffet is p_2 and if the consumer also wants (even though it is not necessary) to have the breakfast in the hotel, s/he will buy a quantity of r buffets in accordance with his/her demand

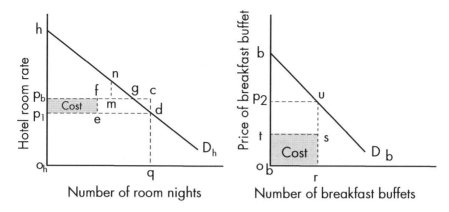

Figure 4.1 Economic principle of bundled pricing

schedule (D_b). By bundling these two commodities together, even though the area of $p_b cdp_1$ is commonly smaller than the area of $p_2 uro_b$, it still represents an increase in the total revenue of the hotel with one transaction as a transfer from consumer surplus to the realized revenue of the hotel (i.e., the area of $p_b mndp_1$, where the area mng = area cdg). In other words, when a hotel is selling its rooms, the consumer is also charged for the breakfast buffet.

Since the cost of providing a breakfast buffet to any customer is the same to the hotel (i.e., area $o_b rst$ = area $p_1 efp_b$), the profit of the hotel also increases (e.g., by the area of cdef in Figure 4.1). Although this profit may be less than the area of $tsup_2$ in which the breakfast buffet had been separately sold to a customer, the related spending of the customer is now guaranteed instead of allowing him/her to make the choice through free will after s/he arrives at the hotel. In addition, this bundling strategy may allow the hotel to better plan for food quantity (supply) for breakfast, and further reduce the cost for the service.

From the standpoint of many consumers, especially those who may be more inelastic in their demand for hotel rooms and related services like business travelers, they may consider this bundle as long as the bundled price is within their highest willingness and ability to pay. Besides, although a consumer may finally decide to forgo one or more breakfasts during his/her stay at the hotel, s/he may only feel that s/he paid a higher room rate of p_b instead of p_1, and that s/he might still have enjoyed a consumer surplus (the area of $p_b mnh$ instead of hdp_1).

Bundled pricing and price differentiation

Based on the aforementioned examples, it is not difficult to see that bundled pricing is indeed associated with the principle of price differentiation, but the opposite may not necessarily hold. For example, when airlines charge passengers higher prices for business class than economy class, the price differences are also justified by the different in-flight services and food and beverages that are bundled. In contrast, a higher price for a fast-track ticket offered by a theme park which simply allows a consumer to save time and avoid waiting in a long queue to enjoy attractions and other services is solely a form of price differentiation.

Despite the differences between bundled pricing and price differentiation in business practices, the feasibility of identifying and segmenting different consumer groups serves as a common ground to ensure the desired ends (i.e., to raise business revenue) from these pricing strategies. In bundled pricing, a particular group of consumers who may be less responsive (or inelastic) to a higher price charged for a package of commodities (which has a major commodity that they want to purchase and one or more complementary items) instead of paying a lower price to just purchase the major commodity in the package must be clearly differentiable.

In addition, the effectiveness of a bundled pricing strategy in the market may also rely on the consumer being able to easily compare whether the bundled price is actually less than the sum of each item purchased separately. As indicated by Tjan (2010), if customers are offered "simple transactions in which separate and package pricing can be quickly compared" (Tjan, 2010: 2), they may be more inclined to accept and pay for the related bundle of commodities. Otherwise, consumers (especially those who are non-business and budget-sensitive individual travelers) may prefer to pay for separate items when they really want them. In other words, if the price charged for bundled commodities is clearly higher than the sum of the prices of individual items in the package, or the price difference between a major commodity and the package as a whole is evidently larger than the consumer surplus, s/he may not choose this bundle.

Expenditure taxes

Considering that a large proportion of the hospitality commodities traded in the market are non-necessities or luxuries (see discussion related to Figure 1.1 in Chapter 1), it is a common practice of governments to tax the consumption of these commodities as a means to raise public revenue. Since the tax is imposed on the consumption (either on the quantity or the expenditure), the market price of related commodities also changes, hence influencing the buying behavior of consumers and the output decisions of firms.

Definition and impact of expenditure tax

In principle, an expenditure tax is imposed onto a commodity when it is consumed. Thus, the ultimate cost of consumers for enjoying a commodity will increase after this tax. Suppose that the market demand and market supply schedules for the dining services of a restaurant are D and S respectively before the tax; see Figure 4.2. In equilibrium (e), an average price of p is charged by the restaurant for its meals and a quantity of q meals are sold.

If an expenditure tax of $t is imposed onto a meal consumed, the restaurant is supposed to collect this tax on behalf of the government. Based on the number of meals sold, say, in one year, the restaurant is then required to pay the total sum of this tax to the government. However, if the restaurant does not impose this tax to its customers, this tax comes from its own revenue which is similar to incurring an extra business cost. Therefore, the effect from an expenditure tax is similar to an upward parallel shift of the supply curve from S to S+t as shown in Figure 4.2.

Generally speaking, if demand is downward sloping and supply is upward sloping, the expenditure tax is shared between the consumers and the restaurant. Again applying Figure 4.2 as an example, an upward shift of the supply curve after the tax leads to a new equilibrium (e_t). In this new equilibrium, a higher price (p_c instead of p) is billed to the customers so that their quantity demanded will decrease from q to q_t. However, after receiving p_c from serving a meal, the restaurant can actually earn p_s. The total amount of expenditure tax that is paid to the government is measured by multiplying the difference between p_c and p_s and the quantity sold [i.e., $(p_c - p_s) \times q_t$]. For this expenditure tax, the share provided by the consumer is $(p_c - p) \times q_t$, and the share of the restaurant is $(p - p_s) \times q_t$.

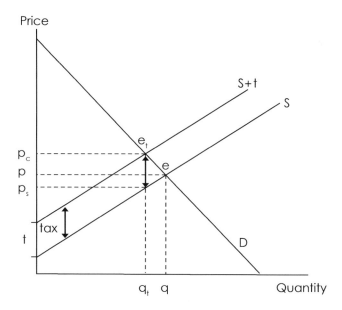

Figure 4.2 Impacts of expenditure tax on equilibrium price and quantity

Price elasticity as a benchmark

A management team of any firm will find it necessary to enquire about the amount of expenditure tax that the company has to pay so that the impact to its total revenue is minimized. If the customers shoulder more of the tax burden in terms of paying a higher price, how would their response, which could be to reduce the quantity consumed, affect the total revenue of a firm? In contrast, if the firm shoulders more of the tax, what is a reasonable amount? To address these questions, the principle of price elasticity is a useful benchmark.

Intuitively, if consumers are more price-elastic in their consumption than firms in their production, the latter may not be able to transfer a greater portion of the tax to its customers, and hence shoulder a higher portion of the tax, and vice versa. In extreme cases, if the price elasticity of supply of a firm is totally inelastic, the firm has to shoulder all of the tax. Conversely, if the price elasticity of demand of consumers is totally inelastic, they have to bear all of the tax.

By referring back to Equations (3.2) and (3.3) in Chapter 3, the ratio of the price elasticity of supply to that of demand ($\varepsilon_p^s / \varepsilon_p^d$) can be simplified by using the notations of Figure 4.1 which is presented in Equation (4.5) below.

$$\frac{\varepsilon_p^s}{\varepsilon_p^d} = \frac{{}^{\%\Delta q_s}\!\big/\!{}_{\%\Delta p_s}}{{}^{\%\Delta q_d}\!\big/\!{}_{\%\Delta p_d}} = \frac{\dfrac{\Delta q_s}{q} \dfrac{p}{\Delta p_s}}{\dfrac{\Delta q_d}{q} \dfrac{p}{\Delta p_d}} = \frac{\dfrac{q_t - q}{q} \dfrac{p}{p - p_s}}{\dfrac{q_t - q}{q} \dfrac{p}{p_c - p}} = \frac{p_c - p}{p - p_s} \quad (4.5)$$

In the last simplified term of Equation (4.5), ($p_c - p$) stands for the higher price paid by a consumer as his/her share of the expenditure tax, and ($p - p_s$) refers to the lower price ultimately received by the firm following the imposition of the tax. The difference between p_c and p_s is then equivalent to the tax submitted to the government (i.e., $t per unit sold as shown in Figure 4.2). Accordingly, the share of an expenditure tax between a firm and its customers is determined inverse proportionally to the ratio of the price elasticity of supply to that of demand, as rewritten in Equation (4.6).

$$\frac{\varepsilon_p^s}{\varepsilon_p^d} = \frac{\text{Price elasticity of supply}}{\text{Price elasticity of demand}} = \frac{\text{Share of the tax by consumers}}{\text{Share of the tax by a firm}} = \frac{p_c - p}{p - p_s} \quad (4.6)$$

For example, if an expenditure tax of $6 is imposed onto each admission ticket sold by a theme park, and if the price elasticity of supply of the tickets is 2 and that of demand for the tickets is 1, the theme park pays $2 while the consumers pay $4 of the tax. That is,

$$\left(\frac{\text{Price elasticity of supply}}{\text{Price elasticity of demand}} = \frac{2}{1} \right) = \left(\frac{\text{Share of the tax by consumers}}{\text{Share of the tax by a firm}} = \frac{\$4}{\$2} \right).$$

In other words, the theme park will raise the price of its admission tickets by \$4, and then pay the remaining \$2 of tax. This example also shows that if a firm is more elastic in its production than a consumer in his/her consumption (e.g., $\varepsilon_p^s = 2 > \varepsilon_p^d = 1$), the firm will shoulder less tax than the consumers. In contrast, if consumers are more elastic in their consumption, the firm will have to shoulder a higher portion of the tax.

Cost structure of firms

While price plays a central role in any production and business decision, the quantity produced or business volume chosen by a firm could be hardly determined if its cost of production is not taken into account at the same time. As discussed in Chapter 1, the output decision of a firm is guided by marginal revenue and marginal cost (see discussions related to Figure 1.3). In principle, a firm will continue to produce as long as the revenue derived from an extra unit of output (i.e., marginal revenue) is higher than the extra cost of producing this unit (i.e., marginal cost). To make this comparison, cost is an indispensable factor for measuring the marginal cost while price allows a firm to assess the marginal revenue.

Total fixed and variable costs

To any firm, the cost of production or doing business is broadly categorized into fixed and variable costs. As the terms suggest, fixed cost will not change over a certain range of output (or period of time), while variable cost changes according to the different quantities or levels of output.

Based on the investment and business decisions made by a firm at the beginning of a time period, some costs like interest payments for capital funds and rental expenses are fixed, say, on an annual basis. These costs may not be neglected nor change once the business commences. In addition, salaries paid to directors and managerial/administrative teams like executive officers and accountants may also be fixed despite business turnover. In other words, within the planned capacity of a production site or a business scale, the sum (total) of these costs is a fixed amount (e.g., a positive amount like f as shown on the vertical axis in Figure 4.3) throughout the entire range of output or business volume (i.e., the horizontal line TFC as shown in Figure 4.3).

Variable inputs have to be used to operate a business on a daily basis. For example, after a hotel starts business with the required fixed assets and business inputs in the first place, different variable factors need to be taken into consideration at the operational level such as front desk employees, concierge staff, and housekeeping positions. Besides, various consumable inputs like electricity, cleaning appliances, and maintenance equipment will be spent in proportion to the occupancy rate of the hotel and use of its related facilities. In principle, if the hotel is not open for business, variable inputs and hence total variable cost is zero. When it is open for business, a total variable cost

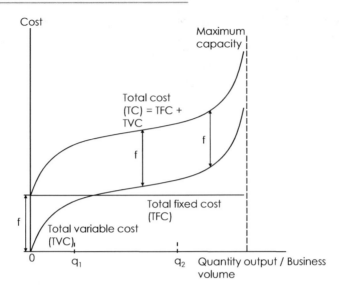

Figure 4.3 Behavior of the fixed, variable, and total costs of a firm

will be incurred and increases as a consequence of the increase in business volume.

When a firm begins to produce or operate, its total variable cost (TVC) increases, which is shown as a steep upward sloping curve in Figure 4.3. This increase slows down (the curve becomes flat) when the output level continues to increase. Yet, when the output level or business volume approaches the maximum capacity of the firm, there is a substantial increase in the total variable cost (the curve steeply slopes upward again). Indeed, the behavior (i.e., the shape) of the TVC curve is consistent with the characteristics and contributions of the related variable factors in the production or business process.

Going back to the example of the practices of a hotel (which could also hold true for a theme park or a restaurant), it can be easily observed that labor cost at the operational level always represents a large portion of the total variable cost. This is because when a hotel opens its doors for business, a given number of servicing employees have to be hired for various positions even if the check-in rate is only 10% or 20% on a very slow business day (e.g., around q_1 in Figure 4.3). Nevertheless, if the occupancy rate increases to, say, 60% or 70%, the related employees would be more "busy" but the hotel does not need to hire extra labor. The extra cost is likely due to money spent on utilities and related consumable inputs. In other words, between a certain range of output (e.g., between q_1 and q_2 in Figure 4.3), the increase in the total variable cost is minimal as the extra services could be largely provided by the current labour pool when they are free and available during non-peak times.

On peak business days like the weekend or public holidays when the occupancy rate is quite high (e.g., greater than q_2 as shown in Figure 4.3), part-time workers may need to hired or current workers may need to be paid overtime which means that the increase in total variable cost is evidently higher. In addition, the maintenance cost (or cost for wear and tear) may also increase as the maximum capacity is approaching. Thus, the increase in the total variable cost of a hotel will be much higher in the peak season as opposed to normal business days.

Since the total cost is the sum of the total fixed cost and total variable cost (i.e., TC = TFC + TVC), the behavior of the total cost curve is represented by a parallel shift of the total variable cost curve upward by the amount of total fixed cost. As shown in Figure 4.3, the distance between the TC and the TVC curves is the same (i.e., a distance of f) at different output levels.

Marginal and average costs

The marginal and the respective average costs could be clarified with reference to the aforementioned behavior of total cost. Mathematically, the marginal cost (MC) is the change in total cost (ΔTC) with respect to the change in quantity output (Δq). As shown in Equation (4.7), since total cost is the sum of the total fixed cost and total variable cost, and the former does not change (ΔTFC = 0), marginal cost can simply be measured by the change in total variable cost (ΔTVC) with respect to the change in quantity output.

$$MC = \frac{\Delta TC}{\Delta q} = \frac{\Delta(TFC + TVC)}{\Delta q} = \frac{\Delta TVC}{\Delta q} \tag{4.7}$$

As marginal cost depends on the incremental cost of producing one more unit of output, the average cost shows on average, the cost of producing each unit of the output when a total of q units are produced. Thus, the average fixed cost (AFC), average variable cost (AVC) and average total cost (ATC) as expressed in Equations (4.8a), (4.8b) and (4.8c) are derived by dividing the respective total cost by the quantity that is produced.

$$AFC = \frac{TFC}{q} \tag{4.8a}$$

$$AVC = \frac{TVC}{q} \tag{4.8b}$$

$$ATC = \frac{TC}{q} \tag{4.8c}$$

Also, since total cost is the sum of the total fixed cost and total variable cost, the same is for the average total cost as shown in Equation (4.9).

$$ATC = AFC + AVC \qquad (4.9)$$

The behavior of these costs in accordance with their characteristics with respect to different output levels is shown in Figure 4.4. First, as the total fixed cost does not change, the slope of the average fixed cost (AFC) shows a downward trend of decline when the quantity output increases (i.e., moving away from the origin to the right in Figure 4.4). For example, at a lower level of output like q_1, the average fixed cost is higher than that at a higher level of output like q_2.

Behavior of marginal cost

Unoccupied (or idle) time (or capacity) of servicing workers due to variable factors like operational labor of a firm when its output level or business volume is low may increase business turnover with a lower additional cost than the preceding unit produced or sold. A primary reason is that any variable factor that is used like labor may have a minimum efficiency level (or ability to

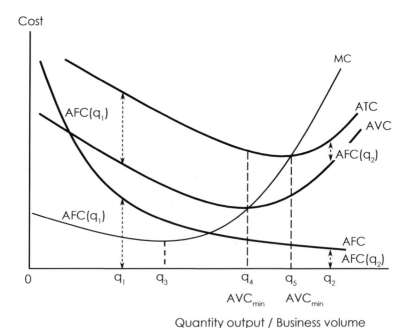

Figure 4.4 Behavior of average fixed, average variable, and average total costs of firm

produce a given level of output) without extra spending (cost). Besides, work efficiency increases with routine incorporated in the work role. In other words, more output can be generated with fewer additional resources needed, and hence the marginal cost is reduced when output or business volume increases from a low level (e.g., below q_3 as shown in Figure 4.3).

However, when the quantity output or business volume continues to increase beyond a certain level (e.g., greater than q_3), the marginal cost starts to increase. This may be due to the decline in efficiency of labor under long working hours or more pressure when workload continues to increase. When the quantity output or business volume further increases, extra variable factors may have to be put into place, and as a result, there is a substantial increase in marginal cost.

Behavior of average costs

As shown in Equations (4.7) and (4.8b), marginal cost represents an addition to the total variable cost when the quantity output increases, and average variable cost which is calculated by dividing the total variable cost by the quantity output. Therefore, the average variable cost continues to fall as long as the marginal (additional) cost associated with the extra units of output are below average. In contrast, when the marginal cost increase is above the average variable cost, the average variable cost is increased. As indicated in Figure 4.4, the average variable cost continues to decline to q_4 when the marginal cost is less than the average variable cost, and increases when the marginal cost is greater than the average variable cost. So the average variable cost is at minimum at q_4 when it is equal to the marginal cost.

$$\text{AVC is at minimum } (\text{AVC}_{min}) \text{ when AVC} = \text{MC} \qquad (4.10)$$

The average total cost (ATC) is the sum of the average variable cost and average fixed cost, and hence the average variable cost curve shifts upward by the amount of average fixed cost at each level of output. Since the average fixed cost decreases when output increases, the gap between the average total cost and average variable cost is somewhat reduced when output increases (e.g., the gap corresponding to q_2 is much smaller than q_1 as shown in Figure 4.4).

Technically speaking, since the average total cost curve is above the average variable cost curve, the marginal cost curve will meet the average cost curve first (e.g., at q_4) and then the average total cost curve (e.g., at q_5, ATC is at minimum). Hence, it is possible that a firm may experience a fall in its average total cost while its average variable cost is increasing (e.g., within an output range between q_4 and q_5 as shown in Figure 4.4).

$$\text{ATC is at minimum } (\text{AVC}_{min}) \text{ when ATC} = \text{MC} \qquad (4.11)$$

Cost, price, and output decision

Given the general behavior of the cost structure of a firm as illustrated in Figure 4.4, it can be easily observed that in any short period of time when a fixed cost cannot be eliminated, a firm will choose an output level of q_4 or higher if the market price (or marginal revenue) equals or is higher than the minimum average variable cost. By choosing any output level higher than q_4 where the marginal revenue equals marginal cost, the revenue received in excess of the average variable cost could be used to cover some of the fixed costs so that net loss can be minimized. Moreover, if the price is higher than the minimum average total cost, the firm will produce more than q_5 (until MR = MC) so that profit can be maximized.

However, if the market price is below the average variable cost, the firm should not produce any more (i.e., should shut down) because any unit produced means an additional loss to the firm on top of its fixed cost. Thus, the portion of the marginal cost curve of a firm that is above the minimum average variable cost curve is indeed equivalent to the supply curve as applied to reflect the output decision of a firm with respect to various prices.

In the short run, a firm will shut down if p (or MR) < AVC.   (4.12)

If the market price for a firm's output is persistently below its average total cost over a long period of time, the firm will shut down and leave the market.

In the long run: a firm will shut down if p (or MR) < ATC.   (4.13)

Break-even pricing

Given the fixed capacity of the hospitality industry (e.g., number of rooms and the facilities of a hotel, or number of tables and size of the kitchen of a restaurant, or geographical area and related facilities of a theme park), a major attribute in the supply of its services is that unoccupied capacity, and hence unsold services on a slow business day, may not be stored so that they can expand their volume of services beyond maximum capacity on a peak day. In addition, it is commonly observed that on a slow business day, the output and price decisions by following the MR = MC criterion may not necessarily allow a firm to derive sufficient revenue to cover its total variable cost of business. For example, as illustrated in Figure 4.5, when MR = MC, the total revenue derived from the business by supplying a quantity output of q_1 (i.e., represented by the area of $P_{MR=MC} \times q_1$) is less than the total variable cost ($AVC_{MR=MC} \times q_1$).

In Figure 4.5, the marginal revenue curve is under the demand curve because to sell more services (like physical products), a non-price differentiating firm has to lower the price to all customers, instead of a new customer only. Consequently, the net increment in the total revenue (i.e., marginal revenue) is the price received from the extra unit sold minus the loss from existing customers who were paying a higher price. In other words, while a downward-sloping demand curve shows the average revenue derived from each unit sold with respect to a particular price, its corresponding marginal revenue curve is underneath, when more is sold by lowering the price (this relationship between a downward-sloping demand curve and its corresponding marginal revenue curve can be found in any economics textbook).

In circumstances of low demand, a break-even criterion instead of a profit-maximization criterion may be more meaningful to the price and output decisions of the firm. Instead of closing the business on slow days, the firm may adjust its price downward from normal days or peak days to a level such that on average, the willingness of customers to pay for the commodity may at least allow the firm to cover its variable cost of business; that is, *a price and output level under which total revenue equals total variable (operational) cost – break-even*. As illustrated in Figure 4.5, a firm can stay in business by setting a price at $P_{break-even}$ and choosing a business volume at q_2.

$$\text{Break-even pricing: price where AR = AVC} \qquad (4.14)$$

In practice, break-even pricing means the lowest average price which is acceptable by a firm if a certain quantity output is to be supplied (or business volume is to be maintained). This provides particular insights to a firm into its price and output decisions when business is slow. When making related decisions, a firm should understand the behavior of its average variable cost with respect to various levels of output.

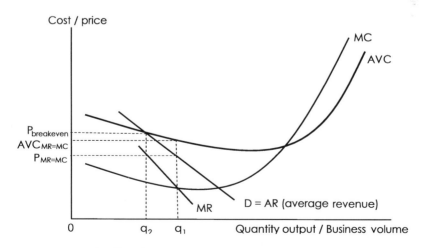

Figure 4.5 Principle of break-even pricing

Did you know? ...

Although revenue management has long been prevalent in the various hospitality industries such hotels, airlines and theme parks, the practice has continued to advance strategically since the beginning of the 21st century. Traditionally, revenue management was largely in the form of inventory management which simply focused on selling more rooms, seats or admission tickets which are the "inventory" of the hospitality firms. Today, this is a highly complex and challenging area to the top management of any hospitality firm with much emphasis on understanding the behavior of consumers and setting the right prices for different market segments, rather than just aiming to increase the quantity sold of the same commodity.

Box 4.1 Price elasticity as measure to optimize price, and hence business volume and total revenue

According to the extensive data in Enz et al. (2004: 24): "offering guests prices that are lower than those of competitors does lead to higher occupancy percentages for the discounting hotel, but these comparatively lower prices do not increase RevPAR performance compared to the competition". In other words, reducing the price in the attempt to increase the quantity sold may not always result in higher total revenue, and therefore is not necessarily an effective means of revenue management.

In their study, Cross et al. (2009: 56) argue that fundamentally, "prices are essentially transparent, hotels will need to consider customer price elasticity and not simply match competitors' prices, with a goal of optimizing prices". By referring to the experiences shared by hotel group leaders on revenue management such as Marriott International, Hyatt, and Carlson Hotels, Cross et al. (2009) indicate that understanding and measuring the price elasticity of demand of hotel customers to the different room rates have been a commonly agreed upon measure by the industries to set their prices right.

In addition, different customer groups in the market could be differentiated through the measurement of price elasticity of demand. This empowers a hotel to price its rooms and related services differently to different customers. Thus, a hotel may be able to utilize its fixed capacity in any given period of time effectively and efficiently, and hence optimize its business volume and total revenue. Nevertheless, it is also evident to the industries that "determining the elasticity of that interaction is a tremendous challenge" (Cross et al., 2009: 67).

Discussion questions:

1   With reference to the discussions in this chapter, explain why lowering room rates "does not increase the RevPAR performance" (i.e., revenue per available room) of a hotel.
2   Think about any two customer groups whose price elasticity of demand for hotel rooms are clearly different on normal days. What are the strategies available to a hotel for establishing prices for these two customer groups respectively so that its total revenue could be optimized?
3   In practice, why is it that "determining the elasticity of that interaction is a tremendous challenge"?

Conclusions and remarks

In contrast to the production of traditional and physical commodities, a unique feature of hospitality is that it is supplied by the "capacity-limited services industries" in which "variable demands and segmentable markets" are associated with business practices (Heo and Lee, 2009: 446). As discussed and shown in this chapter, when demand is "variable" and the market is "segmentable", the principle of price elasticity of demand and the related economic rationale provide useful grounds for firms to approach the related price and output decisions.

Indeed, it is shown that the price elasticity of demand conveys essential information to firms to identify different market segments (in terms of different consumer groups, or different business time periods) for the same commodity. Thus, price differentiation and bundled pricing have become plausible measures to increase total revenue. Besides, to minimize the effects from an expenditure tax to price and the business volume, and hence total revenue, related modifications in the price and output decisions may hardly be effective if the price elasticities of demand and supply are not reasonably assessed.

In addition, it is important to emphasize that the characteristics of a hospitality firm are to provide services with fixed space and number of facilities, so that unoccupied capacity on any one business day does not allow a firm to produce any services in advance for sale in the future. This non-storable feature of hospitality services (in contrast to physical commodities) implies that the criteria (from both the demand and supply sides) that guide the price and output decisions of a firm for the same commodity may be quite different among peak (e.g., the case illustrated in Figure 3.7 in Chapter 3), normal and slow (the case illustrated in Figure 4.5 in this chapter) days.

Overall, it is evident that the attributes of demand for hospitality services as a service-based industry, and the supply structure of hospitality services, have their unique qualities. Therefore, an in-depth understanding and experience from the practices are indispensable for proficiency in applying such principles to related business decisions.

Note

1 To generalize the relationship between the changes in price and total revenue when the price elasticity of demand is elastic and inelastic respectively, some simple mathematical operations are absolutely necessary. Students who feel less than confident with the related calculations that are presented in this section do not need to spend extra time on the related materials. Instead, the related discussions and the general relationships as presented in Table 4.1 are derived from these calculations.

References and further reading

Adhikari, A., Basu, A., Raj, S.P., 2013. Pricing of experience products under consumer heterogeneity. *International Journal of Hospitality Management*, 33 (1), 6–18.

Brue, S.L., Grant, R.R., 2013. *The Evolution of Economic Thought*, 8th, international edition. South-Western Cengage Learning, Boston, USA.

Cross, R.G., Higbie, J.A., Cross, D.Q., 2009. Revenue management's renaissance: A rebirth of the art and science of profitable revenue generation. *Cornell Hospitality Quarterly*, 50 (1), 56–81.

Enz, C.A., Canina, L., Lomanno, M., 2004. Why discounting doesn't work: The dynamic of rising occupancy and falling revenue among competitors. *Cornell Hospitality Report*, 4 (7), 6–25. Available https://scholarship.sha.cornell.edu/cgi/viewcontent.cgi?referer=&httpsredir=1&article=1187&context=chrpubs

Haynes, N., Egan, D., 2017. Revisiting the relevance of economic theory to hotel revenue management education and practice in the era of Big Data. *Research in Hospitality Management*, 7 (1), 65–73.

Heo, C.Y., Lee, S., 2009. Application of revenue management practices to the theme park industry. *International Journal of Hospitality Management*, 28 (3), 446–453.

Kimes, S.E. 1989. The basics of yield management. *The Cornell Hotel and Restaurant Administration Quarterly*, 30 (3), 14–19.

Lewis, R.C., Shoemaker, S., 1997. Price-sensitivity measurement: A tool for the hospitality industry. *Cornell Hospitality Quarterly*, 38 (2), 44–54.

Mak, J., 1988. Taxing hotel room rentals in the U.S. *Journal of Travel Research*, 27 (1), 10–15.

O'Neill, J., Quadri-Felitti, D., 2016. Resort fee and service fees in the U.S. hotel industry: Context and concepts related to partitioned pricing. ICHRIE Research Report, International Council on Hotel, Restaurant, and Institutional Education, June. Available www.chrie.org/i4a/doclibrary/getfile.cfm?doc_id=28

Parkin, M., 2016. *Microeconomics*, 12th edition. Pearson Education Limited, Harlow, UK.

Pekgün, P., Menich, R.P., Acharya, S., Finch, P.G., Deschamps, F., Mallery, K., Sistine, J.V., Christianson, K., 2013. Carlson Rezidor Hotel Group maximizes revenue through improved demand management and price optimization. *Interfaces*, 43 (1), 21–36.

Repetti, T., Roe, S., Gregory, A., 2015. Pricing strategies for resort fees: Consumer preferences favor simplicity. *International Journal of Contemporary Hospitality Management*, 27 (5), 790–809.

Samuelson, P.A., Nordhaus, W.D., 2002. *Economics*, 17th edition. McGraw-Hill/Irwin, Boston, MA, USA.

Samuelson, P.A., Nordhaus, W.D., 2010. *Economics*, 19th edition. McGraw-Hill/Irwin, Boston, MA, USA.

Tjan, A.K., 2010. The Pros and Cons of Bundled Pricing. *Harvard Business Review*, HBR Blog Network, February 26. Available https://hbr.org/2010/02/the-pros-and-cons-of-bundled-p.html

Vogel, M.P., 2009. Onboard Revenue: The secret of the cruise industry's success? In: A. Papathanassis (ed.), *Cruise Sector Growth: Managing Emerging Markets, Human Resources, Processes and Systems*. Gabler, Wiesbaden, Germany, pp. 3–15.

Wood, P., 2013. Price elasticity and demand change indicators. *Hotel Business Review*, October 6. Available www.hotelexecutive.com/feature_focus/3606

5 Macroeconomic environment and business cycles

Objectives and learning outcomes

This chapter is organized to acquaint students with the most basic knowledge on the principles of macroeconomics. The materials presented in this chapter aim to provide students with an indispensable resource for understanding the related periodical releases and reports on the macroeconomic performances of various economies and their changes. As a result, students will have the ability to further develop their skills for academic purposes and/or working in the related industry areas.

The nature and business significance of the topics presented in Chapter 1 (under "Macroeconomic principles"), such as inflation, unemployment, business cycle, and government policies, are further elaborated and discussed in this chapter with first an introduction on the principles of aggregate demand (AD) and aggregate supply (AS). To increase the understanding of students on the role of the government in promoting a sound environment for economic activities, the related principles for government macroeconomic policies (particularly fiscal policy in terms of government expenditures and taxation) are discussed.

In addition, despite advocacy for regionalization and globalization due to the potential economic benefits, their recent progress is not without ambiguities and uncertainties. These might have important influences (both positive and negative) on the practices of the world hospitality industries in many areas. Therefore, another objective of this chapter is to guide students to appropriately evaluate possible influences at both the local and regional/global levels.

The other primary components of the macroeconomic environment – money and the monetary system (including the commercial banks, interest rate, currency exchange rate, and related government policy – monetary policy), will be discussed in the next chapter.

After reading this chapter, students will:

- recognize the major components of the macroeconomic environment;
- understand the principles of AD and AS;

- be able to apply the principles of AD and AS to understand changes in the macroeconomic environment;
- have a good grasp of the causes and impacts of inflation and unemployment;
- understand the characteristics and significance of a business cycle in any market economy;
- understand the arguments that support government fiscal policy and the influences;
- understand the motivation that drives regionalization and globalization and the pros and cons; and
- understand the significance of the related macroeconomic topics to the hospitality industry.

Composition of macroeconomic environment

To adequately prepare for possible challenges and take advantage of potential market opportunities, a good understanding of the composition of the macro-economic environment and its interrelationship with market activities is indispensable to anyone who is at the decision-making level. For example, in a study on hotel employment decisions, Wong (2004: 287) shows that macro-economic factors like the "production index and the gross domestic product" of an economy are as important as "industry-specific factors" to management teams. Besides, Kim et al. (2018) find that there is a significant long-term relationship between the macroeconomic environment and merger and acqui-sition activities in the restaurant industry.

In contrast to microeconomics, macroeconomics focuses on the larger trends in the environment around consumers and producers in the economy. To a large extent, this environment is in fact the aggregation of individ-ual activities that are performed at the different microeconomic levels. For example, *firms* and *households* are the two major components that consti-tute the macroeconomic environment. In practice, while firms are producers (sellers) of commodities, they are also the employers (buyers) of production resources like labor services in an economy. On the other hand, while house-holds represent the consumer (buyers) of final goods and services from firms, they are also the providers (sellers) of related production resources like labor services.

On top of firms and households, the *government* (the public sector) is an indispensable part of the macroeconomy which has significant influence (both direct and indirect) on economic activities with the legitimate power to impose various economic policies. Besides, since money and other forms of monetary and financial resources like credit play an essential role in facilitat-ing economic activities, related organizations in the *monetary and financial sys-tem* (or the *banking and non-bank financial sectors*) are another major component of the macroeconomic environment. In consideration of the growing scale and scope of the financial systems in world economies, and their significant role in supplying financial resources (or products) for firm investment and

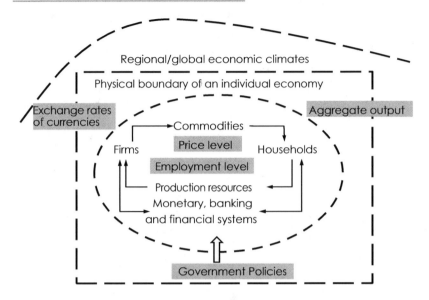

Figure 5.1 Composition of macroeconomic environment

toward household saving, fluctuations in these related sectors may have crucial impacts on the entire economy.

In addition, as most economies in the world are more open in trade (in terms of goods and services, as well as production and investment resources) with other countries, the economic climate at the regional and global levels may affect not only the environment but the real performance of an individual economy. Despite this, the macroeconomic environment is a collection of all elements at the individual level like firms, households, government, the monetary, banking and financial systems, and external factors (as shown in Figure 5.1). The collective forces consequently generate various impacts onto the entire economy. Depending on the nature of the feedback, the current performance of the economy may change in different directions.

As shown in Figure 5.1, the changes in the components identified for an economy's macroeconomic environment are generally measured and reflected by changes at the price level, employment level, aggregate (or real) output, and the exchange rates between domestic and foreign currencies, as well as government policies. To show the possible changes in the macroeconomic environment, the principles of AD and AS are usually applied and used.

Aggregate demand and aggregate supply

As mentioned earlier, the macroeconomic environment is composed of a number of key elements (or variables). First, when studying the economy as a whole, *aggregate demand* (AD) and *aggregate supply* (AS) are emphasized instead of individual demand and individual supply for a consumer, a firm, or a particular market. Simply speaking, AD represents the sum of all individual demands for the total goods and services (real output) in an economy that consumers are prepared to buy at a specific price level, or the price indices that can be measured based on the principle in Equation (1.6) in Chapter 1. On the other hand, AS is the relationship between the total of all goods and services (total output) that individual firms will produce and sell at a given price level, and used to predict the average price level.

Similar to the discussions on individual demand and supply curves (see Chapter 3), the AD curve is downward-sloping and the AS curve is upward-sloping (see Figure 5.2). In contrast to the measurements for individual demand and supply, the unit applied in the vertical axis is the average price level (or price index) of all commodities and capital goods traded in the economy. By the same token, the unit of measurement presented in the horizontal axis is the AD (or real output) from the whole economy within a given period of time (e.g., a month, a quarter, or a year).

Aggregate demand

Since AD can be measured by the total amount of spending (Y) through the real output of an economy within a given period of time, the GDP which is discussed in Chapter 1, and the measurement of GDP as expressed by

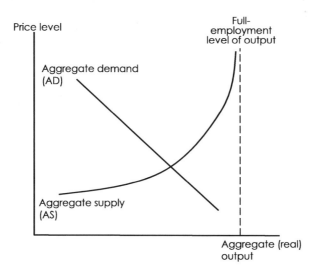

Figure 5.2 Aggregate demand and aggregate supply curves

Equation (1.3) provide a reasonable basis to identify AD, and it is restated in Equation (5.1).

$$AD = Y = GDP = C + I + G + (X - M) \tag{5.1}$$

Generally speaking, Equation (5.1) shows that the AD is measured by the total amount spent by:

1   households in terms of their *consumption expenditures (C)* on final commodities (e.g., spending on necessities like food, as well as non-necessities like hospitality services);
2   firms in terms of their *investment expenditures (I)* on the formation of capital goods (e.g., factories, hotels, information technologies);
3   the government in terms of its *public expenditures (G)* on either final commodities (e.g., public expenditures on medical care for the elderly or national defense products) or capital goods (e.g., public expenditures on infrastructure construction); and
4   the balance between the expenditures of foreign buyers on the real output of an economy (i.e., *exports* of an economy: X) and the expenditures of locals on non-locally produced commodities (i.e., *imports* to an economy: M).

Aggregate demand curve and its changes

Given the context and method of measuring AD, it is obvious that *if there is a decrease in the average price level in the economy, the purchasing power of those with money (including households, firms and the government) increases so that more of the real output would be spent, and vice versa.* In addition, if there is a decrease in the average price level in the output of an economy, foreign buyers may purchase more of the output of this economy. In contrast, foreign commodities become relatively more expensive to domestic consumers so that the amount of imports will be reduced, and vice versa. These simple but essential explanations mean that the *AD curve slopes downward.*

On the other hand, any autonomous changes in the variables of C, I, G, and (X − M) lead to a shift in the AD curve. For example, given the existing price level, if the government decides to increase its spending on final commodities, *ceteris paribus*, the AD curve shifts upward (or outward), and vice versa. In contrast, when more of the local residents prefer to travel abroad, their spending outside the economy on tourism services which are considered to be imports will increase so that as "M" increases, *ceteris paribus*, the AD for domestically produced commodities falls, and the AD curve shifts downward, and vice versa.

Aggregate demand and hospitality industry

The hospitality industry is a major industry, so its relationship with the AD of an economy is interactive and dynamic. The business nature of the hospitality industry (see Figure 1.1 in Chapter 1) means that its real output (together with the outputs produced by other industries and the public sector) not only determines the AD of an economy, but is also determined by the collective AD of an economy. Generally speaking, if the AD of an economy is high (or increasing), it can be inferred that the amount of expenditures spent on the different forms of hospitality services is also high (or increasing).

In principle, if local households want to spend more, say, when their income increases or if they are feeling optimistic about the future, some of their increasing expenditures may be due to eating out or enjoying short local vacations. Also, if the AD increases due to more international tourists, the hosting economy experiences an economic surge from their spending. Accordingly, the increase in consumption expenditures (C) and/or export of tourism services (X) implies that the real output in the hospitality industry will increase.

When the business scale increases, the hospitality industry intuitively increases employment opportunities and spending on capital goods. While an increase in employment opportunities implies that the aggregate income of the economy will further increase and hence the consumption expenditures (C) of households as well, spending on capital goods means that investment expenditures (I) will also increase. Thus, the AD increases in the subsequent quarter, and this may result in a dynamic relationship that gives rise to the parallel growth in both the economy and the hospitality industry.

Aggregate supply

In any given period of time, the total output that firms in an economy plan to produce is determined by the average price level of the commodities, as well as the price level and availability of the resources for production. While the full-employment level of output is in principle fixed in the short run, technological advancements over time may allow an economy to expand its production capacity.

Aggregate supply curve and its changes

Since firms are profit-making entities, an increase in the average price level in the economy may send them a positive signal to increase their output, or will attract more firms to take part in the market. On the other hand, when firms are competing for a given quantity of resources within a certain period of time to increase their output, the aggregate cost of production will consequently increase. These two simple reasons explain the *upward slope of the AS curve* as plotted in Figure 5.2.

Considering the resources endowment in any given period of time in an economy, however, there is a maximum amount of output that could be produced (i.e., the full-employment level of output as shown in Figure 5.2). In other words, when the output of an economy is approaching its maximum capacity, the collective forces of firms to compete for limited resources for production would only lead to a rapid increase in the average cost and price levels, but minimal increment in its real output.

On top of raw materials, production requires the input of labor and capital. In the long run, the limited production capacity of an economy may expand if there is a positive growth in population and accumulation of capital goods. In addition, technological advancements (including improvements in education) will increase efficiency, and hence reduce the average cost of production. As more real output may be derived from the existing quantity of resources (including human resources), or newly invented resources like the use of solar energy instead of fossil fuels or synthetic materials instead of timber or metal, the AS curve shifts downward (or outward).

On the other hand, if factor prices (i.e., costs of production) on average increase for every level of output, the AS curve shifts upward (or inward). Thus, it is commonly seen that as the world price of crude oil increases (e.g., the situation in the 1970s and the 1980s), the AS curve is pushed upward, and hence the inflation rate in economies that rely on importing crude oil as a major input for production rises. Besides, any *external shocks* like earthquakes may damage the production capacity of an economy, and hence shift the AS curve upward.

Aggregate supply and hospitality industry

To a large extent, output from the hospitality industry relies on various intermediate outputs that are produced by the primary sectors like mining and agriculture, secondary sectors like manufacturing and food processing, and other tertiary sectors like banking and finance, and hence input from them. Considering these relationships, business output from the hospitality industry is evidently influenced by the price level of the intermediate commodities acquired from other economic sectors.

Besides, in the business process, the hospitality industry is competing with other economic sectors for direct inputs such as labor and capital goods. Thus, when an economy has low output, more unused factors of production may be available to the hospitality firms at relatively lower costs. On the other hand, if an economy is approaching its full-employment level of output, business costs for the hospitality industry will escalate, especially in terms of labor cost and rent.

On the other hand, if the AS of an economy is pushed inward due to increases in world commodity prices of, for example, crude oil or food items, it is reasonable to acknowledge that while the production cost of hospitality firms will increase, some firms may just terminate business. This implies that the unemployment rate may also increase. In addition, crude oil is a primary raw input for firms who need oil to run their machines and for households toward energy consumption, and an increase in its price not only increases the cost of production of firms, but reduces the real income of households so that they might have to reduce their spending in other areas, including hospitality services. For example, Kasparian (2009) confirms the adverse (or negative) income effect due to an increase in crude oil price on the spending power of French households.

Macroeconomic equilibrium and changes

In any given period of time, interaction between the AD and AS determines the average price level (which may be denoted by a certain price index: PI) and the real output to be spent (Y) by the various economic sectors, and hence the use of related production resources. For example, given that AD is AD_1 and AS is AS_1 as shown in Figure 5.3, the economy is in a macroeconomic equilibrium M^e_1, with an average price level PI_1 and aggregate output Y_1.

When AD and/or AS change, the related curves shift. Consequently, the macroeconomic equilibrium transitions from one state to another, which leads to changes at the price level and in the real output of an economy, as well as the use of production resources.

Consequences from changes in aggregate demand

Suppose that AS is constant in any one period of time, say, for one or two years. An increase in the AD (i.e., the AD curve shifts from AD_1 to AD_2 as shown in Figure 5.3) will change the macroeconomic equilibrium from M^e_1 to M^e_2.

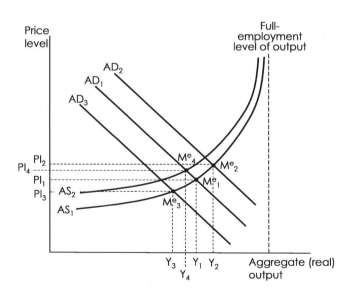

Figure 5.3 Changes in macroeconomic equilibrium

Therefore, both the average price level and real output increase (from PI_1 to PI_2, and Y_1 to Y_2 respectively). In principle, the increase in price level denotes inflation. This is because to spend at the same level of real output (e.g., Y_1) after AD increases (to AD_2), economic participants have to pay a higher price. In other words, this reflects the reduced purchasing power of money.

To meet the increase in AD, firms will increase their use of factors of productions by offering, for instance, higher wages to increase labor employment. In this situation, although the average price level (inflation) has increased, and thus the real output (which increases to Y_2), unemployment in the economy is lower.

In contrast, if AD decreases, say, from AD_1 to AD_3, the average price level in the economy will fall from PI_1 to PI_3, and real output from Y_1 to Y_3. Under this new macroeconomic equilibrium, M^e_3, firms may reduce or withdraw part of their production so that unemployment may increase in the market. If the fall in average price continues when AD declines, the economy experiences a period of deflation.

Consequences of changes in aggregate supply

As discussed, technological advancements and changes in factor prices are the two major factors that lead to shifts in the AS curve. In practice, technological advancements will improve the efficiency of production in the long run, and hence lead to a downward shift of the AS curve. So, the economy may expand its real output at a lower price level. Actually, this is a common long-term trend that is find in most economies around the world.

Occasionally, however, a unique situation that calls for investigation is an increase in the price of commodities like crude oil as discussed earlier, in which the effects shift the AS curve upward during certain periods of time. Shortly after the decrease in AS (i.e., AD remains unchanged at AD_1 while AS shifts from AS_1 to AS_2 in Figure 5.3), it is shown that while price level (inflation) increases from PI_1 to PI_4, real output also declines from Y_1 to Y_4 under the new macroeconomic equilibrium of M^e_4. In other words, a decrease in AS may lead to a more unfavourable situation to the economy than a decline in AD.

In principle, inflation caused by an increase in AD is called *demand-pull inflation*. In this situation, although the average price level increases, so do employment and income levels of the economy so that the economic participants are able to spend (enjoy) more real output. This means that inflation is accompanied by a positive economic growth.

However, inflation caused by a reduced AS because of increased factor costs is called *cost-push inflation*. In this situation, the economic participants have to pay *higher prices for less real output* even though income is reduced. This means that inflation is accompanied by negative economic growth. In economics, this is called the situation of *stagflation* (see, e.g., Moorthy, 2014; Amadeo, 2018).

A short note about the consequences of an increase in AD and AS
Ceteris paribus

  Increase in AD: Price level (inflation) rises and unemployment falls
  Increase in AS: Both price level (inflation) and unemployment fall

A short note about the consequences of a decrease in AD and AS
Ceteris paribus

  Decrease in AD: Price level (inflation) falls and unemployment rises
  Decrease in AS: Both price level and unemployment rise (the situation of
                    stagflation)

Business cycle

Owing to the attributes and practices of AD and AS, any autonomous changes
in one or more of the aforementioned variables (i.e., C, I, G, M, X, factor
cost, technology) that shift the AD or AS curve, or both, will lead to changes
in the average price level in an economy. Consequently, the macroeconomic
performance in terms of real output (e.g., as measured by GDP or its growth),
as well as the employment level change. Over time, the cyclical fluctuations following the changes in AD and/or AS constitute the business cycle of
any market economy. In principle, a business cycle consists of four different
phases: 1) *upswing (or recovery)*; 2) *peak*; 3) *downswing (or recession)*; and 4) *depression* (see Figure 5.4).

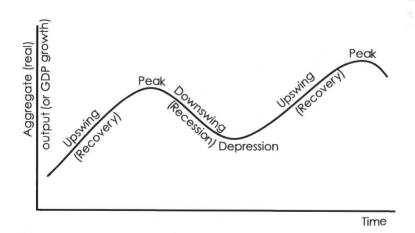

Figure 5.4 Pattern and different phases of a business cycle

Upswing and peak phases

Generally speaking, after an economy slumps for a certain period of time, it may approach a stage in which the firms have to renew some of their fixed facilities and capital goods while households have to replace some of their durable and semi-durable goods. The autonomous increase in consumption and/or investment expenditures then allows the economy to recover and gives impetus to an upswing.

As price and employment levels increase, the economic atmosphere becomes optimistic to households, firms, and investors. Following the initial rebound, there are more positive expectations of the various sectors of the economy, which further stimulate economic activities – while employment and income in the economy continue to increase, so does price level (inflation).

Subsequently, when the economy is approaching its full-employment level of output, further increases in economic activities may be largely reflected in the higher price level (including inflated commodity prices and higher wages in the labor market) instead of proportionate increases in real output and employment. In this situation, the economy is booming and at the peak of the business cycle.

Downswing and depression phases

During a high upswing period, positive expectations are commonly reflected in the rapid increase of households and firms in consumption and invest-ment expenditures (e.g., as reflected in the increasing value of C and I in AD) respectively. Nevertheless, when the economy is peaking, firms and investors may start to wonder when the economy would reach capacity. In addition, the spending of households on durable and semi-durable goods may have also accumulated to a considerable level. Thus, the likelihood that households and firms may reduce their spending increases when the economy has been expe-riencing growth for a longer period of time.

In the end, a slowdown in consumption and/or production activities will reverse the uptrend of the economy which transitions to a downswing (or recession) phase. In economics, a recession is the situation when the GDP of an economy declines for two consecutive quarters (or six months). When the economy declines because AD is reduced, the macroeconomic variables also move in the opposite direction of the peak. For example, following an initial decline in the AD and price level, the profits of firms are reduced and they may then decide to reduce production level and hence the number of employed labor. This implies that the aggregate income of the economy, and hence expenditures will further decline. As the downswing phase proceeds, the economy will enter into an even "worse" situation (i.e., depression or the bottom) in the existing business cycle. Generally, a depression may last for a certain period of time (from several months to quarters) before the econ-omy recovers and starts to swing up again in the subsequent cycle (note: a depression that lasts for many years like the situation in the 1930s as dis-cussed in Chapter 2, is called a *great depression*).

In economics, comprehensive analyses of the factors that are responsible for and lead to the actual performance of business cycles in different eras and different economies, as well as the different lengths of the cycles are common and essential for economists (see, e.g., Arias et al., 2007; Dejong et al., 2000; Greenwood et al., 1988). In this introductory text, however, only some of the more simple business and public implications will be discussed.

Business implications

In practice, changes in the reported values of related macroeconomic vari-ables like inflation, unemployment, GDP growth, and trade balance (includ-ing interest and currency exchange rates, which will be discussed in the next chapter) in the different phases of a business cycle convey essential market information to firms and households, as well as investors and the govern-ment for their related decisions in the economy. To any individual business firm, appropriate assessments of the impacts from the changing economic environment are essential to their business performance and sustainability of their growth, as they may have little influence or control over their economic environment.

Recently, some studies have emphasized the influences of the business cycle on the hospitality industry, especially recessions, and suggested possible pro-active strategies for hospitality firms to better prepare for the related exter-nal shocks. For example, a study by Pearce and Michael (2006: 201) reports that "over 500,000 companies have failed in each of the recessions that have occurred in the U.S. since 1990". By referring to a variety of evidence, they point out that "to position for recession, firms can seek to be active in multi-ple geographies, industries and markets" (ibid.: 203). In fact, the reason that a multi-regional or multi-national firm may be in a better position to deal with a recession is that the business cycle across various regions or nations may not necessarily be synchronized (except in the event of a widespread global recession/depression).

A study by Provance (2009) identifies the adverse impacts from nation-wide recessions on the hospitality industry in Las Vegas, and the interactions between the macroeconomic and the microeconomic environments for some of the major casino resorts. In particular, the influence of the economic cri-sis in 2008/2009 on the casino resorts is investigated. When discussing the possible measures for firms to reduce the negative impacts of the recession, suggestions from Pearce and Michael (2006) are also cited and further elabo-rated (Provance, 2009: 35).

Besides, Lee and Ha (2012: 332–335) explore the macroeconomic fac-tors that significantly affect the performance of full-service restaurants in the US during various recession periods between 1976 and 2007, and show from a comprehensive review of the existing research work that the business performance of hospitality firms is in general highly correlated to the business cycle. They refer to Enz (2009) and emphasize that "the restaurant industry is relatively more volatile to changes of external economic conditions as compared to the rest of the economy" (Lee and Ha, 2012: 333). This is largely owing to the fact that as disposable income declines "in a recession, consumers tend to significantly reduce their spending on travel and/or dining out" (ibid.).

In an upswing period, spending increases on hospitality services and related goods and hence the scale of the hospitality industry also follows suit. When the boom is reversed, however, firms in this industry are usually the first among those that are affected. Thus, a good grasp of the attributes and experiences that are associated with business cycles serves as essential grounds for hospitality firms to proactively respond to changing macroeconomic environments.

Macroeconomic policies

Despite the fact that orthodox economists ardently support free markets, government interventions have never been negotiable in economic history. In the classical *Principles of Political Economy* written by John Stuart Mill in 1848 (Mill, [1848] 1998), the role of the government in an economic society is comprehensively discussed from taxation to social welfare and education (ibid.: Book V). In economics today, two common arguments speak to government intervention: 1) *market failure* and 2) *the business cycle*. In the former, social interests may be possibly overlooked since the markets are composed of individual firms and households who are largely, if not absolutely, after their own interests (e.g., profit and individual pleasure respectively). For example, pollution and over-consumption of non-replenishable resources on Earth, as well as the issue of equity between the rich and the poor in society require government intervention. This is commonly accepted as an essential part in any economy today to ensure the effective use and allocation of economic resources, as well as the distribution of output.

Business cycles and government intervention

In the latter argument for support of government intervention due to *business cycles*, it is mainly suggested that in different phases of a business cycle, government intervention may help to stabilize the volatilities in an economy so that better economic welfare to the community could be ensured. In economics, a systemic formulation of principles to advocate for government participation in managing business cycles has been put forth by British economist John Maynard Keynes in his *The General Theory of Employment, Interest, and Money* (Keynes, [1936] 1953). Actually, this book was released during the terrible times of the Great Depression in the 1930s when unemployment rates were soaring to unprecedented levels.

It was observed in the economy during the Great Depression that autonomous spending by households and firms was imperative for the economy to revert back to an upswing trend but this did not take place for years. Accordingly, Keynes ([1936] 1953) argues that the actual spending by the private sectors might not always be sufficient to stimulate the needed AD that would pull an economy out from depression and subsequently, reduce high unemployment rates. Accordingly, an external force such as that from the government is important to counter the unfavourable effects of the different phases of a business cycle.

Aggregate demand management policies

As suggested by Keynes and his economist peers, governments can modify AD through *fiscal policy* – that is, apply government spending (G) and taxation (T) policies to change the pattern of autonomous spending in an economy. Therefore, AD can be manipulated for the sake of providing a more stable environment for households and firms to perform their economic activities. For example, it is commonly suggested that the government should adopt an *expansionary fiscal policy* to increase its spending and/or lower income tax during a recession so that AD, as measured by using Equation (5.1) can be increased (or its decline can be slowed down). By increasing government direct spending in, say, various economic commodities or public construction projects, the revenue of firms and income of households will also increase so that in the subsequent rounds, consumption expenditures (C) and investment expenditures (I) may both increase.

On the other hand, if taxes that are imposed on the income of households and firms are reduced when the economy is in a recession, then the reduction in their disposable income may be less detrimental so that their ability and willingness to spend may revert back to a certain level. In comparison to direct government spending, however, the effect of tax reduction on AD may experience a time lag because it may take time for people to realize the tax reduction or receive a refund from their pay check.

Once the momentum that reverses the downward trend starts and accumulates, the process will directly and/or indirectly continue so that the economy has the chance to recover from the economic depression. In economics, the continuous impacts from an autonomous change in G, C, or I to the changes in AD is call the *multiplier effect*. That is, an initial increase in the autonomous spending by one economic sector (e.g., the government or firms) will lead to additional increases in the spending of other sectors (e.g., households and firms) in the subsequent rounds of consumption and production activities. Consequently, the ultimate effect which is measured in monetary value is larger than the initial change (mathematical discussions on the multiplier effect can be found in most economic textbooks and will not be addressed here).

In contrast, when inflation is surging and spending in the private sectors continues to boom, the government may consider applying a *contractionary fiscal policy* to reduce public spending or increase taxes. Doing so may be helpful in reducing the inflation pressure, especially for low-income groups, and also the risks from any unexpected sharp reversals in the economy from the boom. Despite the controversy on the effectiveness of contractionary fiscal policies (see, e.g., Hansen, [1941] 2010; Taylor, 2000) in the empirical literature across different nations and periods of time, adjustments made by a government in its fiscal policy may be an important signal to the economic participants on the possible state of the macroeconomic environment and its possible changes sooner or later.

Fiscal policy and hospitality industry

While expansionary and contractionary fiscal policies aim to manage/stabilize AD in different phases of a business cycle, public spending and tax policies in general may interact with the macroeconomic environment to a much larger extent. By referring to the characteristics of the hospitality industry and its simple relationship with an economy (as discussed earlier in the "Aggregate demand and hospitality industry" section in this chapter), a better developed and more stable macroeconomic environment will not simply facilitate business turnover in the industry, but generate positive feedback which may in turn contribute to the sustained growth of the economy.

For example, a study by Benchabane (2016) confirmed that the modern and rapid development of the tourism industry in Dubai has largely benefited from extensive government-funded investments on infrastructure and related social facilities. In turn, "tourism generates a powerful multiplier effect on the economy" (Benchabane, 2016: 2). In many tourist destinations, public spending on the development, renovation, and upgrading of infrastructures such as internal and external transportation systems, as well as communication, energy, water, sewage, and sanitation facilities are essential for the sustainable growth of their hospitality industries. These may also provide crucial information to firms and investors when they are assessing the prospects of related markets in different nations.

Regionalization and globalization

Here, the macroeconomic variables C, I, and G as provided in Equation (5.1) that exemplify the practices of a macroeconomy have been elucidated, and the trade factors in an open economic environment: import (M) and export (X) will be discussed in this section. Although international trade is one of the earliest topics in economics, its significance to the world economies has been largely promoted by a number of public efforts at the intra-/inter-regional and world levels since World War II. One of the landmarks in regional trade cooperation is unarguably the efforts carried out by the related European nations to establish the European Coal and Steel Community (ECSC) and European Economic Community (EEC) in the 1950s (see Chapter 2).

Other well-known organizations for regional economic cooperation include the Association of Southeast Asian Nations (ASEAN) which was initially founded by Indonesia, Malaysia, the Philippines, Singapore, and Thailand in 1967; and the North American Free Trade Agreement (NAFTA) between the United States, Canada, and Mexico in 1994. At the inter-regional level, perhaps the most active organization is Asia-Pacific Economic Cooperation (APEC), which was established in 1989. At the world level, countries under the General Agreement on Tariffs and Trade (GATT), which went into effect in 1948 to reduce certain trade barriers (mainly tariffs and quotas), was evidently an attempt to facilitate world trade. To improve the organization of the GATT in line with the new trends of world trade, it was formally replaced by the World Trade Organization (WTO) in 1995.

In principle, the seeds of regionalization (or globalization) are sown and planted when physical and policy barriers in trading economic commodities are reduced (or removed), and/or there is the movement of production factors like labor and capital goods across the borders of various nations in a region (or globally). As this process continues (which indeed, has been ongoing and found in the world economies since the mid-20th century), the widespread outcome observed is the diffusion of commonly perceived or agreed standards and quality of commodities by households and firms across different nations.

Pros and cons in a more interactive world

In practice, there may not be a single definition for either regionalization or globalization. Although these two phenomena share common grounds and some general qualities, their focus may not necessarily be the same when they are applied to a particular social, political or economic context. Nevertheless, they convey a clear message to the world that interactions between people and firms in different forms are becoming more prevalent. To this end, when firms of one nation are able to enter into the markets of another nation with fewer barriers, consumers now have the choice to not simply purchase locally produced commodities, but spend money on a variety of commodities produced overseas that have lower prices. In economics, this implies the inevitable consequence that would come along with the process of regionalization or globalization, which is an increase in market competition.

In a more open and interactive world, however, a major dilemma that has been observed is the imbalance in trade between the well-developed and the emerging nations (e.g., the US–Japan and US–China trade deficits). In fact, this dilemma is largely due to the structural differences between the nations (which in itself is a complex issue and therefore outside the scope of this book), and the accumulated momentum from the imbalance in trade has ultimately led to the return of protectionism in the world economies. For example, various measures were enforced by the US government in the second half of the

2010s to hold back trade and economic cooperation with Asian and European countries like China as well as some of the EU member nations. As a result, the conventional belief in the effectiveness of globalization and its prospects has been called for a critical review by both academics and practitioners.

Globalization of hospitality industry

Parallel to the progression of regionalization/globalization, a number of public and semi-public organizations have been founded or restructured for the purpose of facilitating travel and tourism activities around the world. Among those organizations, the Pacific Asia Travel Association (PATA), which was established in 1952, and the World Tourism Organization (also abbreviated as WTO or UNWTO, as it represents a United Nations agency that promotes world tourism and related affairs since 1974) are widely known. Besides these, some other organizations, like the World Travel and Tourism Council (WTTC), which was formed in 1990, are actively facilitating world travel and promoting tourism businesses by coordinating related forums and releasing periodical information for the reference of the industries.

Compelled by the related international organizations (both the government and private sectors), positive feedback effects have evidently contributed to the international expansion (globalization) of the world travel and tourism industries, as well as the hospitality industry as a whole. In the global context, while multi-national firms may have to retain their identity (especially around service quality and royalties with their global customers), effective adjustments in their business practices and routines from the home markets to fit into the various culture and perceptions of consumers in different nations are equally important to their sustainability. On the other hand, local firms may also need to enhance their service quality as an essential measure to ensure their competitiveness in an open market.

For example, in a study on the global strategies adopted by international hotels, Whitla et al. (2007: 781) find that business travelers may expect a "similar range of services" like "internet services, a business centre, 24-hour room service and a gymnasium" when they check in to the same hotel brand around the world. However, local elements should not be overlooked by those hotels, "especially for leisure travelers" (ibid.). In contrast to the hotels operating in the "western countries", business turnovers derived from "food and beverage" instead of accommodations "often make up the bulk of hotels' revenues" in the Asian markets (ibid.). Thus, it is suggested that when the international hotels are developing their properties in Asia, they should strategically include "more and larger restaurant outlets, targeting local diners as well as overnight guests" (ibid.).

In addition to the hotel industry, an effective balance between the originality of a business brand and market-specific elements across different regions (or nations) are commonly considered to be responsible for the success of hospitality firms such as restaurants and theme parks in their globalization process. For example, on top of the trademark effect, sustainability and expansion of McDonald's in Japan, Hong Kong SAR, and Mainland China may also accredit its success to the inclusion of local elements into business practices, as well as its food menu.

Another example of globalization of the hospitality industry is Legoland in Malaysia which opened in 2012. As a well-known theme park in North America (Florida and California) and Europe (Denmark, the UK, and Germany), its arrival in Asia evidently is a puzzling item in the progression of globalization. Nevertheless, its practice also shows its strategy to integrate with local elements to ensure the ultimate success of a hospitality firm in another part of the world. As shown in Illustration 5.1, related layouts and decorations set up at Legoland Malaysia are unique to the societal and religious settings in Malaysia and the targeted visitors from Southeast, Central, and Western Asia. Illustration 5.1 shows the Lego figures of a lady and a child with Muslim attire, and a Muslim prayer room, which clearly exemplify the culturally sensitive decisions of the Lego Group management team to include relevant cultural elements in their attraction when setting up Legoland in a different part of the world.

In a highly dynamic and fast-paced world, the success of a hospitality firm not only requires efficiency of its internal business strategies, but also business decisions that are effective enough so that the firm can position itself in different markets in different parts of the world. While the basic economic components for the macroeconomic environment must be well mastered by the related decision makers, the social and political elements which may have significant influence on the changing climate of the macroeconomic environment are equally important to the industry.

Illustration 5.1 Culturally relevant and sensitive Lego figures and facilities in Legoland Malaysia

Did you know? ...

Despite the differences in the numerical values derived by different studies, a statistically significant relationship between the changing values of the major macroeconomic variables like GDP (or other forms of aggregate income in an economy) and business performance of the hotel industry has been reported. This statistically significant relationship is commonly measured in terms of the demand for hotel rooms and hence the total revenue as reported by the industry at both the aggregate level and the property level respectively. Related findings confirm that to be effective and proactive in formulating (or adjusting) business strategies, decision makers of individual firms should have a good understanding of the influence from changes in the macroeconomic environment to their business.

Box 5.1 Relationship between macroeconomic income and demand for lodging

In a study by Canina and Carvell (2005), the relationships between various income variables derived at the macroeconomic level and lodging demand at the property level (i.e., individual hotels) in the United States are statistically examined. While the income variables include quarterly GDP, personal disposable income and corporate income respectively from 1989 to 2000, the demand for lodging is measured by the number of hotel rooms sold in each quarter of the same period. By applying a comprehensive data set which covered 1,204 hotels in 22 urban markets in the United States, they find that these income variables at the macroeconomic level "are statistically important factors influencing lodging demand at the property level for urban hotels" (Canina and Carvell, 2005: 306).

When applying property level data, Canina and Carvell (2005) find that the income elasticity of demand for lodging as measured by GDP is less than one (0.44). They comment that this is different from findings in which this value is greater than one when aggregate level data are applied, like the study by Wheaton and Rossoff (1998: 68) in which "the data are completely aggregate, reflecting the lodging industry as a whole, and not any particular market segment or strata".

Parallel to the findings at the property level, the income elasticity of demand for lodging as measured by personal disposable income (0.29) "is more than twice as large as" the value as measured by corporate income (0.12) (Canina and Carvell, 2005: 301). In addition, an interesting finding is that the sum of the two elasticities derived from personal disposable income and corporate income is

0.41, which "is insignificantly different from the coefficient on GDP (.44)" (ibid.: 302).

Discussion questions:

1   Discuss the importance for the hotel industry to understand the income elasticity of demand for lodging as measured by GDP, personal disposable income, and corporate income, respectively.
2   Discuss the possible reason(s) that the income elasticity of demand for lodging as measured by personal disposable income "is more than twice as large as" the value measured by corporate income. What would be the business implications?
3   Intuitively, can you think of any reason(s) for the income elasticity of demand for lodging becoming less than one when estimated with lodging data at the property level, but greater than one when aggregate level data are applied?

Conclusions and remarks

The information presented in this chapter has reiterated that in an economy, the average price level of commodities, and total output produced and hence employment rate at any given period of time are jointly determined by the AD and AS. Thus, changes in any variable which enters into AD and AS will modify the macroeconomic equilibrium of an economy and launch a business cycle. To minimize the adverse effects from business cycles to an economic society (especially inflation and unemployment), most economists may advocate that the government implement AD management policies (like the fiscal policy being discussed here). Besides, as interactions between different economies across different regions globally have increased since the mid-20th century, influences from cross-border economic activities and changes in related public interests on the macroeconomic environment of a particular economy are evidently becoming much more significant.

As a major industry sector in the modern economy and worldwide, the performance and progress of the hospitality industry at the national and global levels are undoubtedly interacting with business cycles and the changing internal and external macroeconomic environments over time. The strategic business decisions of hospitality firms may be affected by changes in both the local and international economic environments, as well as related government policies, which are beyond their control. Therefore, proactive planning based on possible changes that may change the existing macroeconomic environment is necessary for a firm to better seize opportunities when the economy is booming, or better resist adverse market conditions when the economy is turning toward a more unfavorable direction.

References and further reading

Amadeo, K., 2018. Stagflation and its causes: Can stagflation happen now? Available www.thebalance.com/what-is-stagflation-3305964

Arias, A., Hanse, G.D., Ohanian L.E., 2007. Why have business cycle fluctuations become less volatile? *Economic Theory* 32, 43–58.

Benchabane, Y., 2016. The key factors of a sustainable and successful tourism sector, the case of Dubai. Yazid Benchabane – Academia.edu. Available www.academia.edu/9324959

Canina, L., Carvell, S., 2005. Lodging demand for urban hotels in major metropolitan markets. *Journal of Hospitality & Tourism Research*, 29 (3), 291–311.

Dejong, D.N., Ingram, B.F., Whiteman, C.H., 2000. Keynesian impulses versus Solow residuals: Identifying sources of business cycle fluctuations. *Journal of Applied Econometrics*, 15 (3), 311–329.

Enz, C.A., 2009. *Hospitality Strategic Management: Concepts and Cases*, 2nd edition. John Wiley & Sons, New York, USA.

Greenwood, G., Hercowitz, Z., Huffman, G.W. (1988). Investment, capacity utilization, and the real business cycle. *The American Economic Review*, 78 (3), 402–417.

Hansen, A.H., [1941] 2010. *Fiscal Policy and Business Cycles*, Routledge Library Edition. Routledge, New York, USA.

Kasparian, J., 2009. Contribution of crude oil price to households' budget: The weight of indirect energy use. *Energy Policy*, 37 (1), 111–114. Available https://doi.org/10.1016/j.enpol.2008.08.015

Keynes, J.M., [1936] 1953. *The General Theory of Employment, Interest, and Money*. Harcourt Brace Jovanovich, Inc., New York, USA.

Kim, J., Zheng, T., Schrier, T., 2018. Examining the relationship between the economic environment and restaurant merger and acquisition activities. *International Journal of Contemporary Hospitality Management*, 30 (2), 1054–1071. Available https://doi.org/10.1108/IJCHM-07-2016-0346

Knowles, T., Diamantis, D., El-Mourhabi, J.B., 2004. *The Globalization of Tourism and Hospitality: A Strategic Perspective*, 2nd edition. Thomson Learning, London, UK.

Lee, K., Ha, I.S., 2012. Exploring the impacts of key economic indicators and economic recessions in the restaurant industry. *Journal of Hospitality Marketing & Management*, 21 (3), 330–343. Available https://doi.org/10.1080/19368623.2011.611752

Mill, J.S., [1848] 1998. *Principles of Political Economy*. Oxford University Press, New York, USA.

Moorthy, V., 2014. *Understanding Stagflation: Past & Present*. McGraw-Hill Education, New York, USA.

Peak, C., 2016. Discovering the relationship between macroeconomic trends and regional theme park performance. Manuscript, Northcentral

University, USA (ProQuest Number: 10252140). Available https://search. proquest.com/openview/6c21dc180e1aa56c25eab5bbfa2e7e51

Pearce, J.A., Michael, S.C., 2006. Strategies to prevent economic recessions from causing business failure. *Business Horizons*, 49 (3), 201–209.

Provance, W., 2009. Recession and its affect [*sic*] on the Las Vegas hospitality industry. UNLV Theses, Dissertations, Professional Papers, and Capstones. Available https://digitalscholarship.unlv.edu/thesesdissertations/564

Schiller, B.R., Gebhardt, K., 2013. *The Macro Economy Today*, 14th edition. McGraw-Hill Education (India) Private Limited, New Delhi, India.

Taylor, J.B., 2000. Reassessing discretionary fiscal policy. *Journal of Economic Perspectives*, 14 (3), 21–36.

Wheaton, W.C., Rossoff, L., 1998. The cyclic behavior of the U.S. lodging industry. *Real Estate Economics*, 26 (1), 67–82.

Whitla, P., Walters, P.G.P., Davies, H., 2007. Global strategies in the international hotel industry. *Hospitality Management*, 26, 777–792.

Wong, K.K.F., 2004. Industry-specific and general environmental factors impacting on hotel employment. *International Journal of Contemporary Hospitality Management*, 16 (5), 287–293. Available https://doi.org/10.1108/09596110410540258

6 Money and the monetary system

Objectives and learning outcomes

In the global economies today, the scale and scope of market exchanges and investment activities are largely facilitated by the use of money in various forms or equivalent forms of money (e.g., financial assets that are denominated in monetary terms). Thus, basic knowledge of the particular attributes of money and the forces that compel money to change in form, as well as the practices of the monetary system itself (which mainly includes the central bank and commercial banks in operations with various forms of money) is essential to any business decision maker. Such knowledge is imperative if a decision maker wishes to apply the related monetary and/or financial instruments from the markets effectively and efficiently to boost the performance and long-term growth of his/her business.

Accordingly, the primary objective of this chapter is to provide a comprehensive resource for students on the related knowledge. Specifically, concepts and principles of money and the monetary system are discussed with reference to the practices of the hospitality industry. In addition, this chapter also aims to increase the awareness of students of the characteristics of government monetary policies (which mainly include the measures that change the supply and interest rate of money in the markets). Also, the impacts from changes in the related policies on the business environment and money in an open economy are elucidated. Lastly, students will become acquainted with the significance of technological advancements in improving efficiency on the usage of money, and the increase in volume and scope of transactions in the monetary systems.

After reading this chapter, students will be able to understand:

- the four major functions of money;
- the composition of a monetary system;
- the basic role and functions of commercial banks in a monetary system;
- how commercial banks create different forms of deposit money;
- the principles and practices of a government's monetary policy;
- the influence of a government's monetary policy on the foreign exchange rate of its currency in an open economy;

- the impacts of technological advancements on the practices of money and the monetary system; and
- the significance of money and different components of the modern monetary system on the practices of the hospitality industry.

Characteristics and functions of money

In any economy where no single individual is producing all of the economic commodities for his/her own consumption, exchanges must take place between individuals in the market. However, if the exchange is a *barter* process, there is little efficiency for the related activities. Besides, determining the market prices and the rates of exchange between different physical goods (never mind services which are intangible) would be extremely complicated when the scale and scope of commodities traded in the markets are continuously increasing. For example, while the direct rate of exchange of ten types of goods could be manageable by the participants in the markets, it would become chaos if the number of goods were to increase to 1,000, 10,000, or more. To eliminate the complications (and even confusion) of exchanges in a barter economy, market participants have historically chosen one or a few particular commodities, such as precious metals, as the common denominator and generally accepted means (i.e., money) for exchange of all other commodities in the markets.

In practice, the evolution and expansion of the usage of money (especially paper money in the form of banknotes) in our economic societies not only facilitate the exchange of commodities, but also provide the necessary environment and incentive for laborers to continuously specialize in their works, hence increasing their efficiency of production. This is because after accepting the work of focusing and producing on one commodity, or even one particular task in the production process of a commodity, the money received (i.e., the wages) by a laborer allows him/her to exchange this money for all other commodities in the markets. Thus, an individual may not be resistant to doing the same task every day or even devote effort to improve the related work efficiency for the purpose of obtaining higher wages over time.

For example, when hotels employ laborers for housekeeping services, the related work efficiency should increase so that, *ceteris paribus*, the average variable cost of doing business could decline when more rooms are sold. In turn, by accepting the housekeeping position and performing routine tasks every day, these employees will receive a pay check (money) and then spend their salary in exchange for various commodities that are useful for daily life. In fact, the trading of housekeeping services between hotel employees and employers with money has constituted and contributed to part of the specialization of production in a modern economy. Today, millions of single exchange transactions are being carried out in the commodity and factor markets, and these can hardly be realized and sustained without the efficient operation of money.

As an essential means for market exchanges, money by itself has also long been a unique economic good traded by related organizations like commercials banks in the markets. In consideration of the wide usage and significance of money in an economy, it has been a common practice that through the central bank of a country, a government would take the responsibility to supervise and regulate the proper functioning and integrity of money that is circulating in its economy and the operations of its monetary system.

Functions of money

There are four major functions of money in economics. Money is a 1) medium of exchange, 2) store of value, 3) unit of account, and 4) means of deferred payment. Indeed, these functions are in line with the primary motivations of using money as described above, and hence are beneficial to the economic well-being of the market participants. Following the rapid progression of the world economies and technological advancements from the mid-20th century, actual expressions of these functions of money (or the forms that they take) have experienced significant changes. Nevertheless, the characteristics/core of these functions remain essentially the same.

Medium of exchange

Probably the most fundamental function of money is that it has to be *widely accepted by the market participants as the means of exchange for any economic commodity*. In the exchange process, money allows a buyer to obtain a commodity whenever s/he pays the amount (i.e., the price in monetary terms) requested by a seller. On the other hand, a seller knows that the money that s/he receives from a transaction would allow him/her to pay for what s/he would like to exchange or use in a subsequent round of transaction, and so on and so forth.

Store of value

As the income and spending of consumers or firms may not take place simultaneously, another function of money is that an economic participant can *store the purchasing power received from the current period of time and spend it in the future*. For example, a person may receive a pay check on a monthly basis but s/he will not spend all of the money immediately. Instead, s/he will spend the money on a daily basis before the next payday, or store (save) part of the money on a continuous basis to ensure his/her spending power in the future (e.g., when s/he is unemployed or retired). To a firm, money allows part of its revenue derived from its business operations to be stored for investment (e.g., increasing the number of fixed properties) and/or reinvestment (e.g., construction or renovation of aging facilities) in the future.

Unit of account

As mentioned earlier, one of the major issues of a barter economy is the difficulty of determining a clear set of direct exchange rates (prices) between different commodities traded in the markets. In contrast, if *all commodities are labeled as a common unit* (i.e., monetary price), the rate of exchange between them can be simply converted by anyone without any complications. This function of money is especially important to the development of the service sector like the hospitality industry. For example, if a seafood dinner set is priced at $80, a one-day theme park admission ticket at $20, and a breakfast buffet in a hotel at $10, the rate of exchange between these commodities in any order could easily be converted by anyone. With a clear monetary pricing system, the markets at the microeconomic level (like the related materials presented in Chapters 3 and 4 respectively) could operate efficiently, which in turn, facilitates an increase in the volume of market exchanges and contributes to the growth of the economy as a whole.

Means of deferred payment

Based on the first three functions, an extended and essential role of money in any modern economy is its function *as a means to back up all economic transactions by credit*. To facilitate the spending of consumers and investment of firms, credit (loans) of various forms is widely used in all modern economic societies. In principle, credit allows consumers and firms to spend first and settle payment later. In the related transactions, money provides an undisputable basis to measure the value of resources that are being spent through credit and the arrangements for repayment instalments (i.e., deferred payments). In addition, the *time value* of resources consumed by credit could also be reasonably measured with reference to the common denominator of money, instead of resources in kind.

A snapshot of money and hospitality industry

To the hospitality industry which provides various services, the proper functioning of money in an economy will definitely facilitate its business efficiency. If different services are priced with a monetary value (e.g., in terms of "dollars"), a consumer can easily make decisions on whether it is worthwhile to spend money on a service by making simple and direct comparisons with all other choices/alternatives.

For example, given the demand for accommodation and catering services when a person travels away from home, the efficiency of his/her consumption spending will increase if s/he can simply carry along some commonly recognized and accepted means (money) of payment. Besides, if services like differently rated hotels and different cuisines are priced/charged by using a common unit, consumers are able to directly make related comparisons and hence make decisions more efficiently (e.g., they can choose whether to have breakfast at the hotel restaurant or a restaurant that is close to the hotel).

On the other hand, as all inputs for businesses are paid in money, a hospitality firm could easily compare the monetary cost and monetary income, and then evaluate whether it is profitable to run the business. In other words, all of the microeconomic decisions made by referring to the principles discussed in Chapters 3 and 4 could be efficiently accomplished with the use of money as the medium of exchange and a common unit for accounting.

In modern economies, the practices of using money in different forms may also allow hospitality firms to cultivate effective business strategies. For example, when hotels are developing their loyalty programs with the intention to increase the number of returning visitors, bonus points awarded based on accumulated spending are one of the primary strategies (see, e.g., Shoemaker and Lewis, 1999: Table 3). In this process, accurately determining the spending and calculating the points to be awarded as a means of payment for future consumption of hotel services could hardly be realized efficiently without the use and proper functioning of money over time. Besides, related transactions and business strategies in the hospitality industry today are evidently facilitated by the application of various forms of non-cash money, such as credit and debit cards and electronic money (which will be discussed later in this chapter). Also, applications of these forms of non-cash money as money itself may also allow firms to obtain valuable information about their customers, and explore their spending behavior for business purposes.

Composition of monetary system

An effective and efficient monetary system needs to be in place to ensure the acceptance of money and facilitate its proper function in the markets. Taking into consideration the wide usage of money in an economy and the need to protect the economic well-being of a nation when using money, governments always exercise their legitimate and legislative power at the top to supervise the practices of their monetary system (e.g., business activities undertaken by commercial banks and other monetary organizations). As an outsider, however, governments will usually authorize an independent organization, that is, the central bank, to regulate and manage this system in the most objective and professional manner.

Major organizations and components

Broadly speaking, the central bank of a country is authorized by its government to issue legal tender in term of currency/cash (i.e., coins and banknotes) that is circulated within the economy. Additionally, the central bank also manages treasury like gold and monetary reserves for the government (the country). In addition, it has the legal right to supervise and regulate the related monetary instruments and activities as conducted by the private sectors, especially by the commercial banks. Most importantly, the central bank carries out the monetary policy to modify the quantity and flow of money, and hence manage the aggregate demand of its economy in the different phases of a business cycle.

Following the money issued and the related monetary regulations/requirements as specified by the central bank of a country, the commercial banks will then promote the efficiency of using money for profit-making purposes. Thus, the volume of market transactions between various economic participants would increase. In this process, commercial banks are the deposit taking organizations on the one side, and lenders of monetary funds on the other side of the market. Commercial banks are able to expand (create) the volume of related deposits in terms of the provision (creation) of credit to others who want and are willing to borrow based on the deposits made by households and firms.

In line with the primary organizations and elements discussed above, the *monetary system in an economy is generally composed of*:

1   *the central bank* which is an independent organization that represents the government;
2   *money (currency)* which is issued by the central bank;
3   *public reserves* (such as precious metals and/or currencies of other countries) and *securities* as managed by the central bank;
4   *a monetary policy* which is implemented by the central bank;
5   *commercial banks* which are profit-making private firms; and
6   *deposit money* and *credit* which are generated (created) by the commercial banks.

The principles and practices of commercial banks and the monetary policy of a central bank will be discussed in the next two sections respectively. Prior to doing so, the factors that have led to the modern development of monetary systems in the major economies globally are highlighted, which provide some information that contributes to the related discussions in the later sections.

Evolution of money and advancement of monetary system

In many European countries like England, France, and Germany before the 1940s (and the United States before the 1970s), money was directly linked and convertible to gold at fixed rates which were guaranteed by the respective governments (i.e., the historical gold standard of money). In other words, the ability of the related central banks to issue money, and hence the quantity of circulating money in the related economies were restricted by the volume of gold reserves (or endowments) in the different nations. Owing to the rapid expansion of world economic activities, however, the limited supply (i.e., the quantity) of money under the gold standard might not be able to cope with the continuous growth/expansion of the related economies. Eichengreen (1992), for example, chooses "Golden Fetters" as the title of his book to reflect the restrictions imposed by the gold standard of money on the world economies, which is also argued to be one of the major factors that led to the Great Depression in the 1930s.

Since then, countries have abandoned the gold standard and adopted an inconvertible system of money (i.e., currencies are no longer convertible to gold under any fixed rate guaranteed by the government) when they issue their legal tender. Under this system, issuing a currency in an economy has largely become a form of trust that relies on the legitimate power and autonomy of the central bank to print the money in accordance with its "reasonable" estimations of the quantity of money that should be issued in any given period of time. As this system further develops, the ability of commercial banks to generate (create) money in the form of deposit money through credit is also seen being significantly increased over time (related discussions will be presented in the next section). In practice, the ability of commercial banks to create deposit money is influenced by the monetary policy of the central bank.

In a system of trust and credit, the practices of money (including its general functions) are influenced by three major and interrelated factors since the issuance of money and its equivalents are no longer restricted (or backed up) by any physical commodity like gold. These include: 1) the *quantity of the money supply* (including currency issued by the central banks and deposit money generated by commercial banks) in the market; 2) the *interest rate* (i.e., opportunity cost or price) of using money by households and firms; and 3) the measures taken by the central bank (i.e., *monetary policy*) to change the overall supply and/or interest rate of money in the economy.

For example, if the quantity of commodities traded in the markets in any given period of time is fixed, and if the quantity of money that is circulating in the markets increases (because the central bank issues more money, and/or the commercial banks issue more credit), there will be a reduction in the quantity of commodities in exchange for each unit of money. In other words, when more money is being injected into an economy, *ceteris paribus*, its purchasing power on average will decrease (or inflation rate will increase). On the other hand, if the interest rate falls, the opportunity cost for households and firms to spend money will also fall so that more money will be spent and injected into the economy. In the interconnected world economy today, the interrelationship between these three factors that may change the practices of money as a medium of exchange, store of value, or means of deferred payment could be complicated (more examples will be presented in the following sections).

Commercial banks and monetary system

In principle, banks have been profit-making entities that accept deposits from individuals and firms with surplus of resources or funds and then grant loans to others who want to borrow. These practices can be traced back histori-cally in many economic societies worldwide. The earliest historical instance of banking dates back several thousand years (see, e.g., Shodhganga, n.d.). In their related businesses, banks mainly earn from the interest differentials between their lending rate and payment back to the depositors. That is, banks earn revenue from charging borrowers a higher rate of interest on average than the rate that they pay to the depositors.

Despite the fact that business activities undertaken by the early banks before the Industrial Revolution like those in England were "commercial" in nature (for example, private and joint-stock banks in England in the 17th and 18th centuries), the organization of contemporary commercial banks clearly evolved and then grew after the late 18th century. Through the active role of the commercial banks in attracting deposits and facilitating monetary transactions in the markets, the efficiency of business activities in the related economies increased over time and hence contributed to economic growth in the 19th century. For example, Wright (2008) concludes that the progression of commercial banking "played a key role in early U.S. economic growth. Commercial banks, savings banks, insurance companies and other financial intermediaries helped to fuel growth by channeling wealth from savers to entrepreneurs".

Functions of commercial banks in monetary system

A major function of commercial banks is their strategic activities that oper-ate and create different forms of money, whether these are in the form of channeling the flow of monetary funds between depositors and borrowers, or facilitating the spending of these two groups in the markets for profit-making purposes. Except for currency (i.e., coins and banknotes) which are issued directly by the central bank, commercial banks are able to issue other forms of intermediate credit that allow their customers (individuals and firms) to make use of such credit as money.

Promoting direct spending through related deposits

Traditionally, by allowing individuals and firms to open *savings (or other similar types of) accounts* as a means to deposit (store) their money, commercial banks also provide *checking accounts* (also called *demand deposits*) simultaneously which allow the depositors to spend their money by signing checks (a form of *deposit money*) issued by the banks. Accordingly, when a check is signed by an account holder to settle a transaction, this becomes his/her authorization to the related bank to transfer the specified amount on the check to another account.

Thus, the efficiency and incentive of consumers to spend are largely pro-moted by the availability of checks. For example, when a person is taking a short vacation in another city, s/he has no need to budget and withdraw a lump sum of cash from his/her deposit account in advance, but simply hold a small amount on hand for precautionary purposes and a check book in his/her pocket. To pay for the hotel, restaurant and entertainment bills, and other purchases during the trip, s/he can simply sign checks with the related amounts. In other words, a consumer can spend his/her money whenever s/he wants without the need to carry a large amount of coins and banknotes.

Creation of deposit money for spending

Normally, some of the existing deposits in a bank are withdrawn by depositors for spending, but at the same time, new deposits will also be received. In other words, a bank is always able to maintain a positive balance from its deposit accounts as a whole. This allows the bank to lend money or offer credit to promote market transactions. For example, the most simple form of deposit money created by a bank is by approving overdrafts in some of its checking accounts.

Under this arrangement, a person or a firm may be granted a pre-approved maximum amount to spend by signing checks even though s/he or they may not make a deposit of the equivalent amount of money into his/her/their saving (or checking) account in the first place. After spending, the individual who issues the check through overdraft/credit is bounded by the related repayment agreement with the bank to settle the debt (principal interest charged as agreed in advance) within a certain period of time (e.g., a month).

Through this arrangement, a firm that obtains credit from a bank can pay for some of its costs of production like labor and raw materials through checks before there is actually revenue from the outputs/business. Therefore, the production/business activities of firms could be evidently expanded. By allowing firms to issue checks through credit, the amount of deposits in the banking system will increase because, for example, after an employee receives a pay check, s/he will deposit at least part of the funds into a bank, which allows the bank to further expand its credit in a subsequent round, and so on and so forth (this money creation process is elaborated under the "Monetary policy" section below).

Introduction of credit cards as means of payment

Aside from the traditional operations of cash and deposit money, another widespread function of commercial banks in the modern monetary system is the introduction and promotion of the use of *credit cards* as a direct means of payment (an informative article about the progress and general aspects of the operation of credit cards can be found in Wikipedia; see https://en.wikipedia.org/wiki/Credit_card). To a large extent, the advancement of credit card use after the second half of the 20th century has unarguably increased the efficiency of consumption of individuals and corporate consumers in the markets, and hence business turnover of merchants in the world economies. In principle, except for the store of value function, credit cards indeed fulfill the other three functions of money which facilitate consumption activities in the markets (largely in terms of the consumption expenditures or "C" in the aggregate demand of an economy as expressed in Equation (5.1) in Chapter 5), and hence promote the scale of production and contribute to the macroeconomic growth.

In comparison to the practice of checks and the related deposit money, the use of credit cards may provide more convenience and better security to both consumers for spending purposes and merchants who accept them as a means of payment. As the efficiency of consumption has increased with the use of credit cards, so has business turnover in the consumer markets. This is because in order to issue a credit card, the issuer (e.g., a commercial bank) takes the responsibility in advance to verify the ability and credibility of a potential cardholder to settle a pre-approved amount of credit (for example, USD 2,000 each month). Once a person receives the credit card, s/he can simply present the card for consumption and then settle the debt later through some pre-agreed terms. For example, s/he may settle the total amount of outstanding debt on a monthly basis through cash or deposit money. Or, s/he may settle part of the amount spent, and repay the outstanding balance by accepting a pre-determined rate of interest charged on the balance in a later period of time or over a period of time.

Merchants who accept credit cards as a direct means of payment to encourage consumption are usually required to pay a fee to the card issuers for taking part in the network. However, a major attraction is that for each transaction, authorization has to be obtained (e.g., when a card is put through a credit card machine for a transaction, an authorization code is provided simultaneously). Therefore, merchants are sure to obtain payment from the card issuing bank immediately (as a form of deposit money) even though the consumer may not pay the card issuer later. In other words, by accepting credit cards, merchants do not need to worry about handling a large volume of cash in their everyday business activities, nor the risk of receiving bad checks.

In a study by Chakravorti (2003), the benefits and costs to both consumers and merchants that are linked through the development and widespread use of the credit card network around the world are elucidated. For example, Chakravorti (2003: 53) refers to a report by Ernst & Young (1996) in which "83 percent of merchants said that their sales increased and 58 percent said that their profits increased by accepting credit cards" (in the USA).

Other than operations through cash, various forms of deposit money (which are backed up by either cash or credit), and credit cards, the functions of commercial banks in the monetary system have been expanded by rapid advancements in technology since the end of the 20th century. For example, automated teller machine (ATM) cards, debit cards, electronic money (e-money), and online banking have been widely promoted by commercial banks through innovative applications of digital and information technologies (related practices will be discussed in the last section of this chapter).

Commercial banking and hospitality industry

As the traditional organizations in facilitating monetary transactions and one of the major financial intermediaries in the modern economies (financial intermediaries also include investment banks, insurance companies, mutual funds, and any other organization that acts as an agent to provide services for medium- and long-term financial transactions), the various monetary and financial services made available by commercial banks have become the essential nexus to facilitate the practices and continuous advancement of the hospitality industry. In everyday business, for example, a hospitality firm will receive a significant amount of money in the form of cash, and personal and traveler's checks, as well as deal with the other forms of payments like credit cards. On the other hand, the firm also needs to settle various forms of payments for its business operations like wages and business supplies on a regular basis. To manage all of these monetary transactions efficiently (i.e., with the lowest handling costs), a good understanding and use of the services of commercial banks have become indispensable to any hospitality firm in its business.

In addition to short-term monetary transactions, commercial banks have also been a major source of finance for the investment and development of the hospitality industry. Nevertheless, in contrast to other financial organizations that largely raise their capital funds from long-term sources like the issuance of securities and long-term debts, the financial resources of commercial banks are largely derived from deposits and short-term in nature. Thus, financial lending granted by commercial banks are usually in the form of mortgages, which are backed up by related mortgages like the properties that will be developed by the borrowers (the hospitality firms), and regular repayments on the loans are required.

For example, Singh and Kwansa (1999: 422) point out that "commercial banks have been considered the traditional construction lenders" by providing mortgage loans for the development of the lodging industry in the United States. Considering the progress of other financial organizations and the related financial products/securities over time (see, e.g., Gordon et al., 2004), it is anticipated that the traditional role of commercial banks in construction lending may be limited in the 21st century. Nevertheless, these banks "may become more involved in purchasing debt securities rather than making direct construction loans" (Singh and Kwansa, 1999: 422) in the lodging industry.

Principles and practices of monetary policy

As mentioned in the first two sections above, money in terms of cash and deposit money of various forms plays an essential role in facilitating the efficiency of production and market exchanges for goods and services, and hence the growth of modern economies. Based on the money issued directly by the central bank, commercial banks may be able to increase the volume of deposit money and other forms of direct means of payment like credit cards in an economy through strategic measures for profit-making purposes. Following the rapid expansion in the scale and scope of commercial banking after the second half of the 20th century, different forms of deposit money and their equivalent are far more extensive than cash/currency (coins and banknotes) as circulated money in any economy today.

For example, according to McLeay et al. (2014: 15), money is broadly composed of "bank deposits – which are essentially IOUs from commercial banks to households and companies – and currency – mostly IOUs from the central bank. Of the two types of broad money, bank deposits make up the vast majority." They point out that at the end of 2013, 97% of the money that was circulating in the UK economy was in the form of bank deposits. In fact, "those bank deposits are mostly created by commercial banks themselves" (ibid.) to accomplish and facilitate market exchanges, and as particular commodities which allow them to trade for profit in the money market.

In view of the importance of money in economic activities and the ability of commercial banks to create deposit money, it has been routinely argued that to ensure a stable monetary environment for businesses and economic growth, a government should go through the central bank to manage the practices of the monetary system through *monetary policies* – mainly policies that influence the supply of money and interest rate (i.e., cost) of using money in the markets. Through expansionary (or contractionary) monetary policies, the government is able to increase (or decrease) the stock of money, or lower (or increase) the cost of using money in the monetary system, as well as the ability of the commercial banks to create deposit money.

Money supply policy

To be effective in managing and regulating the volume of money that is circulating in the economy, different forms of money must be clearly categorized/defined in the first place so that the policy targets are clear. According to the aforementioned discussions, money in economics can be generally categorized into two forms: *narrow money and broad money*.

In principle, narrow money refers to any means that is ready to serve as the medium of exchange like coins and banknotes, checks (demand deposit) and saving deposits which could be spent immediately or withdrawn as cash in a very short period of time.

On the other hand, broad money refers to deposits which may not be convertible (withdrawn) immediately into a medium of exchange within a certain fixed period of time. For example, time deposits and certificates of deposit with different fixed periods (e.g., one month, or three months, or one year) are held in the banking system.

In economics and for statistics purposes, the money supply is commonly expressed with the notations of M0, M1, and M2 (higher orders like M3 and M4 may also be included when more different forms of monetary funds in the economy are taken into consideration). In principle, a larger number associated with the "M" means the money that could be converted immediately into a medium of exchange is less liquid.

Notations of various forms of money supply

M0: all physical currencies like coins and banknotes issued by the central bank which are circulating in the economy
M1: M0 plus demand deposit (checks of various forms)
M2: M1 plus saving and time deposits

The economic characteristics of the money supply in different economies are indeed the same, especially for M0, even though the exact terms applied that refer to the different forms of money may not be identical. In the United States, for example, M1 includes "currency in circulation" (i.e., M0), balance in the "transaction accounts" (i.e., checking accounts) and "traveler's checks"; M2 is M1 plus the balance in savings accounts and other deposits and money market funds (Schiller and Gebhardt, 2019: 276–278). In the Euro area, M1 is defined as M0 plus "overnight deposits", and M2 is M1 plus "deposits with an agreed maturity up to 2 years" and "deposits redeemable at a period of notice up to 3 months" (European Central Bank, n.d.a).

With reference to the different forms of money supply, the central bank may exercise its legitimate power to manage the related quantities, especially the deposit money that could be created by the commercial banks in the forms of M1 and M2. To do so, two monetary policies are commonly applied. They are: 1) formal requirements for reserves to back up the deposit money being received and created by the commercial banks; and 2) trading government securities openly in the markets.

Reserve requirements

Since the ability of commercial banks to create deposit money is due to the deposits that they directly obtain from individuals or firms, the central bank may regulate their ability to create deposit money by requiring them to hold a reserve ratio (e.g., 5%, 10%, etc.) of the total deposits in terms of vault cash or direct deposits in the central bank.

For example, if a bank receives a direct deposit of $100 and the required reserve ratio is 10%, then the bank can issue a maximum amount of credit in terms of deposit money of $90 immediately. Hypothetically, if the individual who receives this $90 credit spends it all by issuing a check, and it is deposited into the bank directly, then the total amount of deposit money of this bank is increased by $90. Therefore, the bank may be able to create another $81 of deposit money in credit ($90 – $90 × 10% as required reserve, or $90 × 90%) in the next round of lending. If this process continues, the total amount of deposit money that may ultimately be created is:

$100 + 100 \times 0.9 + 100 \times 0.9 \times 0.9 + 100 \times 0.9 \times 0.9 \times 0.9 + \ldots$
$= \quad 100 \times (1 + 0.9 + 0.9^2 + 0.9^3 + \ldots)$
$= \quad 100 \times 10^*$
$= \quad 1{,}000$

* Note: In mathematics, $(1 + 0.9 + 0.9^2 + 0.9^3 + \ldots)$ is a geometric progression (or geometric series). The sum of this series of numbers can be found by $\dfrac{1}{1-0.9}$, or $\dfrac{1}{0.1}$. (Related calculations in general can be found in any introductory textbook for business mathematics). Students may also find related discussions in any economic textbook like the one by Schiller and Gebhardt (2019: 282–283).

In this example, the original \$100 deposit could be increased by commercial banks tenfold to \$1,000 (\$900 is created) as the reserve ratio is 10% (0.1). This tenfold increase is called a *money multiplier* in economics. From the above note, it is clear that:

$$\text{Money multiplier} = \frac{1}{\text{required reserve ratio}} \tag{6.1}$$

Based on the above principle, if the central bank would like to stimulate economic activities by increasing the stock of money (M1 and/or M2) that is circulating within the economy, it may adopt an expansionary monetary policy to reduce the required reserve ratio, say, from 10% to 8%. Accordingly, the money multiplier will increase from 10 (1/0.1) to 12.5 (1/0.08) so that more money could be made available for the spending of individuals and firms. In contrast, if the central bank sees the need to slow down economic activities (e.g., during an inflationary period) by reducing the stock of money, it can apply a contractionary monetary policy to raise the required reserve ratio, say, from 10% to 12% so that the deposit money which could be created by the commercial banks is reduced (for more discussion about the effects of the changes in the required reserve on macroeconomic performance, see, e.g., Federal Reserve Bank of San Francisco, 2001).

Open market operations

Other than reserve requirements, a central bank can also modify the volume of M1 and/or M2 by selling and buying different forms of government securities (e.g., the treasury bill: T-bill of the US and the British government respectively) openly in the market. For example, the central bank can offer to buy back government securities from the banking system to implement an expansionary monetary policy, so that deposits will be made directly by the central bank to the accounts of the commercial banks. As direct deposits increase, more deposit money can be created by the banks in the subsequent rounds. This principle may also apply to the opposite case in which the central bank wants to adopt a contractionary monetary policy by selling government securities in the open market (Investopedia, 2018 provides a short article and video on its website which could be helpful to students).

In many well-developed economies like the USA today, open market operations have been the dominant monetary measure adopted by the related central banks to modify the money supply, since there is a significant volume of government securities traded in the markets. Nevertheless, in many emerging economies like China and those in Southeast Asia, reserve requirements are still widely adopted by their central banks to manage the money supply.

Interest rate policy

Parallel to the policies which modify the volume of money supply, interest rate is another key policy measure which is applied by a central bank to manage the practices of its monetary system. In principle, the interest rate policy aims to change the opportunity cost (or the price) of individuals and firms in using money, and hence modify their existing consumption and investment behaviors respectively.

In practice, a central bank may change the market interest rate through open market operations and/or direct changes in its interest rate to deal with the commercial banks in the market. First, given the demand for money in any given short period of time, the price (i.e., interest rate) of using money in the market will change if the supply of money changes as a result of the open market operations of the central bank. Second, since the central bank is acting as the bank of all the other banks in an economy, if it changes the interest rate (e.g., the federal funds rate in the USA, or the Treasury bill discount rate in the UK) which is applicable to the banks, the commercial banks then have to change the interest rate for their customers in the markets accordingly.

Since most economic activities today are fueled by the use of deposit money, which is generated through credit, changes in the supply of money and interest rate in an economy will undoubtedly lead to significant impacts on its aggregate demand. Therefore, related monetary policy tools have been widely applied by various governments to manage their macroeconomic performance during different phases of the business cycle. For example, shortly after the outbreak of the global financial crisis in 2008, the US government introduced specific large-scale expansionary monetary policies between 2009 and 2012 (which is commonly known as quantitative easing or QE) to increase the money supply (mainly through various measures under open market operations) and lower the federal funds rate to save/stimulate its economy. Between mid-2009 and the end of 2016, the federal funds rate was held below 0.5%. As reported, "to try and stimulate the U.S. economy, the Federal Reserve cut its key interest rate to a range of between zero percent and 0.25%" (Isidore, 2008) at the end of 2008.

Despite the different debates between (and among) the concerned practitioners and academics on the effectiveness and various short- and long-term effects of the QE policies, the US economy did recover appropriately from the financial crisis. During the process, an interesting finding that was identified in a report by Tannenbaum and Bangalore (2015: 4) is that "the leisure and hospitality industry (inclusive of food services and drinking places) shows one of the largest increases in employment by industry during the nearly six-year recovery". In other words, the aggregate demand of the US economy did increase as a result of the expansionary monetary policy put forth by the US government.

Monetary policy and money in an open economy

As discussed in Chapter 1, economic studies on money in an open economy have largely focused on the *foreign exchange rates* between the currencies of different countries. In an open economic environment, many internal and external factors may simultaneously affect the foreign exchange rate of a currency with other currencies. These mainly include the trade position of a country like its trade deficit or surplus with other countries, flows of financial and capital funds into and out of the country, market expectations, as well as any crucial changes in its social and political environments. Besides, the monetary policy of a country is another crucial factor that must be taken into consideration. When the central bank of a country modifies the supply and/or the interest rate of its monetary funds, the demand and supply of its money (including currency and deposit money) in the foreign exchange markets (both local and overseas) will also change, and hence its foreign exchange rates.

Although the monetary policy as implemented by a central bank only represents one of the many factors that may change the foreign exchange rate of a currency, related measures taken by the central bank may convey essential information to the market participants. For example, if the government of a country would like to boost its exports through a "weak currency" policy (i.e., with the aim to maintain a relatively low exchange rate per unit of the domestic currency that could be converted into other foreign currencies), loose monetary policies like a low interest rate and/or easy money supply policies may be adopted by the central bank. *Ceteris paribus*, it is reasonable to anticipate that given the price level of locally produced commodities, if foreigners can exchange more of the country's currency with the same amount of their money than before, they will spend more on outputs from this country.

For example, the Japanese government maintained low interest rate and weak currency policies in 2017, and as such, "owing to the weak yen environments, the number of foreign tourists to Japan climbed in November 2017, by 26.8 per cent on a year earlier" (Japan Research Institute, 2018: 4). Indeed, the increase in inbound tourists in Japan contributed to business revenue in its hospitality industry as a whole. Although many other internal and external factors (e.g., increase in the income of other Asian countries) might be in place to determine this observed result, a related monetary policy taken by Japan's central bank on its currency exchange rate in the international markets was an indispensable factor.

E-money, online banking, and market exchange

As a result of rapid technological advancements, the commercialization of information and digital technologies has rapidly expanded from the end of the 20th century. Among the major milestones, the evolution and rapid expansion of the use of e-money and online banking (or electronic banking (e-banking)) services have undoubtedly added to the efficiency of market exchanges, and hence the business turnover of various firms, including those in the world hospitality industries.

E-money practices

According to the European Central Bank (n.d.b), "[e-money] is broadly defined as an electronic store of monetary value on a technical device that may be widely used for making payments". In practice, *e-money* products mainly consist of the following two forms: 1) "*hardware-based products*" with which the related payments are to be transferred "by means of device readers that do not need real-time network connectivity to a remote server" (ibid.); and 2) "*software-based products*" which generally require an "online connection with a remote server" (ibid.).

Hardware-based e-money

In terms of the first type of e-money product, specific e-money devices (usually cards that have a magnetic stripe and/or digital chip) issued by firms provide the option to convert cash or deposit money or credit into electronic/digital signals and store in such e-money devices. Then, when an individual presents the e-money device as payment for consumption, an equivalent monetary value would be transferred through an offline or online device reader held by the vendor that is processing the transaction. After receiving the monetary value, which is accepted by the electronic device of the vendor, the vendor may retain the funds in an electronic form, or redeem them for cash from the e-money issuer or instruct the issuer to transfer the funds to a bank account (i.e., in the form of deposit money). Usually, the issuing firm of e-money devices is not necessarily a bank or a financial organization. For example, mass transportation firms and chain retail stores have been increasingly introducing various forms of electronic value-stored cards since the end of the 20th century (e.g., the Oyster card in London and the Octopus card in Hong Kong) to facilitate the efficiency of related monetary transactions.

Software-based e-money

The second type of e-money product largely refers to the transactions/transfers of money through various online systems. In principle, these systems are interconnected with the servers of related banks and non-bank e-money operators together in the internet world, which allow instantaneous transfer of money between different accounts. In practice, a registered individual in the system will obtain approval for the authorization to transfer a certain amount online from his/her bank or non-bank account to a designated account (e.g., the account of the merchant where s/he is making a purchase).

The development of software-based e-money has led to a major advancement in the use of money from demand and saving deposits of commercial banks, which is the introduction of debit cards as a direct means of payment. Instead of using checks or withdrawing cash from ATMs, debit cards allow individual consumers to transfer deposit money online from their bank account directly to the vendor's account to settle payments. Aside from some of the more well-known debit cards issued by the Bank of America, Citibank, and Barclays, there has been a rapid expansion in the use of Chinese UnionPay debit cards since the beginning of the 21st century, which is undoubtedly reflective of Chinese consumption activities both in and outside Mainland China through the worldwide online banking system. In fact, the numbers of hotels, restaurants and retail stores around the world which accept UnionPay as a direct means of payment have been increasing in the past decade.

Continuous advancements in e-money

The security and efficiency (convenience) of using e-money for consumption have been promoted to a large audience of consumers, owing to the continuous advancements in technology like radio frequency identification (RFID) and its wide commercial applications. Hence, the spending volume of consumers has increased over time. A good example that exemplifies the popularity of e-money is the rapid expansion of contactless payment systems (e.g., e-payments through Apple Pay and Google Pay). These allow the use of certain pre-approved amounts for purchases which has facilitated applications of hardware- and software-based products through RFID with debit and credit cards (see, e.g., Trütsch, 2014). Indeed, contactless payment has rapidly gained popularity in the well-developed economies like the USA, UK, and Japan, as well as the rapid emerging economy of China since the beginning of the 21st century.

Another remarkable advancement in the practice of e-money since the late 2000s is evidently the innovative applications of mobile technology by commercial banks and all related e-money issuers at both the local and global levels. The innovativeness of this technology has resulted in the merger between hardware-based and software-based e-money products through *smartphone* applications. Today, by installing related apps onto a smartphone, an individual may simply use the phone as a direct linkage to most of his/her bank accounts online, and transfer money to his/her credit cards and other value-stored cards for payment purposes. More impressive is that some apps may allow users to convert readable images of their credit and debit cards into the smartphones, and then present those images through related scanning readers as a direct means of payment (e.g., the impacts of this "cell phone money" on the financial system was explored by Turnbull, 2010).

In the hospitality industry, an interesting and successful case of issuing and prompting the usage of e-money is Starbucks. In November 2001, Starbucks formally issued its Starbucks card, which was clearly a form of hardware-based e-money (see, e.g., StarbucksMelody, 2013). In the beginning, customers were asked to pay by cash or credit card in the Starbucks stores, and the related amount would then be converted into electronic signals which were stored in the card. To encourage the use of this card, bonus points were granted according to accumulated spending. Then, consumers may use the bonus points to directly pay for (offset) the monetary value of their future consumption. Following the commercialization of mobile technology, all Starbucks customers today can simply add monetary value to their card by using mobile apps like App Store and Google Play and spend the value that is stored in their smartphones directly.

Economic and business significance of e-money

Aside from technological features like the internet infrastructure and internet security, the economic advantages of the widespread use of e-money and related transaction channels though online banking are evidently contributors to the increase in efficiency and decline in marginal costs (especially cost of time) of market transactions. Therefore, the frequency and absolute volume of spending of consumers around the world have been largely encouraged through the more convenient ways of carrying and handling money. For example, Runnemark et al. (2015: 290) find in an experimental study that "people are willing to pay more for identical products with debit cards than with cash".

A study by Cobanoglu et al. (2015) on the practices of mobile payment (MP) identifies that "compatibility with lifestyle was the strongest predictor of consumers' intention to adopt mobile payment technology in restaurants" (Cobanoglu, 2015: "Abstract"). They suggest that to be proactive with related business strategies, "the hospitality marketers and technology specialist should first understand their target segments' values and beliefs, then promote MP technology in a way that suit to their values, needs, and lifestyles" (ibid.: "Practical Implications"). Indeed, this argument may also be applicable to other hospitality firms including hotels and theme parks.

Owing to the tide of technological advancements in the global economic societies, the business efficiency of the world hospitality industry in terms of monetary transactions with customers can hardly be improved if e-money and online banking transactions are not managed appropriately.

Did you know? ...

Inbound and outbound tourists between different countries are connected to the foreign exchange rates of their currency. Although the scale of the connections is not identical among the different countries, nor across the different periods of time owing to impacts from many other factors like changes in income, government policies, and transportation facilities, a good number of academic studies have identified that the changes in the foreign exchange rates of a currency with those of the currency of other countries changes the flow of its residents who are traveling to those countries, and inbound tourists from the related countries as well. In general, these patterns are more explicit for short-haul visitors than long-haul visitors (Greenwood, 2007: 272). As a result of the changes in the currency exchange rates, it is reasonable to conclude that the occupancy rate of hotels in the same destinations will also change, and therefore the industry needs to respond effectively to these changes.

Box 6.1 Impacts from changes in currency exchange rates on tourist flow and hotel occupancy

In economics, changes in the currency exchange rates of a country with the currencies of other countries imply that the prices paid by consumers with the currency of their country for commodities consumed directly in other countries also change. For example, suppose that the foreign exchange rate of the British pound (£) against the US dollar ($) changes from £1 = $1.4 to £1 = $1.5 in a year, and if the room rate of a hotel in Orlando, Florida in the United States remains the same, say, at $100 a night, this means that to a British tourist who is visiting Orlando and staying in a hotel there, the room rate in terms of the British pound falls from £71.4 (i.e., 100/1.4) to £66.7 (i.e., 100/1.5) for him/her.

Intuitively, as the actual out-of-pocket expenses of British tourists who are visiting the United States fall even though the listed prices of the related commodities in US dollars remain unchanged, the British may choose to spend more of their holidays in the United States, and vice versa. Indeed, this relationship between changes in the foreign exchange rates and tourist flow is usually validated by related studies.

For example, when the foreign exchange rate of the British pound rose against the US dollar and some other European currencies between 2001 and 2007 (the foreign exchange rate of the British pound rose from around £1 = $1.4 in mid-2001 to around £1 = $2.0 in mid-2007), it was found that "the growth in outbound UK visitors" largely comprised those who were visiting "these destinations" (Greenwood, 2007: 273) (i.e., the United States and other European countries). In contrast, Greenwood (2007) points out that "US and European visitors to and expenditure in Scotland has grown and declined in line with strong and weak exchange rates" (Greenwood, 2007: 272) of currencies against the British pound.

In practice, it is commonly observed that when visitor arrivals to a destination change as a result of changes in the foreign exchange rates, the occupancy rate of the hotel industry will also change. Barrie et al. (2009) verify this relationship with empirical evidence derived from seven tourist destinations (e.g., Las Vegas, Orlando) in the United States and the foreign exchange rate of the US dollar with five other currencies (e.g., Euro, Canadian dollar, British pound, Mexican peso, Japanese yen, and a weighted index of related currencies). Although the statistical impacts and significance derived from the analyses are not identical across the different tourist destinations, Barrie et al. (2009: 45) conclude that in general, the changes in the "exchange rates do affect hotel occupancy" in tourism sites in the United States.

It is evident from the findings of the related studies that to be effective in responding to the changes in the monetary environment in an open economy, decision makers in the hospitality industry need basic knowledge of foreign exchange rates. In addition, management teams in this industry need to pay particular attention to the different possible impacts from changes in foreign exchange rates on tourist flow and hence hotel occupancy rates.

Discussion questions:

1   When foreign exchange rates change, why are the impacts on short-haul visitors in general more explicit in comparison to long-haul visitors?
2   Aside from the strong British pound, what other economic and monetary policy factors might be responsible for "the growth in outbound UK visitors" and the increase in their related spending in destinations in the United States in the first half of the decade of the 2000s?
3   Suppose that you are a marketing manager for a hotel in the UK and recognize that the US government is trying to implement a weak US dollar policy. How would you respond to the potential changes in your business?

Conclusions and remarks

As an important factor of the macroeconomic environment, money and the monetary system are both indispensable in accomplishing and facilitating market transactions for any firm at the local and global levels. In this chapter, the economic functions of money and its practices in general and role in the hospitality industry have been discussed. In addition, the essential role of commercial banks in accepting deposits and then creating different forms of deposit money through credit, as well as the central bank in modifying the money supply and cost of using money in the markets are elucidated. A good understanding of the functions of these macroeconomic components and their influences as well as their changes in the markets are undeniably relevant to concerned business managers and investors.

After almost two decades into the 21st century, the format of money in the world economies has experienced dramatic changes as a result of technological advancements. These include the rapid expansion in the use of e-money through different means such as value-stored cards and online banking systems. Besides, innovative business applications of mobile technology since the late 2000s have and will further increase how money is being circulated in the world economies, and hence change consumption behaviors. Therefore, the intensity of this macroeconomic trend means that any service-based industry, like the hospitality industry, must be proactive to take advantage of related opportunities in order to ensure the sustainable growth of their business.

Lastly, it is important to note that other non-bank financial organizations, like investment banks, as well as financial markets like the security and debt markets, are essential to the capital investment and long-term development of firms in the hospitality industry. However, these are beyond the scope of this book.

References and further reading

Barrie, B., Flanegin, F.R., Racic, S., Rudd, D.P., 2009. The impact of exchange rates on hotel occupancy. *Journal of Hospitality Financial Management*, 17 (1), 33–46.

Chakravorti, S., 2003. Theory of credit card networks: A survey of the literature. *Review of Network Economics*, 2 (2), 50–68. Available www.rnejournal. com/articles/chakravorti_june03.pdf

Cobanoglu, C., Yang, W., Shatskikh, A., Agarwal, A., 2015. Are consumers ready for mobile payment? An examination of consumer acceptance of mobile payment technology in restaurant industry. *Hospitality Review*, 31 (4), Article 6. Available http://digitalcommons.fiu.edu/hospitalityreview/ vol31/iss4/6

Eichengreen, B., 1992. *Golden Fetters: The Gold Standard and the Great Depression, 1919–1939*. Oxford University Press, New York, USA.

Ernst & Young, 1996. Survey of retail payment systems. *Chain Store Age*, January 72 (1), 6A (5), 11A (4), 18A (4).

European Central Bank (n.d.a). The ECB's definition of euro area monetary aggregates. Available www.ecb.europa.eu/stats/money_credit_banking/ monetary_aggregates/html/hist_content.en.html

European Central Bank (n.d.b). Electronic money. Available www.ecb.europa. eu/stats/money_credit_banking/electronic_money/html/index.en.html

Federal Reserve Bank of San Francisco, 2001. What effect does a change in the reserve requirement ratio have on the money supply? August. Available www.frbsf.org/education/publications/doctor-econ/2001/august/reserve-requirements-ratio/

Fung, B., Molico, M., Stuber, G., 2014. Electronic money and payments: Recent developments and issues. Bank of Canada Discussion Paper 2014–2. Bank of Canada, Ottawa, Canada. Available www.econstor.eu/bitstream/10419/129678/1/796719500.pdf

Gordon, P., Marre, D., Bonjour, B. 2004. Understanding the commercial mortgage-backed securities market in the hospitality sector. *Journal of Retail & Leisure Property*, 4 (2), 105–117.

Greenwood, C., 2007. How do currency exchange rates influence the price of holidays? *Journal of Revenue and Pricing Management*, 6 (4), 272–273.

Investopedia, 2018. Open Market Operations – OMO. Available www.investopedia.com/terms/o/openmarketoperations.asp

Isidore, C., 2008. Fed slashes key rate to near zero. CNN Money, December 16. Available http://money.cnn.com/2008/12/16/news/economy/fed_decision/index.htm?postversion=2008121617

Japan Research Institute, Limited, 2018. Monthly report of prospects for Japan's economy, February. Available www.jri.co.jp/MediaLibrary/file/english/periodical/report/2018/02.pdf

McLeay, M., Radia, A., Thomas, R., 2014. Money creation in the modern economy. *Bank of England Quarterly Bulletin*, 2014 Q1, 14–27.

Poon, S., Chau, P.Y.K., 2001. Octopus: The growing e-payment system in Hong Kong. *Electronic Markets*, 11 (2), 97–106. Available https://pdfs.semanticscholar.org/f800/672c1448f0233ae7982444a85cf6d806b774.pdf

Runnemark, E., Hedman, J., Xiao, X., 2015. Do consumers pay more using debit cards than cash? *Electronic Commerce Research and Applications*, 14, 285–291.

Schiller, B.R., Gebhardt, K., 2019. *The Macro Economy Today*, 15th edition. McGraw-Hill Education, New York, USA.

Shodhganga, n.d. Origin of banking – An overview. Available http://shodhganga.inflibnet.ac.in/bitstream/10603/103219/8/08_chapter%201.pdf

Shoemaker, S., Lewis R.C., 1999. Customer loyalty: The future of hospitality marketing. *Hospitality Management*, 18, 345–370.

Singh, A.J., Kwansa, F.A., 1999. Financing the lodging industry in the next millennium. *International Journal of Hospitality Management*, 18, 415–425.

StarbucksMelody, 2013. The Starbucks card: 2001–2013 – Then and now. Available www.starbucksmelody.com/2013/12/20/the-starbucks-card-2001-2013-then-and-now

Tannenbaum, C.R., Bangalore, A.G., 2015. Weekly economic commentary (Quantitative easing comes to the eurozone, U.S. job growth is strong, but wage growth is not). Northern Trust, March 6. Available www.ntrs.com/documents/commentary/weekly-economic-commentary/2015/0306.pdf

Trütsch, T., 2014. The impact of contactless payment on spending. *International Journal of Economic Sciences*, 3 (4), 70–98.

Turnbull, S., 2010. How might cell phone money change the financial system? *Journal of Financial Transformation*, 30, 33–42. Available www.greeneconomics.net/Turnbull-CellPhoneMoney.pdf

Wray, L.R., 1991. *Money and Credit in Capitalist Economies: The Endogenous Money Approach*. Edward Elgar Publishing, Northampton, MA, USA.

Wright, R., 2008. Origins of commercial banking in the United States, 1781–1830. In: R. Whaples (ed.), EH.Net Encyclopedia. Available http://eh.net/encyclopedia/origins-of-commercial-banking-in-the-united-states-1781-1830

Yuvaraju, D., Rao S.D., 2012. Origin, history and functioning of credit card. *Research Scholar*, II (IV), 131–139. Available http://shodhganga.inflibnet.ac.in/bitstream/10603/88898/15/15_origin,%20history%20of%20credit%20card.pdf

Zhou, Z., 2004. *E-Commerce and Information Technology in Hospitality and Tourism*. Thomson Delmar Learning, Clifton Park, NY, USA.

7 Technology and innovation

Objectives and learning outcomes

To be efficient in production or business operations, no firm should neglect the application of technology in any shape or form. Since the mid-20th century, technological progress and technological applications have been remarkable and beyond the imaginative capacity of any academic or practitioner. The advancement of technology is no longer limited to physical forms like machines and computers that are tangible, but have largely expanded to intangible forms in cyberspace such as digital and information technologies, as well as mobile technology since the end of the 20th century. All of these advancements have evidently changed the traditional ways of production and consumption. Therefore, the aim of this chapter is to acquaint students with basic knowledge on the particular roles of technology and technological progress in business practices and industrial development. To strengthen the understanding of students on the related material, evidence, and literature in general and those derived from studies in the hospitality industry will be quoted for illustration purposes and discussion.

Since the end of the 20th century, the growth of the cruise industry has been unprecedented in the world market. The rapid growth and development of this industry indeed provide an interesting and valuable case study to illustrate the importance of innovation in the hospitality industry. By elucidating the innovative features and the business model that is being used in the development of the contemporary cruise industry, the intention here is to inspire students to come up with further ideas on possible applications of the relevant (but not necessarily exhaustive) experiences in the cruise industry to promote the business efficiency of other traditional sectors in the hospitality industry.

After reading this chapter, students will be able to:

- understand the economic notion of technology and changes in how technology is being recognized by economists and intellectuals in the field over time;
- understand the influence of technology and technological progress on business practices and industrial development (including the hospitality industry);

- identify the nature and interrelationships among inventions, technology, and innovations;
- understand the essence and importance of innovation in economics and in the particular context of the hospitality industry;
- gain an awareness of the role and importance of information technology in the business practices and development of the hospitality industry;
- understand the specific innovative features that have led to the success and rapid growth of the contemporary cruise industry; and
- recognize the relevant experiences in the cruise industry for the development of other sectors in the hospitality industry.

Economic notion of technology

As pointed out in the previous chapters, the advancement of technology will reduce the production costs of firms (i.e., shifting the individual supply curve outwards or to the right). On the other hand, the rapid growth of technology since WWII, and the further advancements and commercialization of digital, information and mobile technologies since the end of the 20th century have also explicitly changed the demand behavior of consumers over time (i.e., the individual demand curve shifts upward). Despite the cyclical fluctuations at the macroeconomic level, all of the changes are reflected in the long-term increases in aggregate supply (i.e., increase in the production capacity of an economy) and aggregate demand (i.e., economic growth) in the world economies.

In other words, advancements in technology over time have unarguably improved the material well-being of human society (although the effects may not be equally distributed or felt by everyone, or every individual economy globally). Thus, ensuring ongoing improvements in technology globally and more importantly, effectively applying the different forms of technologies have been the common interests of all economic participants (including firms, households and governments) because these collective actions as a whole are the major driving forces for economic development.

In economics, formal studies on the role and influence of technology and its impacts on economic activities are largely found in the literature after the 1950s. This could be due to the long-term changes in the methods of production that were adopted by firms, and the consumption behavior of households as a result of the second Industrial Revolution, and then further advancements after WWII (as discussed in Chapter 2). In the hospitality industry, application of the related economic principles has been more prevalent in studies in the 1970s that focus on the role of technology and technological advancements toward business efficiency and modern development of the hospitality industry.

Connotations of technology in early economics

Following the industrial development in Western Europe in the mid-18th century, the significance of technology and technological progress/advancement has been clearly acknowledged, albeit in indirect (or implicit) discourses by economists. Between the first and second Industrial Revolutions (i.e., sometime between the 1750s and 1920s), the concept of *technology* in economics largely referred to the invention of machines and related human-made fixtures and their continuously expanding stock which were *broadly categorized as capital* (i.e., a component of "capital" which contributed as a major factor of production). Consequently, firms who bought these sorts of capital goods were able to increase their productivity by increasing the scale and scope of the division of labor in their production process (see, e.g., Smith, 1998, Book I, Chapter I; Book II, Chapters III and V).

As a matter of fact, the contextual notion of applying the term "capital" to encompass the routine role and functions of technology in economics persisted for over a century in the intellectual world. For example, the notion of technology was still reflected through advancements in capital until the first contemporary economics textbook was published by Alfred Marshall in 1890 (Marshall, 1997). While the contemporary concepts of demand and supply were for the first time comprehensively elaborated (e.g., with a clear introduction on the demand and supply curves and their changes, as well as the concept of market equilibrium), the expression of technology was depicted as nothing more than a simple influence on the position of the supply curve resultant of "the invention of a new process or of new machinery" (Marshall, 1997: 279). In other words, technology was still simply viewed as a factor input of firms, like natural resources or labor, for producing economic commodities.

Changing views and emphasis on technology in the 1950s

Unlike the focus of classical economists like Smith and neo-classical economists like Marshall, some of the other intellectuals including the institutional economists dedicated significant effort to investigate the various factors that influence the different ways that the world economies have developed to shed new light on studies in technology. Instead of simply accepting physical technology as a given input factor (or a type of "resource") that is used by firms, which determines their methods of production and productivity, the dynamic and interactive roles of technology in an economic society were being emphasized and explored. For example, in an early article, Ayres (1953) deliberates that the existence of technology is not part of "(n)ature" and it is important for economists to recognize and explore the "technological process by which the industrial economy was coming into being" (Ayres, 1953: 279) in economic theories.

Then, in a book published decades later in 1974, Ayres further explains that "*technology* includes mathematical journals and symphonic scores no less than skyscrapers and assembly lines, since all these *are equally the product of human hands as well as brains*" (Ayres, 1974: 278; my emphasis). From this standpoint, the philosophical thoughts of economists around the notion of technology have clearly evolved from the conventional view that technology is a type of resource or physical tool of firms for production purposes to interest in exploring human decisions on why a particular technology is invented, or being used by firms, or contributed to industrial changes, or being further developed over time (or replaced by another technology after a certain period of time). In other words, rather than taking the view that technology is simply physical capital which is provided to firms, the dynamic and interactive relationship of technology with the choices made by market participants are emphasized. Besides, influences from the culture and the legal system of an economic society on how firms choose to use or develop technology, and how households receive different forms of technology are now gaining the attention of economists in the field and guide the principles in their studies.

As for other economists who use statistical analyses to examine the significance of technology and its functions in industrial development, many of them have started to emphasize the impacts of capital investment in technology by an industry or a firm on productivity changes. For example, in the book *Economics of Technology*, Granstrand (1994: 3; my emphasis) defines the economics of technology as "*the field of inquiry that focuses on the causal nature of the interactions between changes in various technologies* and natural sciences on one hand *and economic changes of various kinds* on the other". Grandstrand (1994) includes a study by Carlsson et al. (1993) in Chapter 2, who in principle, comprehensively examine and evaluate the influences from the automation technology adopted and upgraded by Swedish factories over time toward their economic performance. Generally speaking, positive impacts are found on their productivity and economic growth as a result.

Following the rapid use of industrial and commercial applications in technology areas, as well as more explicit interactions between consumers and technological commodities in the markets, more related studies have also been carried out to explore these interrelationships over time. For example, Thirtle and Ruttan (1986: 1) said that while "the primary focus of early studies on technical change and productivity growth was simply to measure the contribution of technical change, relative to conventional resources, to growth in output", increasingly more "serious efforts were being made to explore the influence of economic forces on technical change" since the mid-1960s. In their study, the market forces in terms of demand and supply and their changes that bring about technical changes are examined/mathematically and theoretically validated.

Technology and the service industries

In retrospect of the aforementioned economic notion of technology, it is clear that formal studies on the economic role and functions of technology in the service industries as a whole (not specifically a particular service industry like the hospitality industry) have been largely absent in the economics literature before the 1950s. Despite the fact that increases in the scale and scope of the service industries, like finance, health care, and hospitality, have been the focus of some of the economists in their studies, most have only attempted to look at the reasons that have led to an explicit shift of employment in the traditional agricultural and manufacturing industries to the service industries. Thus, influences from the related changes to the productivity of an economy and hence, its growth and development, are explored. Kravis et al. (1984: 188), for example, review the primary literature on these related topics which were published between the 1930s and 1970s.

In view of the rapid growth in the economic outputs of the service industry, Kravis et al. (1984) carry out a comprehensive statistical analysis to examine and determine the factors that are responsible for increasing employment in the service industries of the world's major economies like the USA and UK, and hence the aggregated contribution of the industry to their economic growth. With reference to the available literature, they mainly test "three sets of factors" (ibid.: 196) which may affect the decisions of consumers to spend their income on either physical commodities or services, and hence affect employment in the service industry in meeting the related demands. In principle, the three sets of factors include "income elasticities", "technology", and interactions between "income elasticities and the technological factors" (ibid.: 196–197). It is found in their study that "the driving force behind the expansion of service employment ... is the evolution of technology rather than the change in wants associated with rising income" (ibid.: 210–211). Indeed, the related findings explain a phenomenon discussed earlier in their study, in that without advancements in technology which have led to the availability and widespread use of "radio broadcasting and later TV broadcasting" (ibid.: 197), consumer expenditures in music and performance services might not have increased in the 20th century, and hence promoted employment in the related service sectors and their contributions to economic growth.

Technology and growth of hospitality industry

Following the widespread applications of technology by the hospitality industry like hotels and restaurants since the 1990s, it is obvious that related topics of study by economists and other interested academics in other disciplines who apply different economic approaches are on the rise. Aside from a common interest in exploring the statistical influences from the use of technology on changes in productivity or efficiency of a hospitality firm (or a particular sector), the role of technology is investigated by examining the different contextual layers. That is, the role of technology in facilitating the provision and delivery of services due to changes in the service quality, and innovative ideas that parallel the notion that related changes are indeed "the product of human hands as well as brains" (Ayres, 1974: 278).

For example, the interrelationship between institutional change and development of the hospitality industry in the USA in the 1970s is explored by Ingram (1998), who argues that while "existing organizations" may be more restricted by the "inertia … to incorporate the new technologies" (Ingram, 1998: 261), "new organizations are relatively free" (ibid.: 262) in adopting new technology of various forms to ensure that their competitive edge is maintained. Indeed, rapid expansion of the hospitality industry through the development of new properties by existing large firms in different regions and countries, as well as newly established firms in the markets have been seen as the major drivers that promote technological growth over time. Thus, technological progress in the hospitality industry is evidently the consequence of the instigation of institutional changes by new mindsets which is carried out throughout the industry over time. In addition, Ingram (1998) examines and confirms the practical impacts from changes in the institutions of hospitality education in the USA with the provision of qualified and professional human resources (i.e., human capital), who in turn lead the long-term changes (development) in the industry. Although Ingram (1998) does not directly say so, it is clearly conveyed that the organic integration between physical technology made by human hands and intangible technology invented by human brains leads to the continuous growth of the hospitality industry. Indeed, this may serve as the basis for exploring the importance of innovation in economics and its implications on the substantial advancements made in the hospitality industry in the 21st century.

Among the numerous advancements in the hospitality industry that have been realized by incorporating physical technologies of various forms, one of the most notable is the introduction of automation into business operations. Largely, automation not only improves the business efficiency of hospitality firms in their internal operations (similar to physical production in factories), but also the delivery of related services to their customers. For example, various forms of automation systems have been (and will continuously be) introduced by hotels with the intention to increase the efficiency of routine housekeeping tasks and cost control though energy saving. Besides, automated check-in systems have also been increasingly adopted by hotels and airlines to allow their customers to save time, as well as reduce the labor costs of related routine business operations.

According to Ivanov et al. (2017: 1501), applications of cutting-edge technologies through service automation and robots have been found "in hotels, restaurants, events, theme and amusement parks, airports, car rental companies, travel agencies and tourist information centres, museums and art galleries". By the mid-2010s, the "penetration" (ibid.: 1506) of related technologies was observed to increase over time although applications of "automation and robotic technologies" in the hospitality industry (e.g., hotels) are still limited in scope and scale. It is anticipated that "other robot types may enter this industry segment, such as robots washing and folding laundry" (ibid.) over time.

Invention, technology, and innovation

Following the aforementioned discussions on the economic notions of technology in different eras and research studies on related topics, the dynamic role of technology in contemporary industrial development can be further explored through the principles and essence of innovation. Indeed, this concept provides pragmatic grounds to gain more and better insights from the technological side into the interacting forces that have really led to the rapid growth of the hospitality industry in the 1990s, and its likely path of development ahead in the 21st century.

From both historical and practical standpoints, new ideas and technologies serve as instruments (means or intermediaries) that provide more opportunities for firms to improve their methods of production and therefore increase their productivity. Besides, new or variants of existing commodities would also be introduced over time. Nevertheless, it is humans who choose to invent new ideas or are inspired by the available technologies (i.e., opportunities) to facilitate the efficiency of production and then provide input and feedback for successful changes (technological advancements). Thus, these interactive forces between inventors and practitioners/users of technology lead to industrial and economic developments in the various economic societies. Throughout the process, the selection of different possible combinations of technologies that will be (or are being) invented and applying them to business practices are referred to as the economic notion of innovation. Broadly speaking, *innovation involves the generation and application of a new idea, which is realized through a process that combines and/or produces different technologies with related production resources, into a real and workable solution, and hence promotes new and more efficient ways to improve economic activities.* Indeed, innovation is a major determinant of industrial growth and development.

Innovation characteristics and arguments for innovation

In economics, comprehensive analyses of the essence of innovation has been largely carried out and credited to the intellectual works of Joseph Schumpeter in *The Theory of Economic Development* in 1934 (Schumpeter, 1983). In Chapter II of the book, Schumpeter critically argues that it is the "entrepreneurs" and not the "capitalists" in general who are leading the ongoing development of an economy and its industries. In this process, a major economic function of an entrepreneur is his/her innovative ability to "carr(y) out new combinations" (Schumpeter, 1983: 78) for improving production efficiency. In addition, Schumpeter clearly differentiates between invention and innovation in the sense that "as long as they are not carried into practice, inventions are economically irrelevant. And to carry any improvement into effect is a task entirely different from the inventing of it" (ibid.: 88).

In continuing Schumpeter's intellectual and inspiring work, extensive research studies have been carried out by economists and scholars in the area of economic/business innovations. Sener et al. (2017) propose three major views (neo-classical, Schumpeterian, and evolutionary views) based on the perspectives of different economists in the extant literature to examine the nature and practices of innovation. Among these different views, Schumpeter's arguments on the relationships between invention, technology, and innovation are recapped and explicitly emphasized as three phases:

i   Invention as a creation of new ideas which are systematically turned into technologies;
ii   Innovation as commercialization of invented ideas into marketable forms of production;
iii   Diffusion as disseminating new ways of 'getting things done' through the different layers of production.

(Sener et al., 2017: 206)

Interrelationship and dynamics in industrial development

From the standpoint of practitioners (or applied economists), new ideas which could successfully lead to new combinations (inventions) from the use of existing technologies are necessary to ensure the growth and development of an industry over time. On the other hand, if investments intentionally made by firms in research and development (R&D) activities generate new technologies, and increase the production and business efficiencies of the related industries, their growth and development could also increase as a result. Regardless of which of the two innovative processes (or their combination to varying degrees) is used, the process itself will still be largely one of trial and error in the markets. Therefore, feedback from practitioners is important, and allows revisions of the original ideas or plans, as well as contributing to changes in the existing technology. Thus, it might not be feasible to provide direct or one-way causal relationships among invention, technology, and industrial/economic growth that is generally applicable for the different economic societies. To a large extent, the relationships among invention, technology, and innovation in the industrial development process are interrelated and dynamic.

For example, Schmookler and Brownlee (1962) conduct a statistical analysis on the relationship between technology invented in the USA and the growth of the related industries in the first half of the 20th century (i.e., the statistical relationship "between industry size and inventive activity" (Schmookler and Brownlee, 1962: 173)). They find and conclude that the "progress in technical knowledge in an industry can be an effect as well as a cause of the rate of industry growth" (ibid.: 176). In other words, Schmookler and Brownlee (1962) show or confirm interactive and dynamic relationships between invention, technology, and industrial development. That is, while the growth in new technology based on inventions in any given period of time may promote (lead to) industrial development, this growth may also be due to the investments that are being made throughout the process of industrial development.

In these relationships, innovation is the primary driver of inventive activity and transforms the outputs (i.e., technologies) into new or improved consumable commodities in the markets, hence promoting industrial growth and development. Since the 1950s, the central role of innovation in many firms in driving the invention of new technologies and then commercializing the newly produced commodities or related commodities with added value has been increasingly more pronounced.

For example, Shapiro (1986) examines the impacts and significance of innovation on the introduction of new products, and hence the development of new firms and new industries are clarified with reference to Schumpeter's arguments. Shapiro (1986) defines innovation as the recognition of firms (i.e., the entrepreneurs) of the "latent need for the good" (Shapiro, 1986: 29) of the consumers "that existing goods cannot perform" (ibid.: 28). Consequently, new ideas for inventing new products or adding value to the capacity of existing products led to the introduction of new products that were widely found in the markets in the 1950s. Evidence cited includes the development of the "calculator[s]" from "tabulating equipment", to "electro-mechanical calculator[s]" and "electronic calculator[s]" (ibid.: 28), as well as "telephone, television, and computer" technologies (ibid.: 29). Indeed, it is identified that while innovations have provided new opportunities that allow for the establishment of new firms and new industries in the markets, their practices provide further insights to explain the innovative function of entrepreneurs in theories of economic development per Schumpeter.

Innovations in the hospitality industry

So far, it is evident that parallel to economic studies on technology, the initial focus of economists in terms of innovation was also largely on the various types of secondary industries (primarily the manufacturing industries that produced different physical goods). Notwithstanding, the rapid expansion of the hospitality industry in the world markets has caught the attention of both economists and the academia, which has also motivated them to explore the significance of innovation in the modern development of the hospitality industry as well as their interactive dynamics since the 1970s. While the practices of the hospitality industry are not the same as those in the secondary industries and other traditional service industries like banking and finance, the principles and economic notions around technology and innovation may still be largely (although not necessarily absolutely) applicable.

It is commonly observed that in the process of providing hospitality services, new ideas have been proposed by the industries (e.g., resorts, theme parks, and restaurants) that apply and "mix and match" various forms of existing technologies, especially information and mobile technologies with a variety of physical technological products in the 21st century. Indeed, successful innovations have clearly been favourable for business appeal and toward service quality, as well as increasing the range of selection (with new products and services) for consumers, and hence the competitiveness of related firms in the markets.

Innovations in tourism and related industries

Since the 1950s, innovation has been an indispensable factor that has contributed to the growth of various tourism industries like hotels, restaurants, theme parks, museums, and other similar attractions. Generally speaking, innovative activities carried out on a continuous basis have added to the variety of related tourism services, and hence enjoyed by tourists in world markets. In close pace with the innovations in manufacturing products, innovations in the tourism industry and the ways that they provide related services to tourists have continued to cultivate and complement the "latent need" (Shapiro, 1986: 29) for various services by tourists. In addition, new ideas and "new combinations" have also produced a wide range of new tourism commodities for tourists to enjoy while on their trip away from home. For example, the exterior and interior designs of hotel resorts and restaurants usually add to the visual pleasure of tourists, thus reinforcing their experience as an added value of their spending.

Through a comprehensive review of the related studies, Hjalager (2010) concluded that innovations in the tourism industry have covered a wide range of different areas since the 1990s. In particular, the modern development of tourism has been evidently stimulated and advanced by the continuous efforts and investments of the industry in "product, process, managerial, marketing and institutional" (Hjalager, 2010: 1) innovations. In terms of tourism products and services, Hjalager (2010) concluded from the related studies that in the hotel industry (including both well-established and new hotels of various scales), innovative ideas that introduce and improve the quality of hotel services, such as the "gastronomy, animation, infrastructure, wellness facilities" (ibid.: 2) over time have ensured that new and positive experiences are provided to visitors. Hjalager (2010) even cites an interesting example on the extent of innovativeness, for example, "adding a summer season to winter sports destinations may be considered a far-reaching innovation" (ibid.). Generally speaking, Hjalager (2010) clearly conveys that while the function of entrepreneurship per Schumpeter contributes as the principal determinant which leads to innovation, various "technology-push/demand-pull" (ibid.: 4) factors interactively inspire innovations in the industry and facilitate the efficiency of the innovative process in tourism development.

In addition to domestic tourism, cross-country traveling and direct spending by tourists (i.e., international tourism) have received much attention from tourism and related hospitality firms over time. Throughout the process of internationalization in tourism, innovations have been crucial in framing business practices and the ways that the industries have developed (i.e., their development paths) since the 1990s. Williams and Shaw (2011) indicated that the essence of innovation and internationalization in tourism can be examined based on three propositions: 1) "internationalization can be understood as a form of innovation" (ibid.: 29); 2) "successful internationalization is dependent on innovation" (ibid.: 30); and 3) "internationalization requires firms to have superior knowledge compared to those operating only in the domestic sphere" (ibid.: 31).

These three perspectives clearly demonstrate that in comparison to the concept of innovation per Schumpeter (1983), Sener et al. (2017), and Shapiro (1986), internationalization in tourism requires new ways of thinking. This is especially evident in the third proposition. Having a particular sense about the world markets (instead of an individual domestic market) and related technical knowledge ensure the effectiveness, and hence the success of new ideas that target international tourism. For example, to carry out new ideas for introducing tourism products and services that address the latent needs/demand of tourists, and provide more spending options for those who are traveling across countries, a good understanding of the different cultures and cultural differences serves as the initial grounds for innovations. A good example is the opening of Legoland in Malaysia as discussed in Chapter 5 (see discussions related to Illustration 5.1), which demonstrates the successful application of innovation in the internationalization of a theme park as a tourist destination.

Innovation in the restaurant industry

Since late 2010, innovative applications of information and mobile technologies have become widespread in the hospitality industry, but this is especially the case in the restaurant industry, as many restaurants are using such technologies to improve their business efficiency. Specifically, the innovations adopted improve the quality of the restaurant service and facilitate communication with customers, which increase business turnover and reduce business costs over time. For example, Illustration 7.1 shows the innovative settings of a Japanese sushi chain restaurant in Hong Kong, which is not only welcomed by (and exciting to) most customers, but also increases its business efficiency and turnover.

Schumpeter's notion of innovation is clearly demonstrated in Illustration 7.1. First, the "new combinations" are interesting and effective, which include the use of touch-screen mobile devices and technology, central processing system (instantaneous communication between the customers, kitchen, onsite attendants, and cashier), mechanical equipment (the conveyor belt), interesting interactive menu (electronic menu), and fancy serving presentation (Japanese bullet trains).

Through these "new combinations" that apply or use both hard and soft technologies, this restaurant can reduce a few (perhaps even many) staff members who have high wages, which is often the case in most urban areas (especially commercial areas in the city) or address a staff shortage problem, which is the case in developed cities like Tokyo and Hong Kong. This example shows that average business costs might be reduced by using innovation in business operations.

Delivery of food with Japanese bullet
train model placed onto food
conveyor belt

Touch-screen food menu

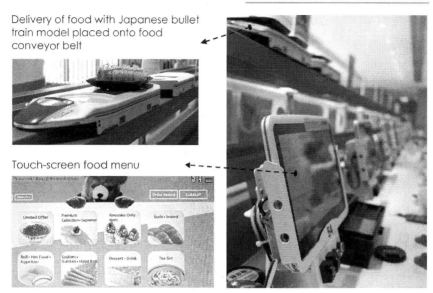

Illustration 7.1 Use of technology in Japanese sushi chain restaurant

Second, whenever the food menu needs to be modified, the restaurant could simply change the information at almost no marginal cost, versus reprinting in hard-copy format, which is costly. Therefore, the use of innovation in providing dining services clearly saves labor and operation costs, so that the restaurant could very well pay off the debt of the fixed costs for using the innovations in a short period of time.

Third, ordering through these "new combinations" might prevent the likelihood of errors in ordering or miscommunication between customers and servers during peak hours, and hence improve the service quality, and business efficiency and turnover

On the demand side, consumers do not have to face pressure of time to decide on their order with the servers standing in front of them and waiting for their order, or call for the server to order extra food. Instead, they can order and add to their order at their leisure (even ordering one dish at a time by using mobile devices when they are almost full). Accordingly, the average amount spent by consumers may ultimately increase. In other words, the spending behavior of consumers in this type of restaurant before and after the innovations are put into place differs. Besides, word of mouth from current customers about the overall improved service quality during the consumption process may also attract new customers.

Information technology and the hospitality industry

To facilitate the provision of services and ensure that the quality of services provided (through different means such as by staff personnel or related products and fixtures) are able to meet and reinforce the positive perception of consumers during the consumption process, an effective and efficient communication mechanism is indispensable for the continuous growth of the hospitality industry. Owing to the need for continuous and timely communication with consumers, advancements in information and mobile technologies would offer a new means (or act as an instrument) for the hospitality industry to increase its business efficiency and expand its market size (i.e., stimulate demand) toward its long-term growth.

Before the 21st century, printed materials (e.g., menus and promotional leaflets) were almost the only means that the hospitality firms used to communicate with their current and potential customers. However, writing, designing, printing, and updating the materials were costly to the firms, especially smaller firms like family-run hotels and restaurants. For example, leaflets sent through the mail was a common tactic for restaurants, hotels, resorts, and theme parks to promote their services to the general public and attract their interest so that they would spend their money on the related services there. However, special promotions for a particular season or to celebrate certain festivals, or the addition of any new services required the rewriting, redesigning, and reprinting of new leaflets, which would be sent out by mail again. Therefore, this business model obviously incurred a high monetary and time cost to the firms in order for them to communicate with their customers. On the demand side, it might not be easy for the consumers to obtain extra information that would assist their spending decisions after receiving the related information in printed format.

Changes in practices

Zhou (2004: 5) said that the

> hospitality and tourism industry ... is an information-rich industry, it depends heavily on finding and developing new means to distribute travel and hospitality products and services, marketing information to consumers, and providing comfort and convenience to travelers. Similarly, consumers are constantly seeking new sources of information to help them make decisions before purchasing travel services to make their trips more satisfying.

As a matter of fact, following the popularization of the internet since the mid-1990s, and the widespread commercialization of digital information technology and its applications through mobile technology devices like notebook computers and smartphones since the first decade of the 21st century, related applications used by hospitality firms have evidently facilitated their distribution of information to consumers.

As mentioned previously, Hjalager (2010: 2) insightfully said that the primary innovation that acts as the "backbone" for the modern development of tourism and its related industries is information and communication technologies (ICTs). Indeed, ICTs allow service providers to create new channels and media that facilitate effective communication with their existing and potential consumers, and hence has been considered to be a propellant of growth in the business efficiency of the hospitality industry since the mid-2010s.

By using related information and mobile technologies, it is evident that the market behavior of the consumers have also significantly changed over time. For example, consumers can search for available hotel rooms and compare room rates at any time; that is 24 hours a day, 7 days a week (24/7) with the use of the internet. This flexibility means that travelers are more inclined to plan for their trips (both short- and long-haul). Zhou (2004: 3) refers to information in 2003 from the US Travel Association, and points out that "travelers used the Internet in 2002 to get information on destinations or to check prices and schedules, growing about 400% over three years". This has directly led to "a remarkable double-digit growth" in the "online booking" of hotels (ibid.).

Besides, even though one may not initially have had any preference in mind, the sheer volume of information that is disseminated through various channels may indeed catch his/her attention or provoke his/her desire to consider the many alternatives for the vacation ahead. Therefore, applying the basic principle of demand here, we can say given that a person in this case has the financial resources to pay for related hospitality services, his/her willingness to address the demand is potentially increased, owing to the advancement of information technology.

Interactions between firms and consumers

In addition to the changes in the business practices and the behavior of consumers, before- and after-sales communication through the internet can indeed generate considerable feedback and attention for continuous and innovative changes in the industry. Firms are not only able to act in a timely manner or even immediately to the consumption decisions of their customers by using the internet, but might also be able to obtain valuable information about them. Based on the collected information, firms can then gain a better understanding of the desires and spending behavior of the consumers, and their changes over time. Accordingly, firms would have more practical and reliable grounds to support the invention of new concepts for hospitality products and services that would stimulate the spending preferences of consumers.

On the other hand, consumers can access a considerable volume of information through the internet on a 24/7 basis following widely accessible internet infrastructures and rapid advancements in information technology in many economies around the world at the end of the 20th century. As a result, they can easily compare the prices of the same (or very similar) hospitality products and services directly, as well as the various experiences or ratings shared by other consumers on websites. In other words, consumers could now access much more knowledge on the different hospitality products and services over time even though they may not have actually used the product or service themselves. In addition, their opinions or desire for hospitality consumptions as posted on websites or webpages may indeed show their latent demand on the one hand, and generate/stimulate the acknowledgment of others on the other hand. The latter could very well produce new demand forces in the market. To this end, it is obvious that mastering of the information technology is a guiding principle for any hospitality firm to interact effectively and efficiently with its customers in the 21st century. Besides, this constitutes as pragmatic grounds for stimulating business innovation toward industrial development.

Olsen and Connolly (2000: 31) refer to the opinions of two of the top "think tanks" in the industry at the end of the 20th century and reiterate the view that "technology will accelerate the consumer's ability to reshape the product and services that make up what has been known as the hospitality industry and that this will change the competitive landscape more than most realize". In addition, they also point out that the anticipated advancements in information technology mean that consumers may have "little product loyalty" (ibid.) in their consumption process. This may be due to the simple fact that after paying for a hospitality commodity (which is not a necessity) one or a few times, it is only human nature to look for something similar and/or better in quality and/or a better deal so that new consumption experiences could be derived (this is a simple rule in economics to raise one's utility from consumption).

Following nearly two decades of advancements in information technology which have been facilitated by the further development of internet infrastructures (e.g., use of optical fiber) around the world and other associated technologies (e.g., advancements in mobile technology), business operations in the hospitality industry have undoubtedly shown fundamental changes as expressed by Olsen and Connolly (2000). For example, the advent of internet platforms like Trivago and hotels.com have led to fundamental changes in the pricing and selling models in the hotel and airline industries, including how they communicate with their customers and the approach that they take for new products and services over time.

Cruise industry – Innovative entity of hospitality industry

The modern development and rapid expansion of the cruise industry in Europe and North America since the 1970s are coveted in the world hospitality industry. Despite the long history of cruise ships, which could be traced back to the 1880s, its contemporary development as an alternative option for vacationing was largely launched in the 1960s. Extensive efforts were made by the cruise industry to innovate itself as a new and attractive "destination" for vacationing by incorporating/applying different cutting-edge technologies. Throughout this process, it is observed that the cruise industry is not simply meeting demands in the market, but also stimulating and creating new demand, as well as improving its business efficiency over time.

A short history of the cruise industry

The general consensus in the literature is that ships constructed with large carrying capacity to provide long-distance transportation services for cargo and passengers between England and the United States in the late 1880s marked the formal establishment of the cruise industry (see, e.g., Grace, 2008). Indeed, it was the advancement and widespread application of a new technology, the large-scale steam engine at the beginning of the 19th century, that led to the construction of cruise ships.

In the 19th century and the first half of the 20th century (except during the two world wars), the development of the cruise industry mainly focused on improving the quality of service for those who had to spend a few days traveling across the Atlantic Ocean between Western Europe and North America. Generally speaking, passengers were largely immigrants (including the rich and the working class) who were traveling from Europe to North America between the 1870s and the 1900s, and then more leisure travelers emerged post-WWI and pre-WWII. In other words, the cruise industry was largely organized to provide unique on-board hospitality services like accommodations, food and beverages, and simple entertainment for passengers who had to spend a few days on the ocean to travel to their destination.

However, owing to technological advancements which contributed to the rapid growth of the airline industry, demand for cruise ships as a means of transportation was falling by the end of the 1950s. As Grace (2008) says, "Increasing air travel and the first non-stop flight to Europe in 1958, however, marked the ending of transatlantic business for ocean liners". Therefore, it can be concluded that as a transportation-based industry, the decline of the cruise industry was caused by the substitution effect of the rise of the airline industry.

Innovations, revival, and rapid growth of the cruise industry

Following its rapid decline, *a critical turning point of the cruise industry which contributed to its revival is found in its innovative rebranding as a "vacation destination"* instead of simply a means of providing long-distance transportation with a range of related hospitality services for passengers to travel from one place to an end place (the destination). As indicated in an early study by Bull (1996), for example, the new direction of development in the cruise industry since the 1960s is turning cruise ships into "destinations or floating resorts rather than primarily means of transport" (Bull, 1996: 28).

As a vacation destination by itself, cruising means that passengers could be (although not necessarily) boarding and departing at the same place (e.g., the same dock in the same city) after a few days of travel. Nevertheless, passengers are offered opportunities to disembark from the cruise ship to visit different places, and depending on the length of the cruise, this could be a couple of places to several excursions during their journey. One of the most common itineraries of cruise trips organized in North America today is visiting various cities and islands in Alaska and the glaciers. Tourists not only might enjoy close proximity to the glaciers on-board the cruise ship, but can also disembark to take part in short (e.g., half-day) local tours to see a glacier, or enjoy other activities like zip lining or dog sledding in the natural environment. After returning back to the cruise ship, other types of entertainment and hospitality services like movies, swimming in the pool, or fine dining are available for their enjoyment.

Commonly, passengers are given adequate flexibility to decide on what they would like to do and whether they would like to take part in any local excursions by referencing a list of pre-arranged activities during the trip after they embark and check into their cabin on the cruise ship. As depicted in Illustration 7.2, after boarding and then proceeding to enjoy the pool services, passengers may talk about the activities that they actually want to join (or things that they want to do) during the trip.

Illustration 7.2 Cruise ship as a destination itself and also a multi-destination trip

Source: Tochi Leung

Once on the cruise ship, passengers are offered a selection of pre-arranged entertainment and diverse on-board activities for their enjoyment. In addition to the variety of different cuisines that are provided in the buffet lounges and restaurants during the trip, passengers can also enjoy a wide range of on-board facilities like the swimming pool, gym, spa, table tennis, cinema, and shops, as well as other entertainment like concerts, performances, theme workshops, and casino gaming.

During the cruise, passengers are exposed to different scenery. For example, joining an Alaskan cruise means that passengers can enjoy close proximity to a glacier from the outer deck, or in the cafés on the side of the ship, or simply inside their own cabin on the ship. In other words, passengers are given many choices or the freedom to experience the trip and the attractions, such as the glacier; e.g., sharing the moment of excitement with others on the outer deck (see Illustration 7.3), or having a more private experience by viewing the glacier in a café on-board, or enjoying the moment with family in individual cabins.

In addition, passengers may also be given the option to disembark from their "floating hotel resort" through small "shuttle boats" (like the one shown in Illustration 7.4) to take part in short-haul tours on some of the coastal islands and cities during their voyage. When the passengers are on such tours in different places, they simply take their backpack without having to check in/check out of their cabin, and do not need to carry the souvenirs around that they had purchased on their previous stops. For those who are not interested in any of the stops (local tours) or change their minds and do not wish to disembark, they simply stay on the cruise ship and take part in other on-board activities.

Therefore, it is evident that the most unique and innovative feature (business model) of the modern cruise industry is its "all-inclusiveness" as a multi-destination vacation with one simple check-in and one check-out procedure.

Illustration 7.3 In close proximity to a glacier on an Alaskan cruise

Illustration 7.4 Local tours departing from the "floating hotel resort" on small "shuttle boats"

Besides, to reinforce the experiences of the passengers and continue to increase business efficiency, the most common and increasingly prevalent practices undertaken by the cruise industry are to use innovative applications and develop related technologies over time.

For example, Gambino (2012) explains that cruise ships are continuously incorporating "the latest gadgets into their services and updating their ships with cutting edge features". In practice, the "cruise lines have adopted innovations such as electric engines, hydrodynamically efficient hulls" (ibid.), which not only save on operation costs, but also provide more consistent and comfortable experiences to passengers on the entire trip. In addition, innovative applications such as facial recognition technology used on-board to provide digital photo albums and interactive menus on iPads in the restaurants, as well as installation of "5D theater" facilities by some of the cruise liners have undoubtedly reinforced the on-board experiences of tourists. These ensure a "wow factor" and positive feedback from the passengers, so that the likelihood of repeat visits and recommendation to others through word of mouth are increased. Indeed, these innovative applications of technology by the cruise industry have been widely accepted by tourists, and therefore the reason for the rapid growth of this industry since the beginning of the 21st century.

Implications of growth of the cruise industry

To a large extent, the experiences of the cruise industry based on its use of innovative technology might be unique to the nature of this industry.

Nevertheless, the valuable implications to the hospitality industry as a whole and the related industries should not be overlooked. This is especially the case in an increasingly dynamic and globalized economic environment, as the need to understand the importance of innovation in relation to technology and culture is relevant to any firm in the hospitality industry. Although the practices of the business firms in the cruise industry may not be the same owing to the industry culture, they share some common principles in their business operations. For example, the function of entrepreneurship in the creation and promotion of new services or new ways to deliver services is not only essential for ensuring the long-term growth and development of the hospitality industry, but would undoubtedly add to the variety of the services that could be enjoyed/experienced by consumers, and hence contribute to their material well-being from the related spending. Ultimately, the related dynamics might contribute to interactive growth with other industries and the macroeconomy.

Entrepreneurship and innovation should be culture-oriented

As mentioned earlier, the argument raised by Schumpeter (1983) that entrepreneurship is the primary force which leads to industrial and economic development has served as the guiding principle for studies related to the economics of technology and innovation thereafter. In addition to the literature that has been cited in this chapter, this simple yet essential principle is undoubtedly demonstrated by the successful reform and revitalization of the cruise industry, and its rapid growth in the 21st century. Nevertheless, a comparison of the practices of the cruise industry in North America, Europe, and Asia evidently show that the business features and components included on the routes in different continents/regions are not the same.

The differences are due to the differences in culture and demographics of the primary consumer groups, so that both on-board and related port services for different routes that are operating in North America and Europe may require different creative angles. These differences may be even more substantial as the industry is expanding to Asia. A statistical study by Chen et al. (2016), for example, found that the motivation of the passengers from Asia for taking a cruise is different from that of passengers from the West. To a large extent, they find that Asian cruise passengers are "escaping and bonding" rather than motivated by the desire to increase their self-esteem or learn, as is the case with Westerners (ibid.: 247). Also, if the intention to cruise is to escape from daily life and bond with their travel partner(s), the passengers are largely looking for "relaxation and stimulation" from their routine lives so that they are "most demanding" on "the 'basic', 'recreation' and 'ports' facilities" (ibid.). Thus, Chen et al. (2016: 250) conclude that the "primary focus of cruise companies in conquering the Asian markets should be on ship-based facilities".

Based on the findings in Chen et al. (2016), there is little doubt that at the practical level, innovation is an inevitable necessity for the continuous growth and development of the cruise industry for inventing and introducing newly combined types of commodities to satisfy cruise passengers for different routes around the world. In this process, *an understanding of the culture and recognition of the cultural differences in different markets are the first steps in the quest for pragmatic innovation by firms*. This reinforces the aforementioned argument that in the service-based hospitality industry, culture is the essential factor and even the catalyst for other related industries like the hotel, restaurant, and theme park industries in their business innovations. Owing to the trend of regionalization and globalization as discussed in Chapter 5, for example, it is evident that when a hospitality firm approaches other new markets, or wishes to attract customers from different places to visit their property and enjoy their services, recognition of the cultural differences of consumers in the different markets is the necessary first step to ensure the effectiveness of the related business innovations.

Same principles, different practices

In the above discussion, the general notions of entrepreneurship and innovation (which lead to technological progress), plus the particular considerations given to culture and cultural differences as the guiding principles for the advancement of the hospitality industry have been further elaborated. Nevertheless, the specific practices of these principles are not the same when they are applied by different industries in different markets in which the contextual settings are not alike. Indeed, these differences may be reflected from the different characteristics of the different cruise ships. To impart a unique impression to the tourists/passengers, cruise ships are clearly differentiating themselves by using different designs for the hulls, internal décor, layout and composition of on-board facilities and entertainment, on-board services provided by crew members and servers, route arrangements, as well as port and connection services at the various tourist spots.

Through continuous innovation, product differentiation (i.e., the components that are actually put together for a tourist trip are different) between different cruise ships or by a cruise ship over time will provide different tour experiences to the passengers. Thus, this is a necessary item for the different cruise lines to position their particular business objectives in various market segments. In addition, cruise lines may find it helpful to offer different pricing strategies (e.g., bundled pricing and price differentiation as discussed in Chapter 4) to improve their business performance over time. To this end, it may be worthwhile to emphasize that these practices of the cruise industry could inspire (but of course not be duplicated by) other land-based firms in the hospitality industry.

For example, a common trend observed in the hotel industry is that individual hotels (not just the large hotel resorts or multi-national hotel chains) are increasingly differentiating themselves through continuous innovation of their hospitality products and services. In the process, distinct features offered in their properties (e.g., simple but unique animation in the lobby and hotel rooms through cost-efficient application of technology), which target a certain market segment (i.e., consumer group) and the returning customers may require some innovative thinking. This is also applicable to other hospitality firms.

For business purposes, however, innovations should be implemented with particular attention to the market environment. For the different industries and firms in different markets that are operating in different time intervals, the contextual settings of a particular market, availability and capacity of technology, and technological changes may determine the feasibility of a new idea, and hence its ultimate success. In other words, the practices of each industry could be quite different and a one-size-fits-all approach would not be feasible, even though they might be guided by the same principles.

Expansion of industry chain

It is evident that a comprehensive industry chain has been established due to the innovative approaches in the development and operation of the cruise industry, and this chain will continue to grow with respect to the expansion of the cruise industry over time. For example, all kinds of on-board consumable fixtures, appliances, and goods, as well as the provision of a mass variety of recipes to serve thousands of passengers (without taking into consideration the hundreds or possibly thousands of crew and staff members on the ship) for a trip could hardly be realized without credible and stable provision of supplies from a wide range of suppliers. More importantly, if there are any changes (new ideas) that are introduced to repackage the products or improve the services in one or more areas, timeliness and reliability of the upstream suppliers in modifying their outputs are important to successfully carry out the related changes.

On the other hand, to reduce the average fixed cost, and therefore the average total cost in providing cruise services to tourists/passengers, optimizing the occupancy rate for every trip is unarguably the most important objective that ensures the profitability of a cruise ship. Thus, in addition to the sales and marketing departments of affiliated cruise lines, cooperation of the cruise liner with different land-based travel agents and online travel platforms has been on the increase. Indeed, a widening network over time will also expand the industry chain of the cruise industry.

According to a report released by CLIA Europe (2018) on the economic contributions of the cruise industry to the European economies in 2014, the total amount of "direct expenditures" provided by this industry in Europe was €16.6 billion (ibid.: 4), of which €4.55 billion was spent on the

> construction of new cruise ships … €6.97 billion in spending by cruise lines with European businesses for goods and services in support of their cruise operations … €3.64 billion in cruise passenger and crew spending … . €1.48 billion in wages and salaries plus benefits.
>
> (ibid.)

The distribution of these expenditures among the different related industries clearly show that the continuous growth and development of the cruise industry rely on the inputs from other industries. In turn, expenditures on the inputs from those industries contribute to their business performances, and hence the macroeconomic growth of the related economies.

Given the need of the cruise industry to provide a large selection and variety of hospitality services within a given amount of space (i.e., within the limited space of the cruise ship) and add to the experiences of the cruise tourists at the same time, the business practices of land-based hotels, restaurants, and theme parks may not exactly be the same in comparison to the cruising business. Nevertheless, like the cruise industry, not one of these industries is able to produce all of the components needed for their business operations. This implies that if innovation is to take precedence in the hospitality industry, the related industry chain has to expand over time. That is, maintaining close relationships and connections with the supporting industries is an indispensable part of realizing innovations and new developments in the hospitality industry.

Did you know? ...

Innovation in tourism is important not only in general for inventing new tourism products (like destinations, related facilities, and consumable goods), but more importantly, creating new and fulfilling experiences for tourists throughout their trip. As many tourism markets worldwide are probably now maturing after decades of development and rapid growth since the 1950s, innovation is considered to be a common means for the industry to reinvent itself and rebuild some of its attractions, and hence stimulate repeat visits and cultivate new demand. Nevertheless, putting innovation into practice may require the industry to have an in-depth understanding of the advantages of innovation in tourism and the areas that should receive attention and focus.

Box 7.1 Essence and practice of innovation in tourism

Weiermair (2004) deliberates on the nature of innovation per Schumpeter in the context of the tourism industry in his study, and recommends that the different crises (including social, political, and environmental crises) should be a top item of the agenda of the tourism industry in the 21st century (ibid.: 54). He states that innovation is still an important topic that needs to be comprehensively addressed by the industry owing to the rapid advancements in technology, especially information technology in the world markets since the 1990s.

While affirming the importance of innovation for the continuous growth of tourism, Weiermair (2004: 58) stresses that it is "important not to imitate innovative effects made elsewhere, but to build on a company's or destination's own strength and core competencies". Instead, proactive applications of "new information and communication systems" (ibid.) to gain insights into a particular market are necessary to ensure that the new idea(s) would actually work during the quest to innovate.

By referring to the business characteristics and practices of tourism, Weiermair (2004) further argues that innovation in this industry should be emphasized in the areas of first "product innovation" and then "process innovation" (ibid.: 63). That is, to a tourist, s/he is paying for a package of tourist services and products throughout her/his trip which is composed of a bundle of fixtures, physical goods, and intangible services. Moreover, all of these components contribute to the experiences of the tourist that are derived from the consumption (payment) of the package. Thus, innovation of tourism products like offering accommodation facilities of a higher quality, food and beverages with more variety, and touring activities of different combinations will motivate some of the tourists to repeat their trip, and at the same time attract new visitors.

While the interest of tourists to choose a trip could be stimulated through innovative communication channels and measures, on the other hand, tourism is a process that starts by searching for tour information to making lump sum payments in advance for the perceived leisure, and then the actual participating in trips away from home, and finally returning home. Throughout this process, the perception of the visitor prior to the trip could indeed be reinforced through innovations adopted in tourism products and services, and the consideration of the entire trip such as the overall service quality through effective applications of related technologies.

Discussion questions:

1   With reference to the principles that are discussed in this chapter, elaborate on the reason(s) why it is "important not to imitate innovative effects made elsewhere" for effective innovation in tourism.
2   Discuss how the availability of technology today is helpful for facilitating "product innovation" in tourism.
3   Discuss how the availability of technology today is helpful for facilitating "process innovation" in tourism.

Conclusions and remarks

Technology and innovation are relatively less discussed in comparison with conventional topics like demand, supply, price, money, and banking in economics. Nevertheless, in line with the increasing significance of technological progress in industrial development, related studies have been increasing since the 1950s. In addition to considering the role of technology as part of the capital goods input for production and its routine functions which allow firms to increase their efficiency and productivity, the importance of entrepreneurship in the process of technological invention has been emphasized by a number of economists today and serves as a guiding principle in related studies. Indeed, entrepreneurship in inventing and investing in new ideas and new combinations of existing resources generates the underlying dynamics for technological progress and its contributions to industrial development, which pinpoint the economic notions of innovation.

In the development of the hospitality industry, it is evident that while technological progress provides the necessary instruments for firms to innovate their business, innovations in turn generate new forces which demonstrate that there is the need for continuous advancements and inventions in the related technologies. Indeed, progress and applications of information technology have largely promoted business innovations and hence the development of the hospitality industry since the 1990s. On the other hand, advancements in information technology and popularization of the internet have also clearly modified the behavior of consumers which have generated significant interactive forces that have reshaped the practices of the hospitality industry (including hotels, restaurants, and theme parks) over time.

As a conspicuous case for innovativeness in development and use of cutting-edge technology worldwide, the cruise industry and its practices further underline the significance of entrepreneurship in technological advancement and industrial development. This is an important factor in ensuring the continuous growth of the hospitality industry in the dynamic and globalized business environment today. As compared to the innovations in the secondary industry and other traditional service industries like banking and finance, experiences derived from the practices of the cruise industry highlight the importance of understanding culture and cultural differences in the different markets. Without such knowledge and proactive thinking in the first place, innovation by itself may not be sufficient to ensure that a new hospitality commodity is created for the market, one that would be widely accepted by the targeted consumers, and hence its ultimate success.

In this era, the development of technology and information technology continues to accelerate, so that every firm and each consumer are surrounded by a vast volume of information. To the hospitality industry, carrying out innovations effectively and efficiently is definitely a challenge for the leadership of the related firms, but might also instigate new business opportunities and interactive dynamic processes that contribute to their growth.

References and further reading

Ayres, C.E., 1953. The role of technology in economic theory. *The American Economic Review*, 43 (2), 279–287.

Ayres, C.E., 1974. *Toward a Reasonable Society: The Values of Industrial Civilization*. University of Texas Press, Austin, TX, USA.

Bull, A.O., 1996. The economics of cruising: An application to the short ocean cruise market. *Journal of Tourism Studies*, 7 (2), 28–35.

Carlsson, B., Taymaz, E., Tryggestad, K., 1993. Factory automation and economic performance: A micro-to-macro analysis. Paper presented at The Wallenberg Symposium on Economics of Technology, Marstrand, Sweden, August 18–22, 1991. Available www.ifn.se/wfiles/wp/wp384.pdf

Chen, J.M., Neuts, B., Nijkamp, P., Liu, J., 2016. Demand determinants of cruise tourists in competitive markets: motivation, preference and intention. *Tourism Economics*, 22 (2), 227–253.

CLIA Europe, 2018. Contribution of cruise tourism to the economies of Europe 2017. Cruise Line International Association, Europe. Available https://es.cruiseexperts.org/media/2971/2017-europe-economic-impact-report.pdf

Gambino, A., 2012. Technology innovation in the cruise industry. Business 2 Community. Available www.business2community.com/travel-leisure/technology-innovation-in-the-cruise-industry-0265040

Grace, M.L., 2008. A brief history of the cruise ship industry. Available www.cruiselinehistory.com/a-brief-history-of-the-cruise-ship-industry/

Granstrand, O. (ed.), 1994. *Economics of Technology*. Emerald Group Publishing Ltd., Bingley, UK.

Hjalager, A.M., 2010. A review of innovation research in tourism. *Tourism Management*, 31 (2010), 1–12.

Ingram, P., 1998. Changing the rules: Interests, organizations, and institutional change in the U.S. hospitality industry. In: M.C. Brinton, V. Nee (eds), *The New Institutionalism in Sociology*. Russell Sage Foundation, New York, USA, pp. 258–276.

Ivanov, S.H., Webster, C., Berezina. K., 2017. Adoption of robots and service automation by tourism and hospitality companies. *Revista Turismo & Desenvolvimento*, 27/28, 1501–1517.

Kravis, I.B., Heston, A.W., Summers, R., 1984. The share of services in economic growth. In: F.G. Adams, B.G. Hickman (eds), *Global Econometrics: Essays in Honor of Lawerence R. Klein*. MIT Press, Cambridge, MA, USA, pp. 188–218.

Marshall, A., 1997. *Principle of Economics*. Prometheus Books, New York, USA.

Olsen, M.D., Connolly, D.J., 2000. Experience-based travel: How technology is changing the hospitality industry. *Cornell Hotel and Restaurant Administration Quarterly*, 41 (1), 30–40.

Perucic, D., 2007. The impact of globalization on supply and demand in the cruise industry. *Tourism and Hospitality Management*, 13 (3), 665–680.

Rodgers, S., 2008. Technological innovation supporting different food production philosophies in the food service sectors. *International Journal of Contemporary Hospitality*, 20 (1), 19–34.

Schmookler, J., Brownlee, O., 1962. Determinants of inventive activity. *The American Economic Review*, 52 (2), 165–176.

Schumpeter, J.A., 1983. *The Theory of Economic Development: An Inquiry into Profits, Capital, Credit, Interest, and the Business Cycle*. Transaction Publishers, New Brunswick, NJ, USA.

Sener, S., Hacioglu, V., Akdemir, A., 2017. Invention and innovation in economic change. *Journal of Economics, Finance and Accounting*, 4 (2), 203–208.

Shapiro, N., 1986. Innovation, new industries and new firms. *Eastern Economic Journal*, 12 (1), 27–43.

Smith, A., 1998. *An Inquiry into the Characteristics and Causes of the Wealth of Nations* (A Select Edition). Oxford University Press, Oxford, UK.

Swann, G.M.P., 2009. *The Economics of Innovation: An Introduction*. Edward Elgar, Cheltenham, Gloucestershire, UK.

Thirtle, C.G., Ruttan, V.W., 1986. The role of demand and supply in the generation and diffusion of technical change. Economic Development Center (Bulletin Number 86–5, September 1986), University of Minnesota, Minneapolis, MN, USA. Available https://ageconsearch.umn.edu/bitstream/7522/1/edc86-05.pdf (Reprinted in: Thirtle, C.G., Ruttan, V.W., 2001. *The Role of Demand and Supply in the Generation and Diffusion of Technical Change*. Routledge, New York, USA.)

Veblen, T., 1912. *The Theory of the Leisure Class: An Economic Study of Institutions*. Mentor Books, New York, USA.

Weiermair, K., 2004. Product improvement or innovation: what is the key to success in tourism? In: OECD (ed.), *Innovation and Growth in Tourism*. OECD Publishing, Paris, France, pp. 53–69.

Williams, A.M., Shaw, G., 2011. Internationalization and innovation in tourism. *Annals of Tourism Research*, 38 (1), 27–51.

Zhou, Z., 2004. *E-Commerce and Information Technology in Hospitality and Tourism*. Delmar Learning, Clifton Park, NY, USA.

8 Sustainable development

Objectives and learning outcomes

In any industry, development is commonly expressed in terms of business capacity such as the different scales of expansion in the related properties, fixtures, and employment, and of course, the dynamics from its innovations over time. The growth of an industry is commonly measured in monetary terms such as changes in the monetary value of its outputs throughout different periods of time. On the other hand, the dynamic interactions between the growth and development of an industry with the environment and ecosystem of a society in which it is situated need to be explored for sustainable development, for instance, in the hospitality industry. The rationale for a closer look is because after decades of rapid growth and development in the hospitality industry and the negative impacts on the environment that have subsequently snowballed, sustainable development has become an increasing topic of concern of the various communities involved. As a major and rapidly growing area of concern and interest in the world economies, sustainable development is an inevitable issue that requires the attention and proactivity of the leaders of related firms.

In this chapter, the concept of sustainable development in general and its relevance to the hospitality industry in particular are elucidated. Some of the particular concerns of various societies are also identified. The purpose of doing so is to familiarize students with knowledge related to sustainable development and hence allow them to gain an awareness of the importance of this topic to the operations and business decisions geared toward increasing the growth and development of the hospitality industry. Thus, the association between growth and development in the hospitality industry and their impacts on the natural environment will be identified and elaborated.

In addition, the principles of related public policies as implemented by most governments around the world to ensure that the sustainable development of their economies as a whole are discussed. The implications of these policies on the practices and sustainable development of the hospitality industry are further elaborated so that students would gain a comprehensive view of the related issues. Moreover, common efforts that are being carried out by the industry to ensure its sustainable development and its contribution to the world economy as a whole are provided. Finally, the prospects and challenges faced by the hospitality industry in its sustainable development endeavors are explored.

After reading this chapter, students will be able to:

- see the inter-dependence of economic growth and development and the differences between them;
- understand the notion of sustainable development;
- understand the social and economic concerns around sustainable development;
- recognize the impacts (externalities) produced from the growth and development of the hospitality industry on economic societies;
- understand the economic principles behind public policies and general regulations enforced to safeguard sustainable development;
- understand the possible impacts of related public policies on the practices of the hospitality industry;
- recognize the common efforts made by the hospitality industry to sustain its own industrial development; and
- recognize the challenges that the hospitality industry faces in its sustainable development endeavors.

From economic growth and development to sustainable development

To people in various parts of the world today, the terms "climate change", "global warming", "greenhouse effect", "deforestation", and "soil erosion" are very familiar. Indeed, all of these environmental issues have not been simply part of natural circumstances, but the consequences of the economic growth and development of the world economies. On the one hand, economic growth and development improve the material life and economic well-being of individuals in any society, but the related activities might indeed exhaust a range of different kinds of resources (both renewable and non-renewable) and cause ongoing deterioration of the environment on the other hand. Although the concept of development in economics is in principle commonly referred to as improvements in the quality of outputs or increases in capacity for production, the adverse effects of economic development to the environment might not have been taken into full consideration by mainstream economists to discredit the related benefits of development. In fact, after a decades- or even century-long expansion of the world economies, the uncertainties of whether economic growth and development could be sustained without further aggravating nature and the ecological environment, and hence adding to social conflict (i.e., issues around the concerns of sustainable development) are clearly on the rise.

Addressing and reducing the uncertainties around sustainable development in the real world, (either at the macroeconomic or industrial level) are intricate topics. Nevertheless, the first step in comprehending the related issues is to gain a clear understanding of the differences among economic growth and development and sustainable development, as well as their interrelationships in practice. An awareness of the matrix of sustainable development activities is particularly important to those who are interested in entering and working in the hospitality industry in this era.

Revisiting concepts of economic growth and development

As shown through Equations (1.4) and (1.5) in Chapter 1, economic growth shows the changes in the monetary value of the outputs of an economy (e.g., in terms of gross domestic product or national income) from one period to another (e.g., monthly, quarterly, or annual growth respectively). This is also applicable to the measurement of the growth of an industry or a firm. Under this generally accepted principle, there is always a direct measurement to express whether an economic entity is growing (i.e., increase in physical quantity/scale) or otherwise.

On the other hand, development is characterized by changes in quality of life over time. For example, it is expected that the standard of living and quality of life of a community would improve through economic development. Owing that economic development is qualitatively measured, it is rather an abstract concept which cannot be necessarily determined by simply using a universally accepted formula or quantitative approach. Although some international organizations have attempted to formulate some objective measurements to reflect the development of a society over time, these are largely limited to a set of quantitatively measurable criteria.

For example, the United Nations Development Programme releases the Human Development Index (HDI) annually, which provides statistics of various countries to show the changes/improvement in the social and economic welfares of people living in an economic society over time (e.g., United Nations Development Programme, 2016: Tables 1 and 2, 198–205). To construct this index, three sets of measurable variables are employed. They are:

> Life expectancy at birth [which] reflects the ability to lead a long and healthy life. Mean years of schooling and expected years of schooling [which] reflect the ability to acquire knowledge. And gross national income per capita [which] reflects the ability to achieve a decent standard of living.

> (ibid.: 3)

Generally speaking, the HDI can provide an objective measurement of economic development because when an economy is developing, the quality of life of its people will improve, so that on average they might live longer and enjoy more social and economic outputs, including education. When people receive more education (or become better educated), their productivity will also increase, which will lead to an increase in the national income. Indeed, an increase in the HDI also implies that people in an economy are able to enjoy more hospitality services, which parallels the related discussions provided in Chapter 2. Nevertheless, this index might not be all inclusive, such as the neglect of the quality of the environment which would actually affect the real and potential changes in quality of life of people or the world from one generation to another.

Despite the abstractness associated with economic development, it is not difficult to see its interrelationship with economic growth. Generally speaking, while growth generates surplus or profit (e.g., financial resources) for related investments in new properties and innovative ideas so that the process of economic development can be carried out smoothly, development then expands capacity and improves efficiency, as well as the composition and quality of economic development in the following periods.

Essence of sustainable development

In economics, sustainable development is a relatively immature area which has been largely promoted due to the increasing public concerns of the adverse effects from economic growth and development to the environment, and the impacts of environmental changes to economic societies that occur cyclically. Since the 1970s, economists who have explored topics related to sustainable development mainly focus on two areas. The first area of interest emphasizes the economic impacts of related public policies that attempt to protect the natural environment from economic growth and development, which is commonly referred to as environmental economics studies. For example, topics like the impacts from pollution reduction schemes enacted by a government on the business costs and growth of the hotel industry have been investigated by environmental economics researchers.

The second area of interest involves the necessary measures that need to be taken to preserve the natural environment (or natural capital) from the practices of economic growth and development, which is commonly referred to as ecological economics. Actually, academic journals like the *Journal of Environmental Economics and Management* (since 1974) and *Ecological Economics* (since 1989) represent the formal recognition given to related studies in economics. For example, the economic significance of applying new or renewable production resources or energy by the hotel industry are explored and detailed to ensure a balance in the growth and development of today and the future.

Concerns and fundamentals of sustainable development

In ecological economics, sustainable development has been commonly considered to be addressed by a comprehensive report called *Our Common Future*, published by the World Commission on Environment and Development (WCED) in 1987. In this report, it is clearly argued that "Previously our main concerns centred on the effects of development on the environment. Today, we need to *be equally concerned about the ways in which environment degradation can dampen or reverse economic development*" (WCED, 1987: 35; my emphasis). Many researchers in this field have made reference to the definition of sustainable development in *Our Common Future* as the *"ability to make development sustainable – to ensure that it meets the needs of the present without compromising the ability of future generations to meet their own needs"* (ibid.: 8, cited in Kates et al., 2005: 2; my emphasis).

Nevertheless, as a topic of study that involves a wide range of considerations for environmental issues and their interrelationships with economic growth and development, some discussions or stances could be normative and abstract. Thus, early studies in sustainable development were not spared from criticism. For example, Lélé (1991) has been critical that studies on

> sustainable development (SD) ... the mainstream of SD thinking contains significant weaknesses. These include an incomplete perception of the problems of poverty and environmental degradation, and confusion about the role of economic growth and about the concepts of sustainability and participation.
>
> (Lélé, 1991: 607)

Suggested principles for sustainable development

Despite controversy around related studies, sustainable development is clearly different from conventional economic growth and development. For example, Daly (1990) argues that sustainable development is different from the simple measurement of economic growth and involves more issues than traditional discussions in development. In general, *sustainable development is subjected to two principles*; one is that the *"harvest rates should equal regeneration rates"*, and second, *"waste emission rates should equal the natural assimilative capacities of the ecosystem into which the wastes are emitted"* (Daly, 1990: 2; my emphases). In other words, when outputs from an economy are expanded after extracting more natural resources which are renewable, such as plants and living creatures, for related production, the rate in which these resources are depleted should equal the rate that they could be regenerated by nature. In addition, the waste generated from production and consumption that is drained, emitted, or dumped into the natural environment should not exceed the capacity and ability of the environment to absorb such waste. As for the consumption of non-renewable resources, it is suggested that their depletion "must be paired with a compensating investment in a renewable substitute (e.g., oil extraction paired with tree planting for wood alcohol)" (ibid.: 4). Otherwise, sustainable development cannot be ensured.

Sustainable development in contrast to economic growth and development

Based on the aforementioned rationale, it is evident that sustainable development would not emphasize growth. Besides, slow or negative growth under certain circumstances (e.g., a period of industrial restructuring or transition toward better environmental responsibility instead of economic recession) might not necessarily be considered as undesirable, but instead favorable for sustainable development.

On the other hand, although both sustainable development and economic development consider the qualitative aspects of economic activities, their focus is evidently not the same. In principle, sustainable development largely underlines the interactions between economic activities in any period of time and the external environment so that economic development can be ensured (sustained) over time. To this extent, if economic development refers to the activities which lead to the expansion of the production capacity of an economy and the improvement of the quality of life of its community in the time-span of one generation, then sustainable development represents the efforts to ensure that the related activities would not exhaust resources for the use of future generations. In short, if economic development is a long-term concept, then sustainable development is a multi-generational concept.

Negative externalities from progress of hospitality industry

In economics, externalities are the positive or negative influences from market transactions between a producer and a consumer in a third party (which could be another person, firm, or physical or social environment). For example, when supplying dining services to customers, a restaurant dumps its waste water directly into a river without filtering the waste solids to maintain a low cost of operation. In doing so, however, they harm the environment; for instance, fish may die, so that the related output is reduced quantity of fish. This means that an external cost (i.e., a negative externality) is imposed by the restaurant to the environment from their transactions with customers (also other consumers of fish).

The rapid growth and development of the hospitality industry that have been detailed in the previous chapters have shown that this is a productive industry in the world economies. Indeed, increases in the spending of the general public (or the mass working group as indicated in Chapter 2) and innovations by the related industries in hospitality commodities as shown in Chapter 7, have clearly pointed to industrial growth and development. Yet, practices of the hospitality industry may pose challenges to the sustainable development of an economy as a whole and itself at the same time. This is largely brought about by negative externalities like different kinds of pollution that the industry has generated over time. Besides, rapid expansion of the related production and consumption activities may also accelerate the deple-tion of non-replenishable resources on Earth. In turn, adverse feedback effects from the economic societies might curb further growth of the industry today and in the foreseeable future, as compared to the situation a few decades ago.

Thus, it is important that the leaders of any hospitality firm do not simply master the factors that contribute to the growth of this industry and related principles at the business level (e.g., the principles as presented in Chapters 3 and 4), but also those that must be considered for the sustainable develop-ment of this industry. To a large extent, these factors at the social, political, and environmental levels may affect the practices of related firms in terms of their private cost of production, and growth prospects in different markets and hence their business performance. The significance of these impacts on the hospitality industry have been (and will continue to be) the topic of focus of both academics and the related industries in the coming years.

Industrial efforts and dilemmas

It is commonly observed that, since the end of the 20th century, many large and/or multi-national hospitality firms have continuously put forth various efforts to remedy the possible adverse effects produced from their business (e.g., related pragmatics implemented by their corporate social responsibil-ity departments). For example, the *2017 Marriott Sustainability and Social Impact Report* expressed that their goal is "reducing our energy consumption and greenhouse gas (GHG) emissions to reflect our values, increase opera-tional efficiency and do our part to mitigate climate change risks" (Marriott International, 2017: 27). Indeed, introduction of similar measures to ensure business sustainability has been a common trend in various hospitality firms to gain the support of local communities and governments for their business ventures.

Nevertheless, rapid expansion at the scale and scope of existing firms and entry of new firms into the related industries (e.g., tourism and hotel resorts) over time may indeed increase the depth and breadth of the damages to the environment, as well as the rate of natural capital depletion at the same time. As illustrated in the hypothetical example in Figure 8.1, when the business volume of the hospitality industry is n, a certain amount of negative external-ity (say, E_n) is produced in the environment.

Suppose that a government imposes regulations to reduce the current amount of negative externality to remedy the related adverse effects that are generated directly and indirectly from the supplying of hospitality services domestically; say, by r percent within a given period of time. For example, this may include the requirements for firms to install a sewage treatment system and/or imposition of sewage charges. Or, the industry may introduce related programs on their own will, say, to reduce the consumption of energy like the Marriott or the use of disposable utensils. Thus, the negative externality may be potentially reduced to, say, $E_n(1-r)$ in the next period of time (as depicted

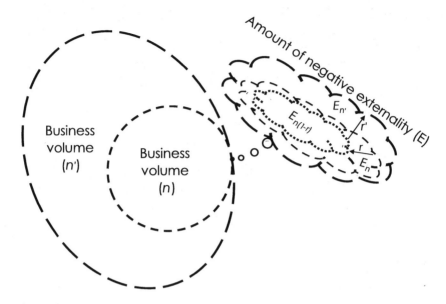

Figure 8.1 Impacts from industry expansion on aggregate amount of negative externalities

in Figure 8.1). However, the scale of the industry could indeed expand rapidly over time (say, from n to n' as shown in Figure 8.1). Consequently, the aggregate amount of negative externalities in the succeeding period is in fact larger than that in the past (i.e., $E_{n'} > E_n$ as the rate of reduction, r is outweighed by the rate of increases in negative externalities, r' caused by the rapid expansion of the business scale and scope of the industry as a whole).

Besides, the aggregate amount of negative externalities could indeed be increased much more rapidly even though the production of the same unit of service by the hospitality industry (e.g., the operation of a hotel room or fine dining) today may generate a smaller amount of negative externality as compared to a decade ago owing to technological advancement. For example, as more hotel resorts are being constructed, more variety in facilities and better quality in service and the hospitality environment are provided to customers. Yet more damage (e.g., air, noise, and light pollution, as well as deforestation owing to the development of the hospitality industry in urban areas) is evidently imposed onto the natural and ecological environment (see Illustration 8.1). To provide a quality indoor environment during the winter season so that visitors can enjoy themselves through various indoor activities like an exercise gym, the industry as a whole with a large and expanding number of hotel resorts is actually consuming a significant volume of energy that is generated by burning fossil fuels. Consequently, pollution that is emitted into

Illustration 8.1 Energy consumption by hospitality industry and air pollution caused by fossil-fuel-generated energy

Source: Tochi Leung

the air is increasing over time, which has aggravated the damage to the ozone layer of our planet.

Wide range of impacts

Recently, various studies have provided evidence to show that modern development in the hospitality industry has indeed accelerated the negative externalities to the environment and the ecosystem. Despite that some firms are putting forth more efforts to reduce the negative impacts from doing business, these efforts are outweighed by the aggregated impacts of the industry as a whole. For example, Jones et al. (2016: 37) point out that to the hospitality industry in practice, "the concept of sustainability provides a teasing paradox", because

> on the one hand, the industry increasingly looks to deploy sustainability within both its marketing messages and the customer experience, while, on the other hand, the headline accent is often on conspicuous consumption, which in many ways, is the antithesis of sustainability.
>
> (Jones et al., 2016: 37)

In the highly competitive local and global markets, enhancing service quality by upgrading and expanding facilities is inevitable and justified from the perspective of the firm. Nevertheless, conflicts between private and social interests in terms of economic activities are clearly evident.

In a statistical analysis on the impacts of the practices of the hotel industry to the environment, Chen and Hsieh (2011: 9) find that "the higher the star rating, the more resources a hotel consumes and the greater are its ecological footprint and environmental impacts". In addition, they find that "food, energy, construction land, textile, and waste" (ibid.) constitute the five major "consumption categories" (ibid.) from the hotel industry, which lead to negative impacts on the environment.

Also, despite that the modern development of the cruise industry has been highly motivated by innovative applications of cutting-edge technologies (as discussed in Chapter 7), the rapid growth in the demand for cruise tours has not only led to public concerns about the deterioration of the coastal and marine environments, but also the related ecosystem. A study by Polat (2015: 443) emphasizes that "Cruise ships are mostly seen as waste producer of the world seas. Big and luxurious ships are real danger for environment protection." Besides, the large increase in number of Arctic cruise tours that include wildlife tourism as one of the itinerary items has resulted in negative impacts to the life of polar bears, and even worse, some of them are reportedly killed after they attacked cruise tourists and/or the tour guides. However, some critics might ask the fundamental question about why polar bears who are living at the North Pole would attack people!

Public policies and guidelines for sustainable development

In consideration of the concerns of various communities around the negative externalities that are being (and will continue to be) produced from the practices of the hospitality industry to the environment and the ecosystem, public policies and guidelines imposed by governments around the world have been on the increase and widening in scope to control the related unfavorable impacts. In principle, the policies and guidelines commonly fall into four main areas: 1) indirect taxation; 2) facility requirements; 3) limitations on waste emissions; and 4) promotion of social awareness. While the policy instruments under the different areas are not the same, they all aim to reduce the over-production and/or over-consumption activities in the markets by emphasizing the social rather than private costs of transactions in the prices of related commodities.

As illustrated in Figure 3.3 in Chapter 3, the interactions between demand and supply in the market determine the quantity of an economic commodity that is produced by firms and purchased by consumers under a unique price that is acceptable to both parties. In the related discussions, the upward-sloping supply curve shows increasing private cost (or marginal private cost:

MPC) of production when more of a commodity is produced. Nevertheless, if negative externalities are involved in the production process, social cost is actually produced which is neglected by both firms and consumers. In other words, the actual cost of producing a commodity to society (i.e., social cost) as a whole is higher than the private cost of the related firms. Thus, the quantity that is produced and consumed in the market is indeed larger than the socially desired amount of production and consumption.

For example, when providing (or expanding) hotel resort services around the world, the water quality of the ocean may be affected to different degrees owing to the sewage that is dumped from the related properties. Thus, seafood output shrinks, and seafood lovers bear a higher price for consumption of seafood. Besides, as depicted in Illustration 8.1, increased consumption of energy of hotel resorts worldwide could add to the amount of carbon emitted into the environment indirectly, and is partly responsible for the worsening climate changes. In other words, the hospitality services provided by the world hotel resorts actually use more resources than disclosed on their company reports. If social cost is also included, the price of the related services will be higher and the transactions in the markets reduced for the purpose of achieving sustainable development.

Indirect taxation

To ensure sustainable development, a government might impose taxes on the amount of negative impacts generated from the production process. Since these taxes are imposed on negative impacts such as the volume of pollution or sewage, and paid by the firms and/or consumers, it is similar to the expenditure taxes shown in Figure 4.2 in Chapter 4. After imposing the taxes, the business cost of firms and price to consumers will inevitably increase. Thus, while some of the negative impacts can be mitigated by the government on a collective basis through taxes, the relative amount of transactions in the market could also be reduced due to increases in the market price.

Figure 8.2 shows that if only private costs are included in production decisions and based on the demand for a commodity (D), p_m is the equilibrium price when the market is in equilibrium (e_m). At this price, firms will produce q_m and consumers will spend on this quantity (i.e., the equilibrium quantity). Nevertheless, if a social cost like pollution is produced from the related market activities and affects other third parties in society, the marginal social cost (MSC) of producing q_m (and hence the price charged) should be represented by p_{ms}, which is higher than p_m. In other words, the supply curve to society (i.e., S_{MSC}) as a whole is to the left (or on the top) of the market supply curve (i.e., S_{MPC}). Thus, if the social cost of producing a commodity is taken into consideration, the equilibrium quantity to be produced is q_s instead of q_m, while a higher price (i.e., p_s) is charged to cover the social cost.

To reduce the social impacts from private business activities, indirect taxation in various forms is commonly estimated based on the social costs and

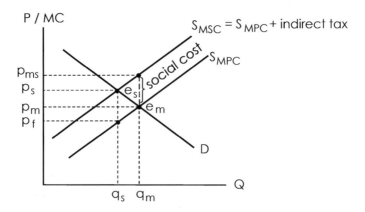

Figure 8.2 Social cost versus private cost of supplying economic commodity

imposed by a government to the related firms. For example, a waste recycling fee and sewage charge might be levied on hotel resorts and restaurants based on their business volume. In principle, the amount of indirect taxes received by the government is equivalent to the area of $[q_s \times (p_s - p_f)]$ as shown in Figure 8.2.

In practice, it could be difficult to precisely measure the social cost of industrial production to the environment, and hence actually identify the difference between p_{ms} and p_m (or modify the market price exactly from p_m to p_s to reflect the preference of society) as shown in Figure 8.2. Nevertheless, a reasonable formulation of the indirect taxes would undoubtedly allow a government to obtain the required resources from the industries based on the negative social impacts on the environment.

Facility requirements

Taking into consideration technological progress, many governments are now requiring firms to enhance their business operations with environmentally friendly facilities. For example, the Ministry of Tourism of the Indian Government issued a requirement in 2014 for hotels to install eco-friendly facilities like a sewage treatment system and equipment to control air, water, and light pollution (Ministry of Tourism Government of India, 2015: 4). Indeed, similar requirements are also commonly found in other countries for their hotel industries (especially in the small tourism destinations located on island states like Sri Lanka and the Caribbean Sea countries).

In addition, governments may also take the lead to enhance the related infrastructures in their country, which then encourages the private sectors to follow suit and revamp their own facilities. For example, "The EU is in the process of updating its energy policy framework in a way that will facilitate the clean energy transition and make it fit for the 21st century" (European Commission, 2018). Under the related proposals, firms might have to upgrade their facilities to match the work done by the government in their country.

Limitations on waste emissions

Parallel to indirect taxation and facility requirements, related policies could also set limitations on the absolute volume of emitted waste by individual firms based on the scale and scope of their business. This could include putting into place a maximum volume of waste water, plastic, and carbon that may be discharged by a firm or an industry during a certain period of time (e.g., on a monthly or an annual basis). In principle, if the waste emission is within a pre-determined volume, a fixed charge (e.g., a fixed amount or amount of indirect tax) could be applied. If a firm emits more waste than its allowable limit, they will pay a higher fee for producing the additional waste, or be subject to a temporary closure.

Among the various forms of waste emissions, the international society prioritizes carbon emissions because continuous and large volumes of carbon emissions from the expansion of economic activities have been identified as the primary source responsible for global warming and related natural disasters like mega storms and wildfires. Thus, governments around the world have entered into agreements (e.g., the Paris Agreement as signed by 174 states and the European Union in 2016) to control carbon emissions in their own countries. For implementation purposes, the involved governments agree on the maximum volume of carbon that can be emitted in a particular year. Based on the cap as agreed, each government will then assign individual quotas to the various industries within its own country. In any given period of time, if a firm (or an industry) maximizes its emission quota, the firm or industry could very likely face the necessity to pay another industry to use its unused quota. Otherwise, they may be forced to suspend production to avoid further penalization.

Promotion of social awareness

Aside from the public demand to include social cost in market exchanges and control the amount of negative impacts from business activities, increasingly more efforts are being put forth by governments to promote the social awareness of the need to preserve the environment. This is usually implemented through the use or support of local media with related environmental protection programs as the means to transfer the ideas and values to the community. For example, some media promotions to reduce the use of disposable utensils and plastic bags are financed by public expenditure budgets to reinforce the awareness of the community to lower white pollution (see Glossary) and plastic waste. Besides, taking into consideration that sustainable development largely requires joint efforts at the regional and global levels, collaborations between governments in different regions and countries are also increasing over time. Related efforts are commonly coordinated through international organizations like the United Nations at the global level, or the European Union and Asia-Pacific Economic Cooperation (APEC) at the regional level.

When promoting social awareness for sustainable development, governments in different countries could also provide joint financial resources to the reputable international, non-governmental and not-for-profit organizations in carrying out their activities and projects. For example, to reduce the impacts of human activities on the natural environment, the World Wide Fund for Nature (WWF), a well-known non-governmental organization, has promoted sustainable development activities in more than 100 countries. To facilitate the related activities, financial support from the governments around the world contribute to around 20% of the operation funds of the WWF. One of the commonly known activities that has been initiated by the WWF is the annual Earth Hour event, which encourages individuals and firms to turn off their lights for one hour on a particular day in March. Other than the energy that is saved, this event has also served as a landmark to promote the recognition of the world communities that they are responsible for conserving the environment. In 2017, firms and individuals in 187 countries participated in this event (WWF, 2017: 11). The WWF also indicated that "countries around the world such as China, Finland and Colombia used the Earth Hour platform to inform and inspire more people to make sustainable choices" (ibid.: 21).

Uncertainties in practices

Despite the receptivity of more countries today toward sustainable development in the world and their respective economies, the effectiveness of their efforts and related policies largely rely on the stage of their social and economic development, as well as their legal practices. In many less-developed and emerging economies, the desire of businesses and the public to pursue economic growth and development over time could indeed inhibit their sustainable development. Consequently, reported economic growth in monetary form could actually be at the cost of reducing their capacity for sustainable development. For example, Guern (2018) estimated that the "lost productivity from death and disease resulting from river pollution and other environmental damage is equivalent to about 4 percent of gross domestic product", despite the related policies introduced by the Indian government to improve the environment in India. In many Southeast Asian countries like Vietnam, Thailand, and Myanmar, recent growths in their hospitality and tourism industries have explicitly damaged their beaches and coastal environment like India.

Prospects of sustainable development in hospitality industry

Following the increase in public awareness of sustainable development, it is undeniable that the hospitality industry has been trying to reduce the socially undesirable effects from their business operations. Related efforts largely reflect their willingness to invest in technologies over time to reduce the negative impacts to the environment. In addition, supportive measures like continuing education and on-the-job training that contribute to the awareness of employees of the importance of sustainable development are commonly adopted by hospitality firms.

As mentioned earlier, rapid expansion of the scale and scope of hospitality businesses could indeed counter the sustainable development efforts of this industry. This is a result of the growing demand (especially the mass demand for leisure and related hospitality services as discussed in Chapter 2), and the desire of local firms in some of the less-developed and emerging markets to entice global tourists to use their hospitality services. Thus, it is commonly observed that in some of the emerging markets, the growth and development of their tourism and hospitality industries have greatly posed obstacles to the sustainability of the related businesses.

Common efforts

Among the various efforts carried out by the hospitality industry for sustainable development, "green hospitality" is commonly promoted to guide competing firms in the major markets. According to Kasavana (2008: 140), the term "green" largely refers to the notion of "eco-friendly businesses", although there is no unique or formal definition of the term. To various sectors in the industry, green hospitality is carried out through the common efforts of the various firms (e.g., hotels, restaurants, theme parks, and cruise ships) to achieve the "three Rs – reduce, reuse and recycle" (ibid.).

In line with technological progress, green hospitality has been largely implemented by hospitality firms through the related "web sites and directories promoting green travel destinations, green hotels, green eateries, green meeting facilities, green convention centers, as well as green suppliers" (ibid.). So it is evident that a wide range of firms in the hospitality industry are putting in common efforts to meet the demand of their communities for sustainable business practices. To a large extent, they are working through a common checklist to reduce their negative impacts to the environment although their business practices are not identical.

In promoting green hospitality, the hotel industry (including hotel resorts of different themes and different scales) is contributing much more in their common efforts toward "green hotels", which can be easily recognized by their customers and the general public. Aside from using various technologies to conserve energy and water, green hotels also implement eco-friendly programs such as efforts "to reuse and recycle soaps and shampoos" (Mohapa-tra, 2016), as well as reducing the use of plastic materials. In New York City (NYC), for example,

> 19 major hotels have pledged to reduce their individual carbon footprint ... to reduce greenhouse gas (GHG) emissions 80% by 2050. It's esti-mated that participation will reduce citywide GHG emissions by 32,000 metric tons and save approximately $25 million in energy costs.
>
> (ibid.)

Indeed, the hotel industry in various major cities around the world are prac-ticing similar programs with the local governments to lower their negative impacts to the environment over time.

Taking into consideration the increasing common efforts and the wide applications of technologies, it is reasonable to believe that many hospitality firms (especially the multi-national firms) are working toward the right path to achieve sustainable development. With the efforts made, the industry in general would not only obtain the approval of the respective hosting commu-nities, but also meet the requirements of the local governments in its continu-ous progress toward sustainability.

The challenges

Despite the common efforts that are being made by the majority of the players in the hospitality industry globally, its sustainable development is still inhib-ited by the reality that many emerging economies continue to pursue short-term profits and the large number of employment positions that could be made available by the rapid expansion of the hospitality industry (especially tourism). To compete for the funds spent on hospitality services in different markets (i.e., in both the well-developed and the less-developed markets), local firms may likely try to find ways to increase their business turnover and reduce operation costs by neglecting the environment. Although some of the governments might take the lead and invest into various forms of clean energy programs, and international firms (e.g., Marriott and Sheraton) could also transfer their eco-friendly practices to the local businesses when they enter the emerging markets, local firms may simply benefit from these efforts rather than taking part in the related programs.

In addition, as Eric Ricaurte, CEO of Greenview in the Mekong Tourism Investment Summit said in 2016, the "Average carbon emissions per hotel room are coming down, but with the tens of millions of new rooms predicted to come to market by 2050 the aggregate emissions of the hospitality indus-try will be massively larger than what they are now" (mekongtourism.org, 2016). Aside from the increase in hotel rooms to the markets in the foresee-able future, a large number are anticipated to be constructed in the emerging markets in Southeast and Central Asia, South America, Eastern Europe, and

Africa. To a large extent, many local firms and the public in those regions might emphasize more on their economic growth after approval of the expansion of the hospitality industry. Subsequently, while the natural environment in those countries might be undermined, related waste emitted into the air and dumped into the ocean would likely inhibit the efforts of the industry in other parts of the world.

For example, Mbasera et al. (2016: 2) summarize from the existing literature that "In Zimbabwe and South Africa, the hospitality sector is facing an increasing burden regarding solid waste, pollution of water bodies and excessive use of energy and water". They find that a large number of hotels in Zimbabwe and South Africa "have no green management policies", which "implies that the implementation of green initiatives is being carried out in a haphazard manner" (ibid.: 4). Indeed, similar issues are found in the emerging markets which require continuous efforts for the industry as a whole to promote and transfer sustainable development initiatives from the well-developed to the emerging markets.

Did you know? ...

To reduce the increasing number of negative impacts produced from economic growth and development on the environment and the ecosystem, collective efforts need to be put forth by governments globally. The United Nations (UN) has recently coordinated voluntary agreements, which many countries have entered as participants to ensure global sustainable development. In turn, this is commonly recognized as a necessary condition for sustainable development at the country level.

The hospitality industry is one of the world's fastest-growing industries and therefore consumes a significant volume and a wide range of resources. Therefore, supportive measures undertaken by the hospitality industry would unarguably contribute to the desired ends for sustainable development. Indeed, as facilitated by major hotel and tourism associations (e.g., the American Hotel and Lodging Association, and the International Tourism Partnership), the hospitality industry has made continuous efforts to reduce its negative impacts on communities and the environment. Nevertheless, one of the fundamental challenges that the industry faces is the rapid increase in its business scale, and hence the increasing amount of negative impacts on the environment.

Box 8.1 Sustainable development requires joint efforts between governments, industries, and consumers

In 2015, the United Nations Development Programme (UNDP) released a list of 17 sustainable development goals (SDGs) as founded and agreed upon by leaders of 193 countries for the next 15 years (which is also titled the "2030 Agenda for Sustainable Development"). Of the 17 SDGs, about one-third are directly focused on the efforts necessary to preserve the environment and resources of this planet. They are:

6   Clean water and sanitation
7   Affordable and clean energy
12   Responsible consumption and production
13   Climate action
14   Life below water
15   Life on land

(UNDP, 2015)

(Other goals include "no poverty", "zero hunger", "quality education", and so on and so forth.)

The latest UNDP report in 2018 on the progress of these goals indicates that on average, countries around the world have been making efforts to meet the SDGs such as improving the water quality and applying clean energy. Nevertheless, much effort is still needed in the foreseeable future. For example, it is highlighted that "the rate of global progress is not keeping pace with the ambitions of the Agenda, necessitating immediate and accelerated action by countries and stakeholders at all levels" (UNDP, 2018: 4). This view is indeed consistent with the aforementioned discussion as presented in Figure 8.1.

To ensure sustainable development, hospitality firms have increasingly adopted the SDGs as the related guiding principles when practicing their business. According to Scanlon (2017), for example, "The largest global lodging companies, American Hotel and Lodging Association members Marriott-Starwood … are working along with other member hotel companies to implement the 17 SDG's in the operations of their lodging properties."

Based on the business practices of the hospitality industry, major efforts carried out by related firms are mainly reflected from their use of new facilities and arrangements that lower the consumption of energy and water, as well as reduce carbon emissions from their business operations. In addition, various efforts are also put forth by firms to reduce the volume of food waste and trash, such as disposable utensils and appliances.

As a return for their business efforts, hospitality firms indeed gain customer loyalty so that business turnover could be increased by the increased number of reservations and return rate of existing customers. Owing to technological progress, more information on the efforts made by a hotel in supporting sustainable development could be easily accessed by customers online. As pointed out by Scanlon (2017), for example, "Trip Advisor travel-booking page indicates to customers the Green Leader Certification using a green leaf logo". Thus, when customers, especially business groups, are selecting a hotel for their stay and related events, they are able to choose the desired property that reflects their responsible consumption of the related hospitality services.

Discussion questions:

1   From the standpoint of an individual hotel, what would be the benefits of following the SDGs of the UN when formulating sustainable development strategies?
2   Despite the fact that many efforts have been made around the world to work with the 2030 Agenda for Sustainable Development, "immediate and accelerated action by countries and stakeholders at all levels" is unarguably necessary. Illustrate this argument with a real-world example from the hospitality industry.
3   Other than water, energy, and waste, what would be some other areas that the hospitality industry could focus on toward sustainable development?
4   Sustainable development plans could be costly to small individual hotels, and hence they might not be supportive of sustainable development. Do you agree with this argument?

Conclusions and remarks

In consideration of the deteriorating global environment and ecosystem due to rapid economic growth and development, sustainable development has been a pressing issue for governments, industries, and consumers of various countries. Owing to the negative impacts that have been induced onto the environment since the Industrial Revolution, the current environmental issues can hardly be resolved by any individual party through a simple approach. Joint efforts are critical to avoid the further worsening of environmental problems and the resultant climate change like global warming, rise in the sea level, and extreme weather, as well as exacerbation of the declining quality of the ecosystem.

As a rapidly growing global industry since the mid-20th century, it is undeniable that the practices of the hospitality industry have resulted in the depletion of a significant amount of the world's natural resources. In improving service quality to customers, the hospitality industry has inevitably produced negative externalities of one form or another to the environment and the ecosystem. Thus, responsible production by the hospitality industry and the promotion of responsible consumption of hospitality services would unarguably contribute to the sustainable development of the world economies, which would in turn safeguard an appropriate and sustainable environment for the further development of the hospitality industry.

Despite the fact that sustainable development requires the efforts of various stakeholders from economic societies around the world as a whole, three basic principles could be adopted by practitioners in the hospitality industry when related business decisions are formulated. They are as follows:

1   Recognition of the possible negative externalities and inclusion of social costs from the business process may likely reduce turnovers and net monetary profit; nevertheless, these are essential and effective means to ensure sustainable development.
2   Under the global context of sustainable development, the expenditures of a firm on environmentally friendly facilities and programs will in turn gain the loyalty of its existing and potential customers, and hence increase its competitive edge in the markets.
3   Effective applications of technology not only increase the ability of a firm to achieve sustainable development, but also enhance its contributions to its economy of which the breadth and depth depend on its business scale and scope.

To ensure the effectiveness of sustainable development efforts, and hence sustainable development of the hospitality industry as a whole, continuously raising the awareness of employees at the operational level of environmental issues is an indispensable process. In other words, it is important for employees who are carrying out the work to provide the related products and services to understand the importance of the related policies that are executed by governments and top management members of the companies. Thus, employees in various positions will actually perceive that they contribute to the sustainable development of the industry, instead of simply doing their job as required. Indeed, a correct understanding of sustainable development of employees will likely increase their motivation to preserve the environment in their own personal life.

References and further reading

Bruns-Smith, A., Choy, V., Chong, H., Verma, R., 2015. Environmental sustainability in the hospitality industry: Best practices, guest participation, and customer satisfaction. *Cornell Hospitality Report*, 15 (3), March. Available https://scholarship.sha.cornell.edu/cgi/viewcontent.cgi?article=1199 &context=chrpubs

Chen, H.S., Hsieh, T., 2011. An environmental performance assessment of the hotel industry using an ecological footprint. *Journal of Hospitality Management and Tourism*, 2 (1), 1–11.

Daly, H.E., 1990. Toward some operational principles of sustainable development. *Ecological Economics*, 2, 1–6.

European Commission, 2018. Clean energy for all Europeans. European Commission, Belgium. Available https://ec.europa.eu/energy/en/topics/energy-strategy-and-energy-union/clean-energy-all-europeans

Guern, C.L., 2018. When the mermaids cry: The great plastic tide. Coastal Care. Available http://plastic-pollution.org (first written and published in November 2009, last updated in March 2018).

Hays, D., 2014. Greening hotels – Building green values into hotel services. *Tourism and Hospitality Management*, 24 (1), 85–102.

Houdré, H., 2008. Sustainable development in the hotel industry. *Cornell Hospitality Industry Perspectives*, 1 (2), 6–20.

Hritz, N., Cecil, A.K., 2008. Investigating the sustainability of cruise tourism: A case study of Key West. *Journal of Sustainable Tourism*, 16 (2), 168–181.

Island Resources Foundation, 1996. *Tourism and Coastal Resources Degradation in the Wider Caribbean*. IRF, St. Thomas, Virgin Islands, USA. Available https://wedocs.unep.org/bitstream/handle/20.500.11822/9250/-Tourism%20and%20Coastal%20Resources%20Degradation%20in%20the%20Wider%20Caribbean-1996Tourism-coastal-resources-degradation-Wider-Caribbean.pdf?sequence=3&isAllowed=y

Jones, P., Hillier, D., Comfort, D., 2016. Sustainability in the hospitality industry: Some personal reflections on corporate challenges and research agendas. *International Journal of Contemporary Hospitality Management*, 28 (1), 36–67.

Kasavana, M.L., 2008. Green hospitality. *Hospitality Upgrade*, Summer, 140–148. Available www.hospitalityupgrade.com/Hospitalityupgrade.com-0093-2016Redesign/media/hospitalityupgrade.com-0093/File_Articles/HUSum08_Kasavana_GreenHospitality.pdf

Kates, R.W., Parris, T.M., Leiserowitz, A.A., 2005. What is sustainable development? Goals, indicators, values, and practice. *Environment Science and Policy for Sustainable Development*, 47 (3), 8–21. Available www.environmentmagazine.org/Editorials/Kates-apr05-full.html

Klein, R.A., 2011. Responsible cruise tourism: Issues of cruise tourism and sustainability. *Journal of Hospitality and Tourism Management*, 18 (1), 107–116.

Lélé, S.M., 1991. Sustainable development: A critical review. *World Development*, 19 (6), 607–621.

Liu, Z., 2003. Sustainable tourism development: A critique. *Journal of Sustainable Tourism*, 11 (6), 459–475.

Lynn, C., 2009. Corporate social responsibility in the hospitality industry. *Hosteur*, 18 (2), 5–10. Available www2.nau.edu/clj5/Ethics/Hosteur-CSR%20paper.doc

Marriott International, 2017. *2017 Marriott Sustainability and Social Impact Report*. Available http://serve360.marriott.com/wp-content/uploads/2017/12/2017_Sustainability_and_Social_Impact_Report-1.pdf

Mbasera, M., Du Plessis, E., Saayman, M., Kruger, M., 2016. Environmentally-friendly practices in hotels. *Acta Commercii*, 16 (1), a362. Available www.scielo.org.za/pdf/acom/v16n1/11.pdf

mekongtourism.org, 2016. Carbon emissions challenge for hospitality industry, August 10. Available www.mekongtourism.org/carbon-emissions-hospitality-industry

Melissen, F., Sauer, L., 2019. *Improving Sustainability in the Hospitality Industry*. Routledge, New York, USA.

Micioni, C.W., 2009. Going green in the hospitality industry. *UNLV Theses, Dissertations, Professional Papers, and Capstones*, 642. Available https://digitalscholarship.unlv.edu/thesesdissertations/642

Ministry of Tourism Government of India, 2015. *Revised Guidelines for Classification/Re-Classification of Hotels*. Government of India, New Delhi, India. Available http://tourism.gov.in/sites/default/files/HRACC%20Guidelines%20for%20Hotels2.pdf

Mohapatra, T., 2016. How green is your hotel: Sustainability in the hotel industry. GreenHomeNYC Blog, December 29. Available http://greenhomenyc.org/blog/how-green-is-your-hotel-sustainability-in-the-hotel-industry/

Nordhaus, W.D., 1993. Reflections on the economics of climate change. *Journal of Economic Perspective*, 7 (4), 11–25.

Nordhaus, W.D., 2006. After Kyoto: Alternative mechanisms to control global warming. *American Economic Review*, 96 (2), 31–34.

Polat, N., 2015. Technical innovations in cruise tourism and results of sustainability. *Procedia – Social and Behavioral Sciences*, 195, 438–445.

Prud'homme, B., Raymond, L., 2013. Sustainable development practices in the hospitality industry: An empirical study of their impact on customer satisfaction and intentions. *International Journal of Hospitality Management*, 34, 116–126.

Ricaurte, E., 2017. Hotel sustainability benchmarking index 2017: Energy, water, and carbon. *Cornell Hospitality Report*, 17 (18), 3–17.

Scanlon, N.L. 2017. The UN's sustainable development goals and lodging practices. *Hotel Business Review*, May 28. Available https://hospitality.fiu.edu/the-uns-sustainable-development-goals-and-lodging-practices

Sloan, P., Legrand, W., Chen, J.S., 2013. *Sustainability in the Hospitality Industry: Principles of Sustainable Operations*, 2nd edition). Routledge, New York, USA.

UNDP, 2015. *Sustainable Development Goals*. United Nations Development Programme, New York, USA. Available www.undp.org/content/dam/undp/library/corporate/brochure/SDGs_Booklet_Web_En.pdf

UNDP, 2016. *Human Development Report 2016*. United Nations Development Programme, New York, USA. Available http://hdr.undp.org/sites/default/files/2016_human_development_report.pdf

UNDP, 2018. *Sustainable Development Goals Report 2018*. United Nations Development Programme, New York, USA. Available https://unstats.

un.org/sdgs/files/report/2018/TheSustainableDevelopmentGoals Report2018-EN.pdf

WCED, 1987. *Our Common Future.* Oxford University Press, New York, USA.

WWF, 2017. *Earth Hour Highlights 2017.* World Wide Fund for Nature, Gland, Switzerland. Available http://awsassets.panda.org/downloads/Earth_Hour_Report_2017.pdf

Glossary

Aggregate demand (AD) [Chapter 5]
Measured by total amount of spending of all economic participants on outputs of economy. In principle, AD equals the sum of consumption expenditures spent by all sectors, including household consumption expenditures (C), fixed capital firm investment expenditures (I), public expenditures of the government (G), and expenditure of foreigners on exports (X), but minus the expenditures of an economy on imports (M). That is, $AD = C + I + G + (X - M)$. $(X - M)$ refers to net exports (NX).

Aggregate demand management policy [Chapter 5]
To achieve the macroeconomic goals of stable growth, low inflation and unemployment rates, and stable foreign exchange rate in different phases of a business cycle, a government may implement policies that change (manage) the aggregate demand. In principle, aggregate demand management policies include both fiscal and monetary policies. See also *aggregate demand*, *business cycle*, *fiscal policy*, and *monetary policy*.

Aggregate supply (AS) [Chapter 5]
The planned total output that firms will produce and sell in an economy at different price levels. In principle, the AS curve is upward sloping with respect to (or positively related to) the average price level in an economy. In any given period of time, the absolute AS is limited by the resources available in an economy for production purposes. Over time, the AS can increase (AS curve shifts outward) due to technological advancements, or decrease (AS curve shifts inward) due to increased factor price or natural disasters or wars. See also *factor price*.

Average fixed cost (AFC) [Chapter 4]
Total fixed cost (TFC) divided by the quantity (q) produced by a firm. That is, $AFC = TFC/q$. Since the TFC does not change within a given quantity of output, the AFC is continuously reduced as output is increased.

Average total cost (ATC) [Chapter 4]
Total cost (TC) divided by the quantity (q) of a commodity produced by a firm. That is, $ATC = TC/q$. Since TC is the sum of the total fixed cost (TFC) and

total variable cost (TVC), ATC = (TFC + TVC)/q (i.e., ATC = AFC + AVC). Owing to the shape of the plotted curves of AFC and AVC, ATC is U-shaped.

Average variable cost (AVC) [Chapter 4]
Total variable cost (TVC) divided by the quantity (q) of a commodity produced by a firm. That is, AVC = TVC/q. In principle, the AVC first decreases when output is increased. This is due to the fact that the fixed capacity installed in a production/business site could be easily combined with (or utilized by) variable factors like labor. However, when output continues to increase, the extra output derived from adding more variable factors to a given amount of fixed capacity will be reduced. This means that after reaching a certain optimal level of efficiency (or combined fixed capacity and variable factors) with the lowest AVC, the plotted curve will slope upwards; that is, the AVC is U-shaped with respect to increases in output. See also *variable cost*.

Break-even pricing [Chapter 4]
Price of a good or service is set so that total revenue simply covers total variable (operational) costs at a certain level of output. In principle, firms use break-even pricing as an important reference to determine the lowest price that they would charge. For instance, when business is slow in certain periods of time, or declining for a short period of time. Break-even pricing would allow operations to continue without additional loss from fixed business expenditures.

Broad money [Chapter 6]
Narrow money plus money that is deposited by individuals into the banking system in fixed terms. Money deposited under fixed terms, such as time deposits and certificates of deposit for one month or three months may not be withdrawn or converted immediately into a medium of exchange for spending purposes. See also *narrow money*.

Budget constraint [Chapter 3]
The purchasing power (e.g., amount of money) of a consumer versus his/her plans to spend on certain commodities (goods or services). Determined by the income or wealth of an individual.

Bundled pricing [Chapter 4]
A package of related consumable goods and/or services that are bundled together and sold for a single price. Although in principle, the bundled pricing of a package of commodities is less than the sum of their individual prices, a firm may experience increased business turnover when more items are sold in a single transaction. As well, consumers might not want some of the products or services in the bundle.

Business cycle [Chapter 5]
Recurrence of upward and downward fluctuations in macroeconomic performance in terms of changes in gross domestic product (GDP), and inflation

and unemployment rates. Every business cycle has four phases: upswing (or recovery); peak; downswing (or recession); and depression. In general, when the business cycle is moving upward, the GDP and inflation both increase while the unemployment rate decreases, and vice versa when it is moving downward. Business cycles are also known as trade or economic cycles.

Casino tourism [Chapter 2]

The organization and provision of large-scale casino gaming facilities to tourists with a wide variety of options. Gaming and hotel resort facilities (e.g., entertainment, shows, and performances) are integrated together in a casino tourist destination. For example, Las Vegas in the United States and Macao in China are the largest and most renowned casino tourist destinations worldwide. Tourists who embark on casino tourism may expect to enjoy related hotel resort services and take part in gaming (although some of them take the trip primarily to gamble). See also *hotel resort*.

Central bank [Chapter 6]

An independent national authority (e.g., the Federal Reserve in the USA, Bank of England in the UK, and People's Bank of China in China) that is responsible for regulating the banking and financial systems in a country. Besides, the entity also coordinates services to facilitate their operations. In addition to issuing the legal tender (i.e., currency) of a country and ensuring its purchasing power in both the domestic and international markets, the central bank carries out a monetary policy to stabilize the macroeconomic performance of its economy, such as inflation and unemployment. See also *monetary policy*.

Choice [Chapter 1]

Taking into consideration the reality that there is scarcity (i.e., limited resources as compared to unlimited wants), an individual or economy has to prioritize alternative uses of resources and then determine the best outcome. Choices are associated with opportunity (economic) costs. See also *opportunity cost*.

Commercial bank [Chapter 6]

A profit-seeking private entity which primarily provides depository and lending services to households and firms. Accepts deposits and lends a portion of the deposits to third parties who seek to borrow funds. Profit is based on the difference between revenue from the interest paid by borrowers and interest payments to depositors. In the process, a major function of a commercial bank is to create the deposit money which facilitates spending and investments in various economic sectors. See also *deposit money*.

Consumer surplus [Chapter 4]

The difference between the monetary value that a consumer is willing to and able to pay to consume a certain quantity of a commodity and what s/he actually pays based on market price. Graphically, this is represented by the area below the demand curve and above the market price at the quantity that is being consumed.

Cost-push inflation [Chapter 5]

The increase in average price level in an economy caused by an increase in the factor price (or input cost) of production. This is commonly due to an increase in the price of raw materials, energy, and/or labor. For example, when the crude oil price soared in the 1970s, the cost of production of many firms increased rapidly, so that the average price of the final commodities in the market also increased. With increased cost of production, some firms may choose to shut down their business. Thus, cost-push inflation may possibly lead to both high inflation and high unemployment rates in an economy. See also *aggregate supply* and *price index*.

Credit [Chapter 6]

A pre-approved amount of money granted by a bank or a financial organization to an individual or firm to spend without an equivalent amount of cash deposit in the first place, and repay the money along with an interest fee within an agreed period of time. In principle, credit stimulates the spending of consumers and firms.

Cross-price elasticity of demand [Chapter 3]

Changes in the demand for a commodity when the price of a related commodity changes. In principle, if two commodities are mutually substitutable, the cross-price elasticity of demand is positive, because when the price of a commodity increases, consumers will demand for more of its substitute, and vice versa. On the other hand, if two commodities are complements, the cross-price elasticity of demand is negative because when the price of a commodity is reduced, consumers will demand more of the other commodity, which is consumed along with the reduced price commodity, and vice versa.

Deficit budget [Chapter 6]

When annual spending of a government (e.g., on social welfare and public investment) exceeds its revenue (e.g., taxes). Generally speaking, a deficit budget is a common expansionary fiscal policy used by a government to stimulate (or stabilize) an economy as it starts to experience a downturn, such as entering a recession period. See also *aggregate demand*, *fiscal policy*, and *surplus budget*.

Deflation [Chapter 6]

The opposite of inflation, in which the average price level of commodities in an economy is reduced. Deflation could be due to reduced aggregate demand during a recession or depression period. Thus, even though the average price level of commodities falls, some households may not be necessarily better off since their income may also fall at the same time. See also *business cycle* and *inflation rate*.

Demand [Chapter 3]

Ceteris paribus, the willingness and ability of a consumer to pay for an economic commodity (good or service) at various prices within a given period of time. In principle, demand for a commodity is generally determined by its price, as well as income and taste/preference of a consumer, prices of related commodities such as substitutes and complements, and government policies like expenditure taxes.

Demand curve [Chapter 3]

A graphical illustration which depicts the relationship between price and the quantity demanded for a particular commodity. Could be a straight line or a curve. Based on the law of demand, in which price and quantity demanded have an inverse relationship (i.e., when price increases, the quantity demanded decreases, and vice versa), the demand curve for a commodity is downward-sloping. See also *law of demand*.

Demand-pull inflation [Chapter 5]

Increase in average prices in an economy caused by a continuous increase in aggregate demand (AD) that outpaces the aggregate supply (AS). Since AD = C + I + G + (X − M), demand-pull inflation is commonly a result of a rapid increase in household consumption expenditures (C) and/or firm investment expenditures (I). As demand-pull inflation is caused by an increase in AD, firms will expand their output so that the employment rate will also increase. Nevertheless, when the economy is at a full-employment level of output, continuous increases in AD will only be reflected in an increase in inflation rate instead of real output. See also *aggregate demand*, *inflation rate*, and *price index*.

Deposit money [Chapter 6]

Commonly refers to demand deposit (or checking account) and savings deposit held in commercial banks. Owners of the related deposit accounts could use the money as a medium of exchange upon demand by signing checks, withdrawing cash, or electronically transferring funds. In any economy, commercial banks can create deposit money by approving loans or credit to households and firms for spending without the need to contribute an equivalent amount of cash deposit in advance. Since loans or credit may be withdrawn in the form of cash that is being deposited into the commercial banks, which is actually money of the commercial banks in the first place, their ability to create the deposit money is capped by the reserve requirement as stipulated by the central bank. See also *commercial bank* and *reserve requirement*.

E-money [Chapter 6]

Digital form of currency used to settle market exchanges and conducted through transmission on physical devices and/or computer networks/internet. Can be in hardware-based or software-based forms. Hardware-based e-money is transferred from cash or the bank account of an individual into a digital format and stored in a physical device like a bank card, and used to settle payments when presented to a card reader installed in a firm (e.g., a shop). Software-based e-money is deposit money that is transferred directly from one account to another through a computer (internet) system by using authorization codes.

Economic development [Chapters 1 and 8]

A process in which the production capacity of an economy is increasing and the quality and standards of living (economic well-being) are improving. In principle, economic development requires continuous long-term investment in fixed capital such as technology and human capital (including education). To a large extent, economic development is a qualitative concept, which is related to but not the same as economic growth.

Economic growth [Chapters 1 and 8]

Changes in the monetary value of the total output of an economy from one period to another (e.g., month, quarter, or year). In principle, economic growth is measured by the percentage of change in the gross domestic product (GDP), gross national product (GNP) or gross national income (GNI) of an economy. The growth can be positive, negative, or zero. To a large extent, economic growth is a quantitative concept, which is related but not identical to economic development.

Elasticity (ε) [Chapter 3]

Measurement of the percentage of change of an economic variable (say, y) with respect to the percentage of change of another variable (say, x). Mathematically, if the "x elasticity of y" is any number a (e.g., 2), this means that when x changes by 1%, then y correspondingly changes by a% (e.g., 2%). The application of elasticity in economics includes the price elasticity of demand (or supply), income elasticity of demand and cross-price elasticity of demand. In absolute value, demand is elastic if $\varepsilon > 1$; inelastic if $0 < \varepsilon < 1$; unitary elastic if $\varepsilon = 1$; perfectly inelastic if $\varepsilon = 0$; and perfectly elastic if $\varepsilon = \infty$ (infinitely large).

Entrepreneurship [Chapter 7]

The act of someone who introduces new ideas and technological changes to the production process which lead to industrial and economic developments. In general, these include feasible new ways that merge existing resources for more product variety and increased production efficiency. In economics, entrepreneurship is the primary factor that contributes to innovation. See also *innovation*.

Equilibrium [Chapter 3]

A situation in which two opposing forces reach a state of balance. In economics, for example, the quantity demanded is negatively related to the movement of price, while quantity supplied is positively related to the movement of price. At equilibrium, the quantity demanded is equal to the quantity supplied (i.e., equilibrium quantity) at a unique equilibrium price. See also *law of demand* and *law of supply*.

Excess demand [Chapter 3]
A situation in which the quantity demanded in the market is greater than the quantity supplied. This is the result when the market price of a commodity is set below its equilibrium price. Excess demand is also called a shortage.

Excess supply [Chapter 3]
A situation in which the quantity supplied in the market is greater than the quantity demanded. This is the result when the market price of a commodity is set above its equilibrium price. Excess supply is also called a surplus.

Expenditure tax [Chapters 4 and 8]
Expenditure taxes are a common form of indirect taxation and imposed on the total amount spent on a commodity. Expenditure taxes increase the actual price for each unit of a commodity paid by consumers and usually reduce the actual price received by the producers. The difference is remitted to the government by the producers based on their business turnover. See also *indirect tax*.

Externality [Chapter 8]
Positive or negative effects generated/imposed from the economic exchanges between two parties to unrelated third parties. For example, pollution generated from the operations of a firm to meet customer demand for hospitality services is a negative externality. This is because the environment and the health of other community members are being adversely affected.

Factors of production [Chapter 1]
All of the inputs required to produce various economic commodities. In economics, there are four factors of production: land; labor; capital; and entrepreneurship.

Factor price [Chapter 1]
Return for the factors of production. In economics, the return for land is called rent; return for labor is wages; return for capital is interest; and return for entrepreneurship is profit.

Fiscal policy [Chapter 5]
A government implemented demand-side policy for macroeconomic management. Carried out by adjusting government spending (G) and/or taxation (T) policies to change autonomous spending patterns, and hence aggregate demand in an economy. In principle, fiscal policies could be expansionary (e.g., increasing G and/or lowering T to stimulate the economy when it is down-turning) or contractionary (e.g., reducing G and/or raising T to slow

down the increase in rate of inflation when the economy is peaking or "over-heated"). See also *aggregate demand*.

Fixed cost [Chapter 4]
The cost to a firm that will not change within a given range of production or output level. Includes capital costs of investing in property and fixtures of a firm. In any short period of time, say, one month or one year, fixed costs cannot be eliminated even if output is zero. See also *variable cost*.

Foreign exchange rate [Chapter 6]
The rate of exchange between the currencies of two countries. In econom-ics, the foreign exchange rate is defined in two different ways. First, it could denote the price of one unit of domestic currency in terms of foreign cur-rency. For example, if the European Union is the domestic economy, its cur-rency exchange rate could be expressed as 1.2 US dollars (i.e., €1 = USD1.2). Second, foreign exchange rate could be expressed as the price of one unit of foreign currency in terms of the domestic currency. For example, if Japan is the domestic economy, its currency exchange rate could be expressed as 125 Japanese yen to 1 euro (i.e., ¥125 = €1).

GDP deflator [Chapters 1 and 5]
A numerical factor that reflects the changes in the average price level of all commodities in an economy for different periods of time. Commonly used to remove the effect of increasing price levels (i.e., inflation) on the reported monetary (i.e., the current or nominal) value of the GDP to obtain the real GDP. In principle, an index (deflator) of 100 which means 100% is assigned to a base year for comparison purposes. For example, if the year 2000 is cho-sen as the base year and the GDP deflator is 142.8 in 2018, then the nominal GDP is $200 billion in 2018, and its real GDP is equivalent to $140 billion $\left(200 \times \dfrac{100}{142.8}\right)$ for the purchasing power of year 2000. See also *nominal GDP* and *real GDP*.

Globalization [Chapter 5]
A process in which social, cultural, political, and economic exchanges are increasing among the different countries worldwide. Although there is no unique definition for globalization which depends on the objective of the dis-cussion, the term could be generally interpreted as the reduction of barriers for people and firms to carry out cross-border activities. To a large extent, increasingly more collaborations between governments after WWII set the stage for globalization while the rapid progression of information technology has facilitated the progress of globalization since the beginning of the 21st century.

Gross domestic product (GDP) [Chapters 1 and 5]

Monetary value of total outputs produced within the boundaries of an economy. In principle, the output value produced also reflects the generated income at the same time. In economics, there are different approaches for measuring the GDP of an economy. A common way to measure the GDP is to use the expenditure approach, which counts all of the expenditures spent by various parties for the outputs of an economy. In this approach, total expenditure equals the sum of household consumption expenditures (C), fixed capital firm investment expenditures (I), public expenditures of the government (G), expenditure of foreigners on exports (X), minus expenditures of an economy on imports (M). That is, GDP = C + I + G + (X − M), which is the same as the formula for aggregate demand. See also *aggregate demand*.

Gross national product (GNP) [Chapters 1 and 5]

Monetary value of total outputs produced by citizens of an economy (a nation). The outputs could be produced within the boundaries of the economy or abroad. In any period of time, since the outputs produced/income generated within the boundaries of an economy could originate from the properties owned by foreigners, and the citizens of a nation could also carry out production on their properties abroad and acquire the corresponding revenue, thus, GNP = GDP + net property income from abroad.

Hotel resort [Chapter 2]

A large hotel-based property that provides a range of basic hospitality services like accommodations and dining, along with specific types of entertainment and leisure services like an amusement park, skiing, and spa services. If casino gaming services are included, the hotel resort is called a casino resort.

Human Development Index (HDI) [Chapter 8]

An annual index released by the United Nations Development Programme (UNDP) to show the development of countries globally based on statistical measurements of three dimensions of quality of life/living standards: 1) life expectancy; 2) mean years and expected years of schooling; and 3) gross national income per capita. In principle, a higher index reflects a higher level of economic development. This index also allows comparisons of the level of economic development among different countries.

Income effect [Chapter 3]

Changes in the purchasing power of a consumer's income when the price of a commodity changes. For example, when the price of a commodity falls, a consumer might be able to buy more of this commodity (and may also purchase more of other commodities) even though his/her income remains the same. See also *substitution effect*.

Income elasticity of demand [Chapter 3]

Percentage of change in demand for a commodity with respect to the percentage of change in income. In principle, change in demand could be measured in terms of the quantity consumed or the total amount spent on a commodity. In economics, income elasticity is a factor for determining if a commodity is a regular or an inferior item; and if it is a normal commodity, whether it is a necessity or a luxury. See also *inferior good*, *luxury*, and *necessity*.

Indirect tax [Chapters 4 and 8]

An indirect tax is levied on the consumption of a commodity, such as the value added tax (VAT) and the goods and service tax (GST). Unlike a direct tax which is imposed onto income (income or corporate tax) and paid directly by the tax payer, an indirect tax is collected by firms or producers from the sale of a commodity and paid to the government on an annual basis. Since an indirect tax increases the market price of a commodity, and consumers will buy fewer of the commodity when the price is higher, this is a common practice in that firms may share this tax with the consumers depending on their possible responsiveness to the price change (i.e., elasticity of demand). See also *expenditure tax*.

Industrial development [Chapter 7]

A process in which the efficiency of production in an industry improves, while its capacity for production is increased. Industrial development requires both technological advancement and innovation. On the other hand, industrial development produces resources for further investment in technologies and innovative ideas. See also *innovation*.

Industry chain [Chapter 7]

A set of industries that are connected to a core industry and carry out their practices. These include the industries that range from supplying raw materials and intermediate products to producing the core industry, as well as the related industries that are linked to this industry for the distribution of the related commodities. For example, cruise lines in the hospitality industry, which add value to the industry chain.

Inferior good [Chapter 3]

When income is increased, there is less money spent on this kind of commodity. That is, the income elasticity of demand for an inferior good is negative. See also *normal good*.

Inflation rate [Chapters 1 and 6]

A measurement of the changes in the average price level in an economy. If the inflation rate goes up, the purchasing power of money falls, and vice versa. In other words, when the inflation rate is increased, consumers are on average paying higher prices to enjoy the same quantity of commodities as compared to the previous periods. High and rapid increases of the inflation rate may not be desired by the stakeholders in an economy, as a stable and low inflation rate demonstrates the continuous growth of an economy. See also *price index*.

Information technology (IT) [Chapter 7]

Largely refers to the applications of digitalized computing technology to store, access, and analyze quantitative data and qualitative information. IT reduces the search costs of both consumers and producers in the markets and hence increases business volume. Under certain situations, IT also facilitates innovation. See also *innovation*.

Innovation [Chapter 7]

A decision and process that combine different types of technologies with related production resources into a real and workable sphere, and hence promote new and more efficient ways to carry out economic activities that lead to both industrial and economic developments. Innovation refines the methods (and hence lowers the cost) of production and introduces new products (or enhances product differentiation) in the markets. Also commonly defined as the "commercialization of inventions". See also *invention*.

Interest rate policy [Chapter 6]

A monetary policy instrument used by central banks to manage the aggregate demand (AD). If the inflation rate is increased too quickly, which means that the AD exceeds the aggregate supply, the central bank may raise the interest rate to increase the opportunity cost of households and firms to spend on consumption and investment, and hence slow down the increase in AD. Thus, the inflation rate could be stabilized or reduced, and vice versa when an economy enters a recession period. In principle, increasing the interest rate is used as a tool under a contractionary monetary policy, while lowering the interest rate is an expansionary monetary policy. See also *monetary policy*.

Invention [Chapter 7]

Creation of new things or ideas, which may or may not necessarily be practical from the standpoint of business or economic applications. See also *innovation*.

Law of demand [Chapter 3]

A negative relationship between the movement of price and quantity demanded. That is, when the price increases, the quantity demanded decreases, and vice versa.

Law of supply [Chapter 3]

A positive relationship between the movement of price and quantity supplied. That is, when the price increases, the quantity supplied also increases, and vice versa.

Luxury [Chapter 3]

When income is higher, spending on a commodity also increases by a higher percentage. That is, the income elasticity of demand for a luxury good/service is greater than 1. See also *necessity*.

M0/M1/M2 [Chapter 6]
Definitions of different forms of money supply in an economy. In principle, the availability of any form of money as an immediate means for payment to settle a market exchange declines as the numeric value of the concerned money supply aggregates increases. For example, M0 refers to all of the coins and banknotes that are circulating within an economy. M1 equals M0 plus demand deposit like checks of various forms. M2 equals M1 plus savings and time deposits. In practice, the composition and detailed breakdowns of M1 and M2 may vary based on the real situation of different economies. In addition, M3 and higher order money supply aggregates may also be included in some of the more advanced economies in which more monetary instruments are used for transactions in the money market.

Macroeconomics [Chapters 1 and 5]
Study of the overall economic performance of an economy and the major factors that influence its performance over time, instead of the individual activities of consumers or firms in the markets. Primary areas of concern include employment, inflation, growth and development, monetary and banking systems, foreign exchange rates of currencies, international trade, business cycles, and government fiscal and monetary policies.

Marginal benefit [Chapter 1]
When an economic decision is made, the incremental benefits enjoyed by the related individual such as utility (i.e., the level of satisfaction) to a consumer, or profit to a firm, or welfare to a society.

Marginal cost [Chapter 1]
When an economic decision is a made, the incremental cost incurred to an individual such as payment made by a consumer, cost paid by a firm, or expenditure of a government.

Marginalism [Chapter 1]
A theory which states that an economic decision (choice) is made by comparing the incremental (i.e., marginal) changes in the benefits and costs associated with the decision. In principle, a marginal benefit (MB) that is greater than or equal to the marginal cost (MC) (i.e., if MB ≥ MC), will allow a choice to be feasible.

Market failure [Chapter 3]
Disregard of social interests when market practices are based on the private agenda of firms and personal interest of consumers (e.g., profit and individual pleasure respectively). Consequently, the allocation of resources and combinations of outputs produced/consumed in the economy become inefficient. For example, pollution and over-consumption of resources, as well as the unfair

distribution of commodities between the rich and the poor in a society. Thus, government intervention is considered to be necessary.

Mass leisure [Chapter 2]
Leisure spent and enjoyed by the mass working groups, which is different from the notion commonly found prior to the 20th century, when leisure was largely provided to the rich (or upper class) and enjoyed by them. Parallel to the immense infrastructure development and technological progress in the world economies, increases in the income of the mass working group from economic growth and development have led to demand for new cultural and leisure activities, which also provide new business opportunities to the hospitality industry.

Mass society [Chapter 2]
The community that is composed of various mass working groups (which commonly include blue-collar and white-collar workers). Mass society has been expanding following the economic growth and development of the world economies since the end of the 19th century. A common characteristic of mass society is that when income of people in related groups increase, they are inclined to spend the money on improving their quality of life in different ways, which include leisure and hospitality services.

Microeconomics [Chapter 1]
Study of economic behavior and the factors that influence the decisions of individual consumers and producers in the markets. Primary topics explored include consumer (i.e., demand) and firm (i.e., supply) behaviors, determining market price, responsiveness (elasticity) of consumers and producers to market price changes and major determinants of demand and supply, the role of the government and its policies in market efficiency, and different forms of market structures.

Modernization [Chapter 2]
In economics, commonly referred to a process through which the output and income derived by an economy transitions from reliance on agricultural production to industrial/manufacturing production (also called industrialization), and then further to the provision of various types of services (or de-industrialization). Throughout this process, the work environment and living standards are improving, while the average income is also increasing.

Monetary policy [Chapter 6]
A demand-side policy for macroeconomic management implemented by the central bank of a country. Carried out by making changes to the supply of money and cost of using money in the markets. Common policy instruments used by the central bank are interest rate policy, reserve requirement, and open market operations. The amount of money available for market exchanges would be increased (or decreased) by executing expansionary (or contractionary) monetary policies. In addition, the cost of using money would also be

lower (or higher). Moreover, the ability of commercial banks to create deposit money would also be enhanced (or limited). Thus, aggregate demand and/or aggregate supply would be stimulated (or stabilized). See also *deposit money*, *interest rate policy*, *open market operations*, and *reserve requirement*.

Money [Chapter 6]

Any means accepted as a medium of exchange in the markets. To facilitate various forms of economic activities, like consumption, production, and investment, money must be able to fulfill three other basic functions including storing monetary value, and functioning as a unit of account and a means of deferred payment. In principle, money includes banknotes and coins that are issued by the central bank of a country, deposit money of various forms and money market instruments like certificates of deposit. See also *broad money*, *deposit money*, and *narrow money*.

Money multiplier [Chapter 6]

The number of times that a commercial bank is able to create deposit money from the cash deposit received. In principle, the magnitude of the money multiplier is determined by the reserve requirement of the central bank. A higher reserve requirement means that when a commercial bank receives a cash deposit, a smaller amount can be lent out to its customers through deposit money, and hence a smaller money multiplier, and vice versa. See also *deposit money* and *reserve requirement*.

Multiplier effect [Chapter 5]

When the autonomous spending of an economic sector (e.g., government or firms) is increased, the income of other sectors (e.g., households and firms) will also increase so that their spending on consumption and production activities will increase in the subsequent rounds, and so on and so forth. Thus, the ultimate effect of an increase in the total income of an economy which is measured in monetary value (e.g., gross domestic product) is greater than the initial change.

Narrow money [Chapter 6]

Commonly refers to any means that can serve as a medium of exchange. This form of money includes coins and banknotes, checks (demand deposit), and savings deposits that can be readily withdrawn to settle payments. See also *broad money*.

Necessity [Chapter 3]

When income increases, spending on a commodity is also increased by a smaller percentage. That is, the income elasticity of demand for a necessity is less than 1. See also *luxury*.

Nominal GDP [Chapter 1]

The monetary value of the gross domestic product (GDP) of an economy, which is calculated by using the current prices of the considered year. Does not account for the effects of inflation on the real value of the outputs of an economy. See also *gross domestic product*, *inflation*, and *real GDP*.

Normal good [Chapter 3]

When income increases, spending on commodities also increases. That is, the income elasticity of demand for a normal good is positive. See also *inferior good*.

Open market operations [Chapter 6]

A type of monetary policy undertaken by a central bank to change the money supply and interest rate as a measure to manage macroeconomic performance. In practice, the policy instrument used by the central bank mainly refers to the buying and selling of government securities (e.g., government bonds) in the market (mainly through commercial banks). If the central bank sells more government securities to the commercial banks, they have to pay for the related securities by reducing their deposit money so that money supply in the market falls, and interest rate may rise, and vice versa. See also *monetary policy*.

Opportunity cost [Chapter 1]

The value of the best opportunity that has been forgone in making a choice (about "something"). In economics, the "best opportunity" might not necessarily be a single item or a simple monetary value although it could be expressed so. For example, when an entrepreneur decides to launch a hotel, the opportunity cost of this decision is not simply limited to the monetary (or accounting) cost of constructing and operating the hotel, but also his/her forgone salary if s/he has been available for work in the market, as well as the forgone interest income if the amount of capital invested in the hotel was deposited into a bank.

Price differentiation [Chapter 4]

Charging different prices for the same commodity to different consumer groups. This is a common and essential pricing strategy by any firm that wishes to maximize its business performance in terms of total revenue. To carry out price differentiation effectively, a firm must be able to identify and differentiate between its consumer groups with different price elasticities of demand, and avoid the likelihood of the transfer of commodities between the different groups who are charged different prices (e.g., student versus adult tickets to a theme park). See also *price elasticity of demand*.

Price elasticity of demand [Chapter 3]

Shows responsiveness of consumers to changes in the price of a commodity. Measured by the percentage of change in quantity demanded for a commodity with respect to the percentage of change in its price, $\left(\varepsilon_p^d = \dfrac{\% \Delta Q_d}{\% \Delta P} = \dfrac{\Delta Q_d}{\Delta P} \cdot \dfrac{P}{Q_d} \right)$.

According to the law of demand, the numerical value of the price elasticity of demand is negative. See also *law of demand* and *elasticity*.

Price elasticity of supply [Chapter 3]

Shows the responsiveness of firms/producers to changes in the price of a commodity. Measured by the percentage of change in quantity supplied/

produced for a commodity with respect to the percentage of change in its price,

$$\left(\varepsilon_p^s = \frac{\%\Delta Q_s}{\%\Delta P} = \frac{\Delta Q_s}{\Delta P} \cdot \frac{P}{Q_s} \right)$$. According to the law of supply, the numerical value

of the price elasticity of supply is positive. See also *law of supply* and *elasticity*.

Price index {Chapters 1 and 5}

A standardized measure that is used to express changes in the average price level of a basket of goods and services in an economy within a given period of time (e.g., a month, quarter, or year). The basket of goods and services usually includes a set of representative items such as food, transportation, housing, hospitality services and so on and so forth. In principle, a price index is expressed as a percentage (e.g., 110 = 110%). For comparison purposes, a base year is used and a price index of 100 is assigned. Thus, changes in the price index over time show the rate of inflation in the economy. This index could also be applied as a deflator to estimate the real level of output of an economy (e.g., the real GDP) from the reported monetary value of a given period. Some common price indexes include the consumer price index (CPI) and retail price index (RPI). See also *GDP deflator* and *real GDP*.

Producer surplus {Chapter 4}

The difference between the total cost of producing a certain quantity of output and the total revenue derived from selling the output in the market. Producer surplus is graphically represented by the area above the supply curve and below the market price at the quantity being sold. In economics, producer surplus also refers to economic profit.

Productivity {Chapters 1 and 4}

A measurement of the average output per unit of input in the production process. Productivity could be presented as a physical unit or monetary value. For example, given the fixed capacity of a firm, if total output produced by employing 10 laborers is 1,000 units (or $100,000 if the market price of each unit is $100), the productivity of each laborer is 100 units (or $10,000).

Quantity demanded {Chapter 3}

The quantity of a commodity that a consumer (consumers in the market) would like to pay for with respect to its price. See also *law of demand*.

Real GDP {Chapters 1 and 5}

Adjustment of the monetary value of the reported GDP in a particular year with the rate of inflation as compared to the previous year or a base year. Real GDP shows the actual change in the output of an economy by removing the effects from the changes in price levels. See also *gross domestic product* and *price index*.

Reserve requirement [Chapter 6]
Minimum percentage of deposit money that commercial banks must hold as cash reserve and cannot be lent as stipulated by the central bank for a certain period of time. This is a common monetary policy measure adopted by the central bank to change the money supply (i.e., the ability of commercial banks to create deposit money) and interest rate, and hence manage its macroeconomic performance. See also *deposit money* and *monetary policy*.

Scarcity [Chapter 1]
Resources on Earth are finite for any individual, household, or firm. Therefore, there is a gap between the amount of resources available and the unlimited wants of people to meet their material desires. This concept constitutes the origins of economic studies.

Stagflation [Chapter 5]
The situation when an economy experiences high inflation and high unemployment rates at the same time. In other words, even though economic growth is reduced or an economy enters a period of recession, the inflation rate remains high or increases. This is commonly the result of cost-push inflation. See also *cost-push inflation* and *demand-pull inflation*.

Substitution effect [Chapter 3]
In economics, when the price of a commodity increases, consumers will find a substitute to replace the commodity so that the quantity demanded is subsequently reduced. In contrast, when the price of a commodity decreases, consumers will buy more of the commodity as a substitute for other commodities so that the quantity demanded is increased. See also *income effect*.

Supply [Chapter 3]
Ceteris paribus, the willingness and ability of a firm to produce a commodity good or service at different prices within a given period of time.

Supply-side policies [Chapter 5]
Government formulated and implemented policies that strengthen and increase the aggregate supply of an economy. Common examples of related policy measures include education and training, as well as public investment in infrastructure.

Surplus budget [Chapter 5]
Lower annual government planned expenditures (e.g., on social welfare and public investment) than planned revenue (e.g., derived from taxes). Generally speaking, a surplus budget is a common contractionary fiscal policy applied by a government to slow down (or stabilize) the economy when it is overheated (i.e., aggregate demand is increasing rapidly and hence inflation occurs). See also *aggregate demand* and *fiscal policy*.

Sustainable development [Chapter 8]

The ability of an economy to increase its outputs without undermining the natural environment and the ecosystem so that the real production capacity of the world economy could be preserved over time. In economics, sustainable development requires firms and consumers to recognize the social cost and negative effects of their economic activities, and hence require both of them to put forth effort in reducing damage to the environment.

Unemployment [Chapters 1 and 5]

The group who is willing and able to work, and actively looking for employment but unable to secure a job. The percentage of this group to the total working population in an economy constitutes the unemployment rate.

Variable cost [Chapter 4]

Cost varies directly with respect to the volume of output. For example, when more of a commodity is produced, a firm has to employ more laborers and spend more on material inputs. See also *fixed cost*.

Waste emission [Chapter 8]

Waste discharged from the private-sector production process to the environment. Common forms of waste emission include carbon, plastic, and sewage emissions. Indeed, waste emission has posed serious threats to the sustainable development of the world economies and various industries. To remedy the related problems, both industries and consumers globally need to put in joint efforts.

White pollution [Chapter 8]

Pollution caused by dumped waste that is difficult to decompose or recycle. Commonly in the form of styrofoam utensils or plastic bags (which are usually white in color). Responsible consumption and production are necessary to reduce white pollution for sustainable development.

Index